Patricia R. Morrison

TWENTIETH-CENTURY
ROSES

'William and Mary', a modern rose in the old-fashioned style

PETER BEALES

TWENTIETH-CENTURY
ROSES

An illustrated encyclopaedia
and grower's manual of
classic roses from the twentieth century

COLLINS HARVILL
8 Grafton Street, London W1
1988

Collins Harvill
William Collins Sons and Co Ltd
London · Glasgow · Sydney · Auckland
Toronto · Johannesburg

THE PHOTOGRAPHS

The majority of the pictures in this book were taken by the author in various rose gardens around the world (see Acknowledgements) and in the display gardens of his nursery at Attleborough, Norfolk. Other pictures were kindly loaned by the following:

Mrs Anne Cocker, Cocker's Roses, Aberdeen, Scotland: 'Clydebank Centenary', 'Conservation', 'Little Prince', 'Remember Me'

Patrick Dickson, Dickson's Roses, Newtownards, Northern Ireland: 'Ards Beauty', 'Anisley Dickson', 'Cider Cup', 'Disco Dancer', 'Len Turner', 'Lovely Lady', 'Peek a Boo', 'Petit Four', 'Sweet Magic', 'Wishing'

Gareth Fryer, Fryer's Roses, Knutsford, Cheshire: 'Mini Metro', 'Sweet Dream'

Douglas and Rosemary Gandy, Gandy's Roses, Lutterworth, Leicestershire: 'Fergie'

Betty Harkness, Harkness Roses, Hitchin, Hertfordshire: 'Armada', 'Radox Bouquet'

Chris and Keith Jones, Tarvin, Chester: 'Lincoln Cathedral'

Hazel Le Rougetel, Liphook, Hampshire: 'Corylus'

The Limes New Roses, Lifton, Devon: 'Geraldine'

Mike Lowe, Nashua, New Hampshire, USA: 'Alexander Girault'

Meilland's Universal Rose Selection, Antibes, France: 'Air France', 'Meillandina', 'Poppy Flash', 'Scherzo', 'Yorkshire Sunblaze'

Vincent Page, Bracknell, Berkshire: 'Albertine', 'Anna Ford', 'Buff Beauty', 'Clarissa', 'Max Graf', 'Nymphenburg', 'Royal William'

BRITISH LIBRARY CATALOGUING IN PUBLICATION DATA

Beales, Peter
Twentieth-century roses.
1. Roses. Cultivation
I. Title
635.9′33372

ISBN 0-00-272807-9

First published by Collins Harvill 1988
© Peter Beales 1988

Designed by Vera Brice
Photoset in Itek Baskerville and Monophoto Photina
by Ace Filmsetting Ltd, Frome, Somerset
and Servis Filmsetting Ltd, Manchester
Colour origination by Gilchrist Bros Ltd, Leeds
Printed and bound in Great Britain by
William Collins Sons and Co Ltd, Glasgow

To Evelyn May, my mother

Wandering I found, in my ruinous walk,
By the dial-stone aged and green,
A rose of the wilderness, left on its stalk,
To mark where a garden had been.
Like a brotherless hermit, the last of his race,
All wild, in the silence of nature, it drew
From each wandering sunbeam a lonely embrace,
For the nightshade and thorn had overshadow'd the place
Where the flowers of my forefathers grew.

CAMPBELL

'Nevada', from Pedro Dot of Spain

Contents

Acknowledgements

It is not until the last words are penned and final photographs selected that one realizes how much more difficult this book would have been to write without the help of family, friends, colleagues and other rose lovers.

Assistance came in many different ways. For their contributions and encouragement my grateful thanks are due to Jack Harkness, OBE, for such a scholarly Foreword and for his help with the proofs, and for his book *The Makers of Heavenly Roses*, a frequent source of reference; Christopher MacLehose of Collins Harvill for initially conceiving the idea, twisting my arm and nursing me through a bad patch; Mark Crean for sensitively dotting the i's and crossing the t's, and Vera Brice for lovingly and artistically interpreting my work into this design. My wife, Joan, and my daughter Amanda and son Richard gave lots of help and support. For holding the fort for an absentee boss, thanks are due to my nursery staff, in particular managers Heather Friend and Ian Limmer.

For allowing me to take photographs of roses, with or without permission, in their gardens or in gardens under their supervision, I am grateful to the following:

Humphrey Brooke, Lime Kiln, Claydon, Suffolk
Henry and Julie Cecil, Warren Place, Newmarket, Suffolk
Donna Fuss, Adviser to The Elizabeth Park Rose Gardens, Hartford, Connecticut
Ken Grapes, The Royal National Rose Society's Gardens, St Albans
Trevor and Dixie Griffiths, Timaru, New Zealand
Mike and Irene Lowe, Nashua, New Hampshire
Clair G. Martin III, The Huntington Botanic Gardens, California
Bill and Lorna Mercer, Bermuda
Keith Money, Carbrooke, Norfolk
Raymond J. Rogers, The Rudolf van der Groot Rose Gardens, New Jersey
Deane and Maureen Ross, Willunga, South Australia
James Russell, Castle Howard, Yorkshire
David Ruston, Renmark, South Australia
Elizabeth Scholtz and Stephen Scaniello, The Brooklyn Botanic Gardens, New York
David Steen, Auckland, New Zealand
Toni Sylvester, Auckland, New Zealand
Graham Thomas and David Stone, Mottisfont Abbey, Hampshire
Lord and Lady Tollemache, Helmingham Hall, Suffolk
Robin and Laurel Walpole, Mannington Hall, Norfolk
Pat Wiley, Roses of Yesterday and Today, Watsonville, California
Miriam Wilkins, El Cerrito, California
Barbara Worl, Palo Alto, California
And to the owners, administrators and head gardeners of the following gardens: Blickling Hall, Aylsham, Norfolk; Harlow Carr, Harrogate, Yorkshire; Hidcote Manor, Gloucestershire; Kiftsgate Court, Gloucestershire; Leeds Castle, Kent; Sissinghurst Castle, Kent; The Royal Horticultural Society, Wisley, Surrey; Queen Mary's Rose Gardens, Regents Park, London.

In addition, I must thank many members of various rose societies for giving up their time to chauffeur me around, and in particular those from the Heritage Rose Society of South Australia, the Heritage Rose Society of New Zealand, the Southwest Regional Heritage Rose Group in the United States, the Bermuda Rose Society and the Canadian Rose Society.

My thanks to John Adlam for his help with the micropropagation section and to those listed elsewhere for lending additional photographs.

'Armada', from Jack Harkness

Foreword

We who love roses were in profit when Peter Beales and Collins Harvill produced between them the book *Classic Roses*. The author was fortunate in his publisher, who printed a handsome volume; the publisher had reason to thank his author, for his uncommon knowledge and experience; and due to the pair of them, we readers enjoyed a sumptuous tour of the roses of previous times.

It is not every expert on old-fashioned roses who can turn with facility to the moderns. There's a partial blindness among rosarians, whereby some who love the old are led by that love to decry the new; and some who welcome new roses with wonder, as well they might, for they are watching creation unfold before their eyes, scoff at the roses of yesteryear. In recent writings a lofty disdain for the Hybrid Teas may be discerned, as though wisdom, virtue and good taste lie in turning one's back upon the rose darlings of other people. To what extent this attitude betrays a dislike for roses or a dismissal of people, let the psychologists decide. The rose visitors I don't enjoy at our nursery are those whose response on being shown a rose is to shake their heads.

Peter Beales, completing the work he began, in supplementing his *Classic Roses* with this account of twentieth-century roses, shows a much more commendable attitude. If it is a rose, he loves it, whether it is new or old, cultivated or wild, dripping with history or newly born. He doesn't shake his head at roses, he nods it. That shows a good heart, open to all the wonders and beauty with which the genus *Rosa* is stuffed, wonders which are still being revealed, beauty that even in my new seedling roses this year stopped the scratched-handed workers with throats dry, eyes moist, and no words to express their thanks to nature for her bounty.

So *Twentieth-Century Roses* joins *Classic Roses* to complete the portrait of the Queen of Flowers by Peter Beales. I look forward to its publication, trusting it to be a worthy companion to its sister. There is a place on my bookshelf waiting for it, not that the Beales books will spend their time on the shelf; they will probably just pass the nights there, I'll be looking them up in the day time.

JACK HARKNESS, OBE, DHM
Southwold
June 1988

Rosa foetida persiana

Preface

When asked to follow *Classic Roses* with a book on modern roses, I at first refused. How could I, I thought, for in that very book I had openly declared my bias towards the older varieties – surely I should not be so unfaithful to my first love?

'Nonsense,' said my publisher. 'Just write about roses.' I again said No and went on growing and enjoying my roses, old and new. Later I said Yes, although with some trepidation, for it had dawned on me that roses are roses and it was I that was prejudiced, not they. For years my garden had been full of both modern and old varieties, all embracing one another; and although in June my roving eye still sought out 'Maiden's Blush' and 'Fantin Latour', by September those two and others of their kin were just fond memories as I flirted with the modern varieties that would take me into winter. Perhaps I have come of age and have realized, despite my taste for quiet colours and enduring commitment to the older varieties, that all that is new is not necessarily less interesting.

In any case, this book is not just about modern roses, it is concerned with the whole of the twentieth century, a century which, so far, has seen more changes in the development of the genus than could possibly have been envisaged by the raisers of the eighteenth and nineteenth centuries as they strove for their ideal of perfection. Equally, these pages have given me the opportunity to express a long-held admiration of modern hybridizers and their work in creating, from the foundations laid by their predecessors, a most diverse and versatile family of garden plants. For roses are not just about shape of flower, colour and scent, important though these factors are; they are about gardens and gardening. By harnessing so many of their attributes, modern breeders have enlarged the role of roses to one which now allows their use in almost any landscape.

In the first section of this book I have tried to piece together, in concise terms, man's fascinating evolution of roses since the year 1900. In the second section, I discuss the various ways these roses can be used and in the third put forward some ideas as to how they can be grown to give their best. By far and away my most difficult task, however, was deciding which varieties to omit as I compiled the fourth part, the Dictionary, for it has meant discarding many close friends in favour of a balance between old and new. Others may well have chosen differently, but individual taste is precisely why there are so many roses to choose from.

Throughout, I have indulged myself in a few digressions and had the audacity, from time to time, to express some personal opinions on subjects on which I know others, whom I respect, hold different views – so be it.

P.B.

May 1988

'Empress Josephine', a beautiful old Gallica

PART I
In Search of the Perfect Rose

The Influence of the Older Classic Roses

Over the centuries, in his search for perfection, man has manipulated the genus *Rosa* to considerable effect. In the process, he has brought forth a wide diversity of fascinating and useful garden plants. From nature's original pure roses, shape, form, colour, floriferousness and different growth habits have all been combined to great advantage, thus providing us with an unrivalled family of plants.

Some will argue that form and scent have been victims rather than triumphs of progress. Indeed, some of the haphazard creations of the early breeders still carry the most graceful forms and wear the most compelling perfumes. Comparisons, though, are unfair for, as in all things, tastes vary. Judgement as to the merits of one rose over another can only be made against very arbitrary criteria.

Much of man's early work in developing the rose is conjecture, but all was not left to the bees. Haphazard though it was, there is little doubt that during the early days of civilization, both in the Mediterranean and in the Far East, deliberate hybrids were raised. Not until horizons broadened and travel became more commonplace did it become possible for makers of roses to harness such a diversity of genes and to mix and match species and varieties fully to release the potential of the genus.

From the beginning of the nineteenth century, breeders' efforts began to be recorded in more detail, and by the end of Queen Victoria's reign it can be seen from these records that they had laid the foundation for today's roses. Such is the importance of this period that it is difficult, if not impossible, to study the genealogy of modern varieties without reference to the extensive range of nineteenth-century literature.

During that era, botanists and plantsmen such as Parks, Fortune and Banks hunted down several hitherto unknown species from the wild parts of China, the foothills of the Himalayas and other regions of Asia and Asia Minor. Hybrids, too, were discovered in ancient gardens of many of those

Hybridizing a rose (see p. 123)

'Old Blush', or 'Common Monthly'

regions, especially China. These found their way to Botanic Gardens and nurseries in the West where they were soon put to stud by eager nurserymen who crossed and recrossed them with a range of European and Middle Eastern species and hybrids to create, not just hundreds of new varieties, but several distinct new groups of both Large-Flowered and Cluster-Flowered roses.

It is impossible even in a summary history of the rose not to mention the Empress Josephine, for it was she who became the first great patron of the genus. Her passion for roses led to a tremendous increase in their popularity and wider distribution. Her patronage of the nurserymen of the day encouraged interest in the development of new varieties, for she was mimicked both in France and in England by her many wealthy and fashionable contemporaries. There can be little doubt that breeders and growers such as Vibert and Desportes grew rich and were kept on their toes by an insatiable thirst for novelty and variety from that affluent section of French society.

Vibert paved the way for the abundant numbers of French rose nurseries during the nineteenth century. Many roses of merit were raised by such famous growers as himself and Desportes, Laffay, Jacques, Hardy, Guillot, Lacharme and Verdier, to name only a few. All made their contribution, together with Englishmen such as Paul, Rivers and Bennett. As the century progressed, fashions changed from the flat, full, quartered blooms so loved

Rose damascena bifera, or 'Quatre Saisons'

'Catherine Mermet', a Tea rose

The Alba 'Semi-plena', probably one of the earliest roses to be cultivated

'The Portland Rose' or 'Duchess of Portland', a variety of much significance in the development of a longer flowering season

'Souvenir de la Malmaison', which dates from 1843

Rosa moschata, which when crossed with 'Old Blush' gave birth to the first of the Noisettes

by Josephine to big-petalled, globular, high-centred flowers. Although still some way from the shape of today's more refined Hybrid Teas, the latter were nevertheless reflections of things still to come.

Such was its appeal as a garden plant that by now the rose was finding its way all over the globe. Settlers in the new worlds from Europe took with them seeds, cuttings and even rooted plants in pots. Plant health regulations prohibit the easy export of roses today, but at that time a rose was a rose, diseases and all. Many kinds flourished, especially the newly discovered 'Chinas' and 'Teas' which thrived in the climates of the virgin, fertile lands. The worldwide dispersion of roses is now taken for granted, but in the days before it was possible to travel the globe their distribution was limited to the northern hemisphere.

Before the long-flowering species and hybrids arrived from China, European nurserymen and rosarians had little material to work with in their quest for remontancy in the genus. The only rose then known to them that repeated its flowering in the autumn was *Rosa damascena bifera* or 'Quatre Saisons'. Although this rose had been established for centuries in Europe, it had originally come from the Middle East together with other Damasks with less free-flowering abilities than *bifera*. There is little doubt that Damask roses were keenly admired by the Romans long before becoming popular further north.

The other groups of roses predominant in Europe, at least from Roman times through the Middle Ages to the turn of the nineteenth century, were the Albas, Gallicas and perhaps Centifolias (see *Classic Roses*, p. 23). Unlike the Damasks, however, they flower only for a short season and most experts believe that very few, if any, of their genes have influenced the development of our modern varieties; although personally I have a suspicion, supported by some threads of evidence, that the Gallicas have played a larger part through the Portlands than they have ever received credit for. Since we are primarily concerned with the twentieth century, however, this book is not the place to go too deeply into such theories. What is certain is that 'The Portland Rose', also known today as 'Duchess of Portland', played an important role. It emerged at the end of the eighteenth century in Italy and

'Baroness Rothschild', an early Hybrid Perpetual

flowered for a much longer period each summer than had hitherto been dreamed of. The Portlands soon became recognized as a distinct group and several very good varieties were introduced during the nineteenth century. Outstanding among them, and in many ways ahead of their time, were 'Comte de Chambord' and 'Jacques Cartier', both raised in France in the 1860s.

Close on the heels of the Portlands came the Bourbons. The first Bourbon, 'Rose Edouard', is said to have been conceived by the infidelity of 'Old Blush', the China, with the Damask 'Quatre Saisons' on the Isle de Bourbon in the Indian Ocean, now the Isle de Réunion. This may well have happened, but there is compelling evidence from India that 'Rose Edouard' was

Top: 'Perle d'Or', a China hybrid. *Below left:* 'Coral Cluster', a Dwarf Polyantha, and *below right:* 'Iceberg', an outstanding Floribunda

growing happily in Calcutta years before that. Anyway the first Bourbon was found, sent to France and put to stud with other roses to produce more and more of its kind. The early Bourbons were a mixed lot. Most were lax and rather ungainly growers and such was their number that many had but a fleeting life, quickly falling by the wayside with only the best surviving among a riot of novelties. Those of real merit have survived to this day. Although I suspect a little tiredness among some, others such as 'Souvenir de la Malmaison' (1843), 'Louise Odier' (1851) and 'Mme Isaac Pereire' (1881) are still very alert and will go on flowering in our gardens for ever.

By the 1830s, as a result of an orgy of cross-pollination between each and every known group, another very important family of Large-Flowered roses had started to emerge which was eventually to rival all others. They became known as the Hybrid Perpetuals. At the height of their popularity, many hundreds of varieties were being offered to a public ever eager for novelty and they remained in demand for almost a century. Like the Bourbons, many varieties were not up to the intense competition and, after a brief spell in the limelight, became lost for ever and are now only names to conjure with in old books and catalogues. Again, as with the Bourbons, several good Hybrid Perpetuals have survived on their merit and those still with us, such as 'Reine des Violettes' (1860), 'Baroness Rothschild' (1868) and 'Mrs John Laing' (1887), are more than equal to the expectations of a present-day rose.

Important though all the old roses were as blueprints for our modern varieties, the Hybrid Tea could not have evolved in its present style without the influence of the roses from the East, for it was these that not only induced remontancy but also created the mould for both petal compositions and their high-centred shapes. The Teas, or 'Tea-Scented' roses, as they were then called, also helped to induce a wider range of colours than had hitherto been possible from within the limited scope of the European species.

Running parallel to the evolution of the Large-Flowered roses are the interesting diversions that occurred from time to time which led to the development of the Cluster-Flowered types. Highly significant was the crossing of *Rosa moschata* with 'Old Blush' to give birth to the first of the Noisettes – a happy occurrence in North America during the first decade of the nineteenth century which led directly to a useful group of climbing roses, more colourful than hitherto, and with larger clusters of flowers. While the early Noisettes were not all remontant, further crosses with other long-flowerers soon rectified this small flaw in their character.

For a long time the floriferous species *Rosa multiflora* had been recognized as a useful short climber, so it was only a matter of time before matings were induced between this species and various remontant hybrids to bring forth the beginnings of the now indispensable Floribundas. Although in modern times it is becoming more difficult to distinguish between them, the Floribunda is considerably more complex genealogically than the Hybrid Tea. Certainly its early stages of development were far less ambitious than the Hybrid Tea, and one suspects that many a seedling was more the result of accident than design. Unlike the larger-flowered types, which were sought after for the individual shape and form of their flowers, and with geraniums, annuals and perennial plants being so fashionable for bedding and massed display, the Cluster-Flowered roses had no particular niche to fill. It was not until well into this century, when gardening became expensive and less formal gardens were in vogue, that the value of bedding roses was fully appreciated and their potential exploited by breeders and gardeners alike. 'Pâquerette' was the first Polyantha, raised in France in 1875. It is said to have been the first direct cross between *Rosa multiflora* and a China rose. What purports to be this rose is still growing today, but there is little evidence that it was ever very popular with nineteenth-century gardeners.

In Victorian times the best loved and most used of the dwarf cluster varieties was 'White Pet' (1879) ('Little White Pet')– the 'Little' was prefixed later – and several hybrid China roses then referred to as 'Polypompons'. They include the much loved 'Cécile Brünner' (1881) and 'Perle d'Or' (1884), each of similar habit and flower form and both, it is thought, out of crosses between Polyanthas and a famous old yellow Tea rose of 1858, 'Mme Falcot'.

Several Polypompons were introduced between 1875 and the early 1900s, but none really caught on until a decade or so later when the short, shrubby, free-flowering 'Dwarf Polyanthas' were born. Considering their popularity, it was not surprising that a discerning breeder should soon cross them with Hybrid Teas to create the Poulsen roses of the 1920s and '30s. While retaining large clusters, these differed from the Dwarf Polyanthas in having larger, individual flowers and more vigorous growth, but sadly none inherited any fragrance from the Hybrid Tea part of their parentage. Although lack of perfume was quite a drawback, this did not prevent breeders all over the world from working with them and their numbers rapidly increased. From the mid-1930s onwards they became known collectively as 'Hybrid Polyanthas'. By the mid-1940s they had eclipsed Dwarf Polyanthas as bedding plants and were even rivalling Hybrid Teas in popularity. Many of the early varieties had been single or semi-double. They were also rather restricted in colour range, being mostly shades of pink and red, but more and more interbreeding and crossing with Hybrid Teas and other types soon changed this and some excellent, very colourful, double-flowered varieties emerged, some even with distinct traces of perfume. Such was their advance that by the mid-1950s, apart from their clusters of flowers, there was little evidence of Polyantha in their appearance and their group name was changed to Floribunda. The Floribunda is more popular than ever now, and several of the 1950s and '60s varieties such as 'Allgold' and 'Iceberg' are still sold in large numbers today.

The Hybrid Teas

The first Hybrid Tea was launched upon the world amid controversy. It was found by Jean-Baptiste Guillot among a patch of seedlings in his nursery at Lyon, France. Immediately he recognized it as 'something different'. Its flowers, held on a strong neck, were freely produced and rather portly in shape, at least until they were fully open; they were also high-centred in the fashion of the Teas of the day and filled out with lots of petals. Its habit of growth was upright and altogether more tidy than the rather sprawling Hybrid Perpetuals. Guillot had no idea of its true parentage but concluded that it was the result of a secret liaison between one of his 'upper class' Hybrid Perpetuals and a Tea rose with a roving eye.

Although clearly seen as 'different' by its raiser and by many of the experts in France, it took several years to convince the Rose Society there that M. Guillot had stumbled upon a rose worthy of distinction as being the first Hybrid Tea. It was named 'La France' in 1867. It took even longer to convince the British National Rose Society that a new type of rose had emerged and it remained classified as a Hybrid Perpetual in Britain until the early 1890s. It was not M. Guillot, his rose or the French Rose Society that eventually persuaded the sceptics on this side of the English Channel, it was pressure from one Henry Bennett, a prominent English raiser, that forced them eventually to accept the new classification. Between 1879 and 1890, Bennett succeeded in raising several distinct varieties from a deliberate programme of crossing Teas with Hybrid Perpetuals and, in his lifetime, raised well over thirty new roses. Several, such as 'Mrs John Laing' and 'Captain Hayward', were clearly Hybrid Perpetuals but most had the characteristics of the new class, Hybrid Teas. For a long time, Bennett fought against the narrow minds of those within both the professional and amateur rose fraternity to convince them that all that was new and good did not necessarily have to come from France. Some of Bennett's roses won major awards; others fell by the wayside; but one in particular, 'Lady Mary Fitzwilliam', when put to stud – unlike her French counterpart, 'La France', which was virtually sterile – proved very fertile and was used extensively by both French and British breeders to produce many more good roses. Credit must go to Henry Bennett for his all-round work on the rose, but it was 'Lady Mary Fitzwilliam' above any other that established his reputation as, beyond doubt, 'Lord of the Hybrid Teas'. Prior to Bennett's day, most of the best British roses had been Hybrid Perpetuals and had come from either William Paul of Cheshunt or Rivers of Sawbridgeworth. Between them, they raised some excellent roses, and although many of their varieties only appeared fleetingly in their catalogues they must receive credit for stalwart

Left: 'La France', the first Hybrid Tea

Below: 'Mme Caroline Testout', raised in 1890 and as a climber still one of the world's favourites

work in helping to provide Bennett with the initial material. By Edwardian times, the Hybrid Teas were quite popular but still had a long way to go before becoming the reliable group of garden roses we know today.

Despite Bennett, however, French breeders were still ahead of the field. In 1890 Joseph Pernet-Ducher raised what still ranks as one of the world's favourite roses, 'Mme Caroline Testout'. Today this rose is better known in its climbing form. Then, as a bush rose, it had no rivals, producing an abundance of large, blowsy, scented, satin-pink flowers on a sturdy, accommodating plant. Few gardens would have been without at least one specimen of 'Mme Caroline'. Pernet-Ducher was a discerning man and selected his introductions carefully, introducing only those which showed improvement of class or were a clear breakthrough in colour. As testimony to this he was also responsible for raising two excellent forcing roses of the era, 'Mme Abel Chatenay' and 'Antoine Rivoire'. With 'Mme Caroline Testout' flaunting herself in gardens everywhere and his florist's roses adorning many a bridal bouquet, his Hybrid Teas had certainly made their mark. Pernet-Ducher's most important introduction, however, was 'Soleil d'Or'. It was this rose, a cross between the clear yellow *Rosa foetida persiana* and the red Hybrid Perpetual 'Antoine Ducher', which brought the first hint of yellow ever to be seen in the Hybrid Perpetuals, thus making possible the many beautiful yellow Hybrid Teas of today. Initially, 'Soleil d'Or' and its descendants were grouped together as a separate class. To honour their raiser they were called Pernetianas. Sadly, they did not make good garden plants for they were addicted to black spot, an affliction inherited from the yellow side of their ancestry. By the early 1930s most Pernetianas had disappeared or, for reasons of convenience in commercial catalogues, had been merged with the Hybrid Teas.

The warm and sunny climate of southern France was the main reason for the French breeders' dominance during the nineteenth century, but roses were becoming big business and the British – fed up with the many French names in their catalogues – started to raise their own new varieties by hybridizing under glass. Henry Bennett had proved that such methods worked and they were soon adopted by others, among them the firm of Alexander Dickson of Newtownards, Northern Ireland. After several false starts, Dicksons were on the trail of some excellent Hybrid Teas and won the first gold medal ever to be given to a Hybrid Tea with a pink rose named 'Mrs W. J. Grant' (1892). One of the oldest of their varieties still available today is the beautiful single 'Irish Elegance', raised in 1905. Since then, the Dickson family have been responsible for some very auspicious Hybrid Teas, outstanding among which are 'Dame Edith Helen', 'Betty Uprichard', 'Shot Silk', 'Hugh Dickson' and 'Grandpa Dickson'.

Soon after Dicksons began breeding, another well-established Irish nursery, Samuel McGredy of Portadown, started with their pollen brush and it was not long before they, like Dicksons, were winning high awards for beautiful roses such as 'Mrs Herbert Stevens', 'Mrs Henry Morse',

'Dame Edith Helen', a Dickson Hybrid Tea

'McGredy's Yellow', 'Picture' and 'Piccadilly'. Not so famous as a garden rose but a name that will live forever is 'Margaret McGredy', raised in 1927 and pollen parent to 'Peace', the most famous rose of all. Both Pat Dickson and Sam McGredy are perpetuating the family tradition by breeding some excellent roses today, although McGredy has moved to the more reliable climate of New Zealand to pursue his craft.

Although these two firms led the way until the beginning of the First World War, other breeders were busy scattering pollen in search of Hybrid Teas both east and west of Ireland. By the time the war was over and things had returned to normal in Britain, competition for the coveted Gold Medal of the National Rose Society was intense. While it may be unfair to make such a judgement, there were too many winners by far: performance on the show bench rather than garden worthiness had become the criterion of success. Names to conjure with from Britain in the 1920s and '30s are 'Mme Henry Bowles' (Chaplin Bros, 1921), 'Rev. F. Page-Roberts' (B. R. Cant & Sons, 1921) and 'Mrs Edward Laxton' (Laxton Bros, 1936).

During the early 1940s, the rose growers of Britain were mindful of other things. Partly by choice and partly by government decree, they devoted most of their time and land resources to growing vegetables and their greenhouses to such things as tomatoes. The gardening public, too, were preoccupied with similar enterprises for the war effort, so selling roses would have been difficult. Once the war was over, however, raisers quickly resurrected their breeding programmes by planting up hybridizing houses with seedlings and introduced the pioneering seedlings which had been lovingly nurtured in some corner plot through those five long years.

In the 1950s and '60s, demand for novelty was insatiable and the Hybrid Tea hit a high point of popularity. To satisfy demand some breeders, it seemed, introduced everything and anything – some not sufficiently tried and tested – that could be remotely called new. Sadly, this disenchanted customers who rightly became fed up with so many Hybrid Teas failing to live up to raisers' promises and they turned either to other types such as Floribundas or away from roses altogether. Fortunately, some excellent varieties emerged from the more responsible raisers during that period of plenty and they have proved themselves by the test of time.

Ironically, considering how fervently professionals had sought the perfect red rose, one of the best came from an amateur, Albert Norman, who raised 'Ena Harkness' for posterity in 1946. This rose was introduced to the world by the famous firm of R. Harkness & Co. of Hitchin at about the time that Jack Harkness was beginning his own illustrious rose-breeding career. Jack's hybridizing followed several different lines, but two excellent Hybrid Teas of his are the shapely 'Elizabeth Harkness' (1969) and the outstanding Hybrid-Tea-like shrub rose 'Alexander' (1972).

Further north near Aberdeen another conspicuous career was getting under way. Aberdeen, now rich as the headquarters of the North Sea oilfields, geographically awkward and climatically inclement, always

'McGredy's Yellow', raised in 1933 and still popular today

Above: 'Ena Harkness', one of the best-loved red Hybrid Teas

Left: 'Grandpa Dickson', one of the finest modern yellows

Below: 'Silver Jubilee', a Cocker rose of distinction

'Just Joey', from Cants, a popular, coppery-orange rose

seemed to me an unlikely place to grow roses, and in those days its economy was based on the fishing industry. In my young days, exhibiting at rose shows, I was always envious of the high quality and size of Cocker's roses; no doubt fish manure helped. Aberdeen is built on land of good heart, and an enlightened city council – inspired partly no doubt by the success of Alex Cocker – has made it a city of roses. 'Alec's Red' (1970) was Alex Cocker's first successful Hybrid Tea, its name chosen by Alec's friends in the trade who tried and tested the rose before its introduction. Disease resistance had always been a high priority for this breeder and his efforts were rewarded in 1978 when 'Silver Jubilee' was launched; no better rose could possibly commemorate Her Majesty Queen Elizabeth II's twenty-five years on the throne.

Since the Second World War, Dickson, McGredy, Harkness and Cocker have each made their own indelible mark on the Hybrid Teas, but they have not had it all to themselves. Other British breeders have been busy too, notable among them Edward B. LeGrice of North Walsham with the still widely grown 'My Choice' (1958), Bees of Chester with the much loved 'Josephine Bruce' (1949), Gregorys of Nottingham with 'Blessings' (1967) and Cants of Colchester with 'Just Joey' (1972).

In their wisdom and after much lobbying from plant breeders, the British Government introduced an Act of Parliament that was to have far

'Ophelia', from William Paul, and *right:* 'Los Angeles', raised by Fred H. Howard of the United States

reaching consequences for the British rose industry. This was the Plant Varieties and Seeds Act 1964. It brought Britain into line with other European countries and with the United States, by allowing breeders to patent new varieties and receive a just return for their efforts, a return directly linked to the virtues or otherwise of their chosen introductions. It was a complex act and received a mixed reception – so mixed that, for a time, harmony within the industry was, to put it lightly, disturbed. After a short while breeders organized themselves into an association with the apt – it seemed to growers at the time – acronym BARB, standing for British Association of Rose Breeders. When it was realized that patenting was here to stay, relations between breeders and growers became friendly again. New varieties are the lifeblood of the industry and no grower should begrudge the breeder of any successful rose a fair return for his work. With several hundred varieties already patented in Britain since 1964, however, and more and more joining their ranks each year, it is becoming increasingly difficult to sort the wheat from the chaff, especially as royalties are levied on plants produced and not on the numbers sold.

Westwards from Ireland in North America the rose had long been very popular and in 1899 the American Rose Society was founded

> To increase the general interest in the cultivation and improve the standard of excellence of the Rose for all people.

A poignant quotation from its constitution for, since its formation, it has done just that and more for the rose, both in its own land and abroad. Its influence is now far-reaching, not least in its responsible role as overseer of the classification and nomenclature of roses worldwide. The following, reproduced from an American Rose Society annual of 1917, is an early communication between the two rose societies of Britain and America. It is so formal and reads almost as though it was their first communication, but I cannot believe that.

> To arrange for complete understanding and interchange, correspondence has been opened with the Secretary of the National Rose

Society. In a letter dated May 5, 1916, Mr. Courtney Page, the Hon. Secretary of the Society, who is also joint editor of the English Rose Annual, writes thus:

> "I am in receipt of your favor of April 16, and the same mail brought a copy of the American Rose Annual. Please accept my hearty congratulations for the publication, which must have meant an unusual amount of work. It is indeed a fine volume. . . . I quite agree that the stimulation you have given will largely help toward the obtaining of new members by both societies. English rosarians are very keen, and those to whom I have shown your annual are loud in its praise. . . . We shall be happy to coöperate."

A suitable reply to this communication brought the following response from Mr. Page:

> "Your letter of May 24 was placed before my Council at their last meeting, and I was instructed to ask you to be good enough to convey to the members of your Society their hearty appreciation, and to express the hope that everything possible will be done to encourage the friendly feeling between the rosarians of the two great countries."

It has not been recently practicable to secure communications from the great French and German rose-growers.

From the limited range of literature I have available it would be discourteous of me to presume too much about American rose history, but rose breeders there have been increasingly active since John Champneys raised the famous Noisette 'Champneys' Pink Cluster' at Charleston in *c.* 1811. At the beginning of this century, the first all-American Hybrid Teas started to emerge. Two in particular are worth special mention since they soon established themselves as favourites on both sides of the Atlantic: 'Los Angeles' was raised in 1916 by Fred H. Howard and named after his home town; the other, 'General MacArthur', was raised in 1905 by a very active breeder of the early 1900s, E. Gurney Hill of Richmond, Indiana. Both varieties can be found growing in Britain today, although the latter is now seen more often as a climber. Another fact from my 1917 American Rose Society annual which indicates the popularity of Hybrid Teas in America at the time is that, of 349 roses listed as raised by American nurserymen, no less than 114 were Hybrid Teas, 27 of which were accredited to E. Gurney Hill. Some, of course, would have been sports. Hill continued to raise roses until well into the 1930s, and since we mention sports his firm was responsible for introducing in 1918 one of the great favourites of the 1920s and '30s, the beautiful pink 'Mme Butterfly', a deeper sport of William Paul's soft pink 'Ophelia' (1912). Millions of these two roses were produced and sold between the wars and they still enjoy nostalgic popularity to this day, despite, I suspect, some loss of vigour from constant propagation. Both roses

'The Doctor', produced by F. H. Howard for the American raisers Jackson & Perkins

were excellent forcers and acres were grown under glass for the cut-flower market of the period.

The fact that European breeders were clamouring to introduce their new varieties to the lucrative North American market did not discourage breeders there from working successfully to produce their own, and many very good roses emerged during those years. My favourite by far is the superbly scented, shapely, deep silvery-pink 'The Doctor' (1936) raised by F. H. Howard and named in honour of Jean Nicolas, a hybridizer for the firm of Jackson & Perkins which, at that time, was probably the biggest and wealthiest rose company in the world. Interestingly, the pollen parent of 'The Doctor' was 'Los Angeles'.

The early 1940s were lean years for European breeders and with the notable exception of 'Peace' the flow of new seedlings westwards across the Atlantic virtually dried up. Shortage quickly created demand and soon many American rose nurseries were busy cross-pollinating with vigour. In the 1940s, '50s and '60s they introduced some vintage Hybrid Teas. The superb 'Diamond Jubilee' (1947) by Eugene Boerner of Jackson & Perkins was one of the best and is still worthy of a place in any modern garden, as is Herbert Swim's shapely 'Helen Traubel' introduced by Armstrongs in 1951. I fell heavily for this rose soon after it came to England and will always forgive her when she pouts and hangs her head. Nothing, it seems, condemns a rose to the sidelines more than a weak neck, but I have never quite understood why so mild an affliction should be considered so serious a fault. Deportment, however, was never a problem for the long-necked 'Mojave' (1954), the free-flowering 'Sutter's Gold' (1950) or the sophisticated 'Royal Highness' (1962), all American roses of distinction, and all from Herbert Swim. Patent rights, fluctuating currency, improvements in introductions from elsewhere and changing demand for other types of roses help to explain why very few newer Hybrid Teas from America are listed in British catalogues today, but many good oldies still flourish in Britain, where they are much cherished by discerning rosarians.

As with perfumes and wines, not to mention language, the world would be a duller place without French roses, for it was the French who not only gave us some of the best old-fashioned roses but also laid the foundations

Top left: The superbly scented 'Diamond Jubilee' and *top right:* 'Helen Traubel', a fine rose from Herbert Swim

for Hybrid Teas as we know them today. The debt owed to men like Guillot has already been acknowledged, but other Frenchmen of similar mould have not been idle in more recent times. Although his most famous achievements were his pioneering yellow varieties, 'Rayon d'Or' and 'Soleil d'Or', Joseph Pernet-Ducher continued to breed excellent roses until the early 1920s. In 1913, amid controversy, he won £1000 from the *Daily Mail* newspaper for his rich coral 'Mme Edouard Herriot'; and in 1924, just before retiring, he gave us the shapely 'Angèle Pernet', to this day worth a place in any garden.

Space does not permit me to cover much of the detail of the prodigious rose fraternity in France during the first forty years of this century, though men like Frances Dubreuil, Charles and Antoine Meilland and others all made significant contributions to Hybrid Tea roses. They all knew one another and, no doubt, had their disagreements, but like rose people the world over each respected the other's work and they were the greatest of friends. Even marriages between families ensued from time to time.

To select one family of French rose growers and breeders from the twentieth century is almost as unfair as choosing a raiser from the nineteenth century and informing the world that he was the best. I would do no injustice in isolating the Meillands for special mention, however, for while there may have been elements of good fortune involved in the raising of 'Peace', there was no such luck in the way they used the wealth this one rose created.

'Peace', without doubt, is the finest Hybrid Tea ever raised and it will remain a standard variety for ever. Roses have never made anyone wealthy, they are a vocation and few vocations make men rich – except in spirit. Those rose growers I know who have become rich have done so by other means than in the pursuit of their profession. Having said this, had Antoine Meilland and his son Francis thought this way in late 1945 they would never have invested the proceeds of 'Peace' in more land, more greenhouses and more staff to breed yet more roses. We must be grateful for 'Peace' and thankful for their investments. Without either, the modern roses would be the poorer. In their time, they also gave us such beautiful Hybrid Teas as 'Michèle Meilland' (1945), 'Grandmère Jenny' (1950), 'Charles Mallerin' (1951) and 'Bettina' (1953), not to mention the long-stemmed 'Baccara' (1954), a red florist's rose which has saved more marriages than all the guidance counsellors of the world put together.

Sadly, Francis died prematurely in 1958 but in his short life had been the driving force behind the building of the biggest and probably the best rose-breeding establishment in the world at Cap d'Antibes. The business is now in the capable hands of the third-generation Meilland, Alain, who introduced 'Papa Meilland', a beautiful dark red, in honour of his grandfather in 1963 and 'Sonia' ('Sweet Promise'), named after his daughter in 1974. The Meilland name will crop up often in these pages, for not only have they created some excellent Hybrid Teas but they have also been world leaders in several other types of roses.

'Peace', from Meillands of France, remains unrivalled among Hybrid Teas

'Angèle Pernet', produced by the redoubtable Joseph Pernet-Ducher in 1924

'Michèle Meilland', a fine Hybrid Tea from the raiser of 'Peace'

'Sonia', also known as 'Sweet Promise' and a good florist's rose, and *right:* 'Crimson Glory', raised in West Germany by Wilhelm Kordes

Twice this century, Germany and the rest of the world have had their differences, but leaving political history aside the world owes many good things to the industriousness and originality of the German race; roses are no exception. German rosarians were not particularly active in the early stages of the development of the rose, and although men like Peter Lambert, who bred the famous 'Frau Karl Druschki', were hybridizing before 1900, it was not until after the First World War that German breeders stamped their mark and began to influence the pedigree of the modern rose. The first of these was Wilhelm Kordes. His work spanned a wide range of types and, in his time, he introduced some very important roses indeed. He is best known for his hardy, shrubby varieties developed from *Rosa kordesii* and for his foundation work in extending the colour range of modern roses through 'Independence' (1951), a rose I could never really take to but whose issue brought forth a multitude of vivid flame and orange colours.

My bias towards Wilhelm Kordes as the world's greatest hybridizer is well substantiated by the roses to his credit, but as a young apprentice, before I had even heard of him, I knew that the raiser of 'Crimson Glory' had to be someone special. Not only was I first taught to cut roses for shows among rows and rows of this variety, but I was also almost intoxicated by its perfume while being shown how to arrange my first-ever bowl of roses at a flower show. Each bloom had to be wired to support a very weak neck, but the raiser himself could not have been more proud of the result. 'Crimson Glory' had been introduced in 1935 and remained popular as the best red until superseded in the 1950s by one of its descendants, 'Ena Harkness'. Floppiness of bloom had been the recurring habit of most red Hybrid Teas, and indeed of Hybrid Perpetuals, since the days of 'Général Jacqueminot', but by 1950 Kordes had solved the problem with 'Karl Herbst' and later in 1964, his retirement year, with the even better 'Ernest H. Morse'. In between those two in 1957 had come the superb 'Perfecta', a lovely mixture of pinks and cream. Wilhelm died in 1976, leaving a wealth of unique rose progeny for his son Reimer to continue the tradition of the Kordes line with excellent Hybrid Teas such as 'Colour Wonder' (1964) and 'Congratulations' (1978).

Not far from Kordes' establishment another German breeder was busy pollinating, one Mathias Tantau, contemporary of Wilhelm and blessed with many of the same attributes. Tantau's early work was largely with Polyanthas and Hybrid Polyanthas, and although he introduced a few Hybrid Teas between the wars, none became very well known. It was not until his son, also Mathias, got to work that quality Hybrid Teas started to emerge from the Tantau nurseries. The first of these was 'Prima Ballerina' in 1957, then in rapid succession such eminent roses as 'Super Star' ('Tropicana', 1960), 'Blue Moon' (1964), 'Whisky Mac' (1967) and 'Duke of Windsor' (1969). Need I say more, for these roses speak for themselves? His latest rose, the excellent white 'Polar Star', was voted 'Rose of the Year' by British nurserymen in 1985.

The agents for all the Tantau roses in Britain during the 1960s were Wheatcrofts of Nottingham, so they were assured of a rousing introduction. There was no better showman than the flamboyant Harry Wheatcroft, whose personality alone sold millions of roses. Harry attracted publicity wherever he went and succeeded in becoming a household name synonymous with roses.

Sheer weight of numbers prohibits mention of all but a few of the great Hybrid Teas raised during this century, and I have given no more than a cursory glance at the work of some of the people behind them, but it would be wrong to assume that only those so far mentioned have created the world's best and wrong also to ignore altogether other parts of the world. Modern roses would be much the poorer without significant contributions from such men as Pedro Dot of Spain with 'Condesa de Sastago' (1932) and 'Angels Mateu' (1934), Louis Lens of Belgium with, among others, 'Pascali' (1963), Verschuren of Holland who gave us the beautiful and well-loved 'Etoile de Hollande' in 1919 and Jan Spek, also of Holland, with 'Spek's Yellow' ('Golden Sceptre', 1948). For some years the Japanese have been working with roses and although their Hybrid Teas are seldom seen in our Western gardens, this is not through lack of fine varieties but simply, I think, that we have many good ones of our own. I could go on, for wherever roses grow the Hybrid Tea is revered and breeders, both famous and unknown, will forever continue to hone its perfection.

Population density and climatic differences influence where roses are bred as well as the distribution of new varieties. Parts of Australia, for example, have an ideal climate for hybridizing. I know some first-class rosarians and nurserymen there, but it is not surprising that in such a large country with a relatively small market they have never considered breeding roses to be a viable proposition – although I can think of no better place for someone to start.

Looking back over those so far mentioned, my own contribution to Hybrid Teas is insignificant. My first was 'Pinta' in 1973, a shapely, smallish-flowered creamy-white with Sweetbriar perfume. It came as a big surprise since, at the time, I was seeking a red. 'Royal Smile' was introduced in 1980,

a blush-white, also with a very strong scent. Over recent winters this rose has not proved as hardy as I would like, but it is beautiful and does well in warmer climates. I declare, somewhat immodestly, 'Anna Pavlova' (1981) to be my favourite Hybrid Tea, even if it is my own. Knowing this rose was shy in producing flowers, I had left it growing in my trial beds for several years, unintroduced, never having the heart to cast it aside. It was spotted one day by my good friend Keith Money, who was then working on his biography of Pavlova. Keith fell for the rose, and, by sheer persistence over several

'Duke of Windsor', a highly scented Hybrid Tea from the West German raiser Tantau

'Pinta', a Peter Beales rose, has the distinct scent of eglantine

months, persuaded me to name it 'Anna Pavlova'. As Keith had christened the rose, I asked him to write a piece about it in our catalogue. He wrote:

> There is a real period charm about the full, slightly frilled petals with their shades of face-powder pink, all set off with the darkest possible leaves, strangely circular. It is quite haunting: the nearest I can get to describing it would be to imagine a picnic of fresh fruit salad with Turkish Delight and served under a flowering May tree.

I know that without his persistence this rose would still be unnamed.

Here, in England, it never produces any great quantity of flowers but to my incredulity and delight a telegram fell on my desk one day in 1985 saying that 'Anna Pavlova' had been awarded a silver medal by the judges at the Genoa Rose Trials in Italy, primarily for freedom of flower. Despite this award it was not until I saw her in full flush at Deane Ross's nursery in southern Australia that it dawned on me that this lady dances much better in warmer climates than she does in chilly Norfolk.

A beautiful soft blush-pink, 'Anna Pavlova' is outstandingly perfumed

The Floribunda Roses

It is difficult to imagine a world without roses, but even with them it would be a much duller place without Floribundas, which are now taken for granted. Imagine our parks without them. Some Hybrid Teas, I suppose, could play their part and act as bedding plants, but few could emulate the summer-long colour and floriferousness of well-grown Floribundas.

The genesis and early development of the Cluster-Flowered rose have been briefly mentioned already and need not be repeated here, especially as I doubt whether those early raisers had any notion of just how far-reaching and significant their haphazard experiments would prove to be. Suffice to say that however little the preconception – from the moment that genes of *Rosa moschata* and *Rosa multiflora* were linked to those of *Rosa chinensis* – the progress of this type of rose was assured. What has evolved, given the curiosity of rose people, was inevitable, for no raiser, however committed to the cabbage-shaped rose, could resist crossing it with a Cluster-Flowered rose in the hope of getting even more, if smaller, cabbage-shaped roses together on the same plant.

The early Polypompons, as they were delightfully called, were rather awkwardly grouped together for they were a mixed bag; distinct in having

Rosa multiflora, one of the species that gave rise to Floribunda roses

clusters of flowers in one inflorescence, but diverse and varied in size, shape of bloom and habit of growth. It was, therefore, not until the early 1900s that enough uniformly distinct characteristics came forth from among them to form a splinter group, the Dwarf Polyanthas. I adore this little group of roses, or at least those still with us today. They have such cheerful dispositions, are very adaptable and never any trouble, except for occasional bouts of mildew for which I can readily forgive them. They enjoyed deserved popularity in the period between the wars when lots and lots were introduced.

Hardiness is an attribute of the Dwarf Polyanthas which is especially useful in northern Europe and Scandinavia where the winters are too cold for many Large-Flowered roses to flourish without mollycoddling. It was, therefore, appropriate and predictable that a Danish nurseryman should be the first to cross such roses with other types. His name was Dines Poulsen, one of a family of rose growers with a nursery at Kvistgarrd. He used as his seed parent a red Polyantha called 'Mme Norbert Levavasseur' and, for his first pollen parent, the rambler 'Dorothy Perkins'. The result was a rosy-pink which he called 'Ellen Poulsen'. This was shortish in growth after its Polyantha parent and cluster-flowered but not too different from the existing range of Polyanthas; nevertheless it was worthy of introduction and proved, as he suspected, very hardy. Dines Poulsen then produced a rose called 'Red Riding Hood' using the same seed parent but this time crossing

'Chinatown', a fine and very double Floribunda from the Danish raiser Poulsen

'Dusky Maiden', from Edward LeGrice, one of the earliest scented Floribundas

it with the Hybrid Tea 'Richmond'. This too proved very hardy, but unlike 'Ellen Poulsen', its half-sister, its habit of growth was much less like a Polyantha.

After this foundation work, Dines' brother, Svend, took responsibility for hybridizing and soon after, using the Dwarf Polyantha 'Orléans Rose' as 'mum' and the Hybrid Tea 'Red Star' as 'dad', raised two outstanding seedlings. These were introduced in 1924; one was 'Else Poulsen', a pink semi-double, and the other was 'Kirsten Poulsen', a red single. Each had largish flowers compared to the Polyanthas and was taller in growth; the flowers, however, like those of their seed parent, were produced in large clusters. They also continued flowering throughout the summer, whereas most of the Hybrid Teas of the day took a rest between their first flush in June/July and their second in September. It turned out – for genetic reasons that we need not go into here – that these exciting new roses were almost sterile and not easy to breed from, but persistence and patience paid off and more of a similar type followed from the Poulsen stable. The most famous is probably the lovely red 'Karen Poulsen' (1932). The Poulsen roses, as they became known, proved very popular and were soon widely grown throughout the world. Although not as well known as some of the others, 'Poulsen's Yellow' (1939) was of even greater significance, for it brought yellow into the colour range of the dwarf Cluster-Flowered roses for the first time. Talking of yellows, I rate the shrubby, well-foliated 'Chinatown' (1963) the best rose ever to come from the family Poulsen, this time from Svend's son Niels, who in the family tradition started to breed roses in the mid-1950s.

Nothing succeeds like success, and soon other breeders were following the 'Poulsen School' by working with roses of this kind. Obviously, when others started, such roses could hardly be classified as 'Poulsens'; so, after some debate, the powers that be grouped them together and reclassified them as Hybrid Polyanthas. They remained thus known for about two decades, but such was their advance and, for very good reasons relating to size of flower, improved colour range and growth habits that they were reclassified in the early 1950s as Floribundas. I well recall this change of name, for it was in 1951 that I first joined the firm of E. B. LeGrice as a new apprentice. Two other Peters were already working there and, on my first day, to help him differentiate when issuing orders, the foreman, cruelly and to my horror, decided that I should be known as 'Floribunda'. Fortunately, this name did not stick; otherwise, being a sensitive lad, I might have turned away from roses forever.

It turned out, however, that Floribundas were to play an important part in my career, for by then my boss, Edward LeGrice, had been breeding these roses with considerable success for several years. 'Dainty Maid', a lovely single pink, was his first in 1940 with 'Dusky Maiden', of which he was particularly proud, following in 1947. A pride not misplaced, for not only is 'Dusky', as he called it, a beautiful rose but it is also scented, proof that the elusive attribute of fragrance would eventually come to Floribundas.

Above: 'Ripples', a variety of notable colour, like many LeGrice roses
Right: 'Allgold', Edward LeGrice's masterpiece and a rose ahead of its time

Edward Burton LeGrice was a fine man and I was privileged to spend some of the most rewarding days of my life fetching and carrying for him as he lovingly hybridized his roses, all the time quietly talking and unselfishly imparting to my eager ear what I now know to be his own, unique knowledge of roses.

After two seasons of writing the labels for each cross he made, I was taught to emasculate the flowers of his seed parents for him. He would give me a list at the beginning of each day of all those he wanted to hybridize and, a little later, humming a hymn tune, would apply the pollen to make carefully thought-out crosses. It was while I was his label boy in the early 1950s that he laid the foundations for some of the unusually coloured roses that he raised and introduced from the 1950s to the early '70s. To get some of these colours, he used, as I can confirm from the bitter experience of having to spell the awkward long names, the whole range of purple and dark red Gallicas, especially those that were generous with their pollen, such as 'Tuscany Superb' from which came some very strangely coloured seedlings and, indeed, some very beautiful ones, for example 'Lilac Charm' (1952), 'News' (1968) and 'Ripples' (1971).

Only a few plants of his masterpiece, 'Allgold', were growing at the North Walsham nursery when I arrived. It had flowered for the first time as a seedling two years before. He knew then that, if the rose stood up to its proving trials, it would be a winner and I recall the many hours I spent cutting budwood of this variety for distribution around the world. 'Allgold' was a few years ahead of its time. It is a sad irony that the man who first mooted the idea of plant breeders' rights in Britain received such small financial returns for his work in producing the first deep yellow Floribunda. I have always felt very proud of 'Allgold', partly I suppose because of the very small part I played in its beginnings, but more, I hope, because it is an ever-present memorial to a man who taught me a lot about life and shared with me his deep love of roses. In 1961 my wife Joan, to my great delight, chose buds of 'Allgold' for her wedding bouquet. One year after 'Allgold's' introduction in 1956 I was compelled to leave LeGrice's establishment for compulsory National Service. At the end of my two years as a soldier I could have gone back, but instead, inspired by Edward LeGrice, I chose to go it alone. Had I returned to work for him, I know I would have learned much more about roses than I will ever know now. 'Father', as he was affectionately known by his staff, died in 1977, leaving my world and the world of many others the poorer for his loss, but the world as a whole much the richer for his roses.

Another memory of my days at North Walsham is of the frequent visits Edward LeGrice received from eminent rose people from around the world. One such person was a big man from the United States named Eugene Boerner, hybridizer for Jackson & Perkins. He, too, worked with Floribundas with considerable success. Jackson & Perkins had large investments in the breeding of roses and, while anyone with limited resources can cross two roses, there is no doubt that the more crosses one can make the greater the likelihood of breeding a winner. If this sounds cynical it is not meant to sound that way, for without the extensive breeding programme of Eugene Boerner and Jackson & Perkins the world would never have enjoyed such superb Floribundas as 'Goldilocks' (1945), 'Lavender Pinocchio' (1948), 'Fashion' and 'Masquerade' (1949), 'Ma Perkins' (1952) and 'Jiminy Cricket' (1954).

Jackson & Perkins led the way, but some very good Floribundas came from other American breeders during the 1950s and '60s. Herbert Swim raised the excellent and colourful 'Circus' (1956) and followed this with, among others, a rose that must rate as the best pink Floribunda ever raised, 'Pink Parfait' (1960). Both were introduced by the Armstrong Nursery, California.

Gordon Von Abrams gave us the lovely 'Golden Slippers' through Peterson & Dering in 1961. One of the best Cluster-Flowered roses ever to be raised came from Dr E. Lammerts of California in 1954. 'Queen Elizabeth' (strictly, 'The Queen Elizabeth Rose') was introduced to Britain by Harry Wheatcroft and immediately took the country by storm. In the United States it is classified as a Grandiflora, a term used there to separate the large-flowered, taller cluster roses from the general run of short varieties. This classification has never been accepted in Britain because its botanical connotations are thought to be misleading, so, although obviously different

'Ma Perkins', raised in the United States by Eugene Boerner for Jackson & Perkins

from most Floribundas, it nevertheless comes into that category here. Endowed with healthy foliage and blooms of superb quality, impervious to all weather and good for cutting, such a rose had to win many friends. Its usage was not immediately obvious, for it was too tall for bedding and too straight and upright for general use as a shrub. Its introduction coincided with a vogue for ornamental hedging, however, and it soon found its true niche as one of the best hedging roses ever introduced and millions have been sold for this purpose worldwide. From time to time it has produced the occasional sport and the white form, especially, is excellent. The pale yellow form is also quite good, but, advantageously at times, seems to be slightly less vigorous (although, considering the number of 'Queen Elizabeth' roses produced since 1954, it is possible that similar sports could have occurred at different times in other places, and such clones could well be of superior vigour).

In order to link the two Floribunda specialists, LeGrice and Boerner, I digressed geographically to America. To return to Britain for a while, men other than LeGrice have bred some outstanding Floribundas. The notable amateur, Albert Norman, gave us the prickly but stalwart 'Frensham' in 1946. He also bred 'Red Dandy' (1959), a rose I always liked but which, sadly, seems now to have disappeared forever. Interestingly, all Norman's red roses that I know of came directly or indirectly from the famous Kordes Hybrid Tea 'Crimson Glory'. Less prodigious in output than some modern breeders but nonetheless successful was Herbert Robinson, who raised,

'Dearest', a scented Floribunda from Dicksons of Northern Ireland and *right:* 'Frensham', by the amateur raiser Albert Norman

among other good varieties, a rose called 'Highlight' from Kordes' 'Independence' in 1957. 'Highlight' never really caught on but deserves a mention for its role as pollen parent to McGredy's famous 'Elizabeth of Glamis'.

In 1967 Jack Harkness sent out his first Floribunda, 'Escapade'. Perhaps because of my preference for quiet colours I consider 'Escapade' and the highly scented 'Margaret Merril' (1977) to be the best of his cluster-flowered varieties. The aptly named 'Yesterday' (1974) is also very good but is usually classified as a shrub. Of his brighter colours, 'Mountbatten' (1982), also better classified as a shrub, and 'Amber Queen' (1984) are two fine roses that are obviously here to stay.

Alec Cocker's time was not totally taken up with Hybrid Teas. Some very good Floribundas have come from his work, the best known of which are probably 'Anne Cocker' (1970) and 'Glenfiddich' (1976). Another very good Floribunda that I rate highly is 'English Miss' (1977) from Cants of Colchester.

Before the Second World War Dicksons of Northern Ireland had built their reputation on Hybrid Teas, but after it was over they did not take long to get back into the swing of things with some notable Floribundas. Their first ones were two richly coloured roses, 'Shepherd's Delight' (1956) and 'Dickson's Flame' (1958), followed soon after by the outstanding 'Dearest' (1960). Of the 135 Floribundas listed in the Royal National Rose Society's current Rose Directory, no less then seventeen are accredited to Pat Dickson. They include such well-known varieties as 'Scarlet Queen Elizabeth' (1963) and 'Sea Pearl' (1964). Dickson's roses have been chosen as 'Rose of the Year' by the British Rose Trades Association on three occasions in the 1980s: 'Beautiful Britain' in 1983, 'Gentle Touch' in 1986 and 'Sweet Magic' in 1988, although the last two fall more readily into the newly evolved group of 'Patio' roses. That other famous Ulsterman, Sam McGredy, has twenty-four Floribundas to his credit in the RNRS Directory. The quiet 'Chanelle' is one of his best, another is the louder and robust

Produced by Sam McGredy, 'Elizabeth of Glamis' has superbly formed flowers

'Escapade', one of the first Floribundas from Harkness, and *right:* the quiet 'Chanelle', by McGredy

'Orangeade' (both 1959). His best known is probably 'Elizabeth of Glamis', named for Her Majesty Queen Elizabeth The Queen Mother in 1964, a beautiful rose which does well when mild winters allow it to make some older wood. The first of his 'hand-painted' roses, the well-named 'Picasso' (1971), was introduced by McGredy just before he moved to New Zealand. His breeding stock obviously did not suffer from the move and a steady flow of worthy varieties has been raised by him, including 'Old Master' (1974) and 'Sue Lawley' (1980).

After their initial work with the Polypompons and Polyanthas, and a little flurry of activity at the turn of the century with varieties such as Guillot's beautiful 'Irène Watts' (1896) and Turbat's 'Yvonne Rabier' in 1910, nothing of any real significance came from French breeders until after the Second World War. Since then, however, they have certainly not been idle, and as with Hybrid Teas, it has been the family Meilland who have led the way. There can be nothing more frustrating to any inventor than ownership of a product which does not sell. So with plant patent rights available in most countries of the world and Floribundas being used extensively for mass planting by local authorities, Meillands set about raising and selling these roses in a big way. They set up a worldwide network of agents and provided them not only with high-quality publicity and promotional material but also with a succession of high-quality new varieties to sell. Meillands are now concentrating more and more on raising fashionable ground-cover roses, but of the Floribundas they have introduced over the years I particularly admire 'Zambra' (1961), 'Frenzy' (1970) and 'Poppy Flash' ('Rusticana', 1971). Another very beautiful French rose I like, not from Meilland but from Delbard-Chabert, is 'Centenaire de Lourdes' (1958). It is a seedling from 'Frau Karl Druschki' but, sadly, it has inherited none of its parent's hardiness.

'Picasso', the first of Sam McGredy's 'hand-painted' roses

De Ruiters of Holland introduced quite a number of Dwarf Polyanthas during the early part of this century and followed these much later with some very good Floribundas. Of their roses I am particularly fond of the beautifully shaped 'Rosemary Rose' (1954). I also like 'Sweet Repose' ('The Optimist', 1955), but this is seldom seen today. Of de Ruiter's roses 'Orange Sensation' (1961) is probably the best known and has stood the test of time with distinction. Another first-class rose from Holland which has lasted well is 'Mevrouw Nathalie Nypels' (1919); it was raised by Leenders and is now better known simply as 'Nathalie Nypels'. A German named Geduldig raised the beautiful, free-flowering 'Grüss an Aachen' in 1909, way ahead of its time. Originally it was classified as a Polypompon but it fits in happily with the modern Floribundas.

With Denmark just across the border, Wilhelm Kordes was well aware of the work of the Poulsens of the 1920s and '30s, so anything they could do he knew he could do too, and probably better – not that he was a pirate; rose breeders the world over use the results of one another's ideas. After all, Poulsen himself had had to make use of other breeders' roses to start his own initial strains. Even before the war, Kordes had raised one or two very good Hybrid Polyanthas and one in particular, 'Rosenelfe' (1939), clearly indicated the way ahead. It had been bred from 'Else Poulsen', which, considering that it was not very fertile, was an achievement in itself. Its pollen

'Centenaire de Lourdes' from Delbard-Chabert and *right:* 'Orange Triumph', an early Kordes Floribunda

Raised by Leenders of Holland, 'Nathalie Nypels' has remained popular for nearly sixty years

parent was a colourful, fully double, lesser-known McGredy Hybrid Tea called 'Sir Basil McFarland' and with it Kordes proved that the petal numbers of the Hybrid Polyanthas could be increased without loss of the larger flower clusters. His other outstanding introductions were 'Pinocchio' (1940) with its mixed ancestry of Hybrid Musk, Hybrid Tea and Dwarf Polyantha – later to prove invaluable in the progeny of many a future Floribunda – and 'Orange Triumph' (1937), more red than orange but with an unrivalled constitution and the longevity of an oak.

The rebuilding of Germany after the Second World War brought roses for landscaping into much demand. With a great deal of work already done and lots of breeding stock available, Kordes was thus well placed to help satisfy a craving for Floribundas which were tailor-made for colouring the new industrial and commercial landscape of Germany, not to mention the gardens, parks and open spaces that were part of the scheme of things there. 'Korona' (1955) was just one exciting, colourful Floribunda that seemed to symbolize the bright new future ahead for its raiser and its Fatherland. When Reimer Kordes took over from his father in 1956 he excelled in Floribundas, with 'Iceberg' (1958), surely the best of its type ever introduced, followed by 'Lilli Marlene' (1958) and 'Honeymoon' (1960), 'Marlena' (1964) and his most recent, the blood-red 'The Times Rose' (1984). I find this rose a little disappointing and still prefer 'Lilli Marlene'.

With so many successful Hybrid Teas coming out of their nurseries one wonders how the two Mathias Tantaus managed to find time for anything else. Judging by the conspicuous succession of Floribundas created by them since the late 1940s, however, they fully realized that time working with such roses was time well spent. Having said this, some Hybrid Teas and Floribundas are now so interbred that it is almost pot luck as to what comes forth when crossing them with one another.

Like Kordes, Mathias Tantau the first was well aware of Poulsen's work in Denmark; although without any conspicuous success, he had been dabbling in Floribundas since the 1920s and '30s. This continued into the '40s for, ironically, Germans were not forced by government decree to stop breeding roses as the British were. It was Tantau's use of two Kordes roses, 'Rosenelfe' and 'Eva', that gave him his first big break with Floribundas. He crossed a seedling from these two with a red rose of his own breeding called 'Heros' which had the famous Dutch rose 'Etoile de Hollande' as one of its parents. The result in 1951 was a rose he called 'Garnette'. Together with its several sports and close hybrids, it is still to this day a major florist's rose throughout the world on account of its hard-wearing and long-lasting qualities. I may be wrong, but I cannot really believe that in making such a cross Tantau was actually aiming for a forcing rose. With foresight or not, he must have been fortunate to observe its qualities while it was growing under glass, for this rose is hardly worth a second glance when grown out of doors. Later, in 1971, Mathias Tantau the younger introduced another successful forcing rose, the orange 'Belinda'. From the early 1950s onwards this firm

'Korona', a bright Floribunda from the Kordes stable

'Paprika', a healthy, colourful variety from Tantau of West Germany

The finely scented 'Norwich Union', the second Peter Beales Floribunda

bred and introduced a succession of successful Floribundas. I well remember the excellent 'Red Favourite' (1954), which seems to be lost now, and
'Anna Wheatcroft' (1958), a lovely, bright salmon single which I used without much success in my own first attempts at breeding, although it did yield
for me a pleasing little salmon rose, the first I ever introduced, called 'Penelope Plummer' (1970), which never caught on as I had dreamed but is still
cherished by me as my first. Other excellent Floribundas from the Tantau
stable are the vigorous 'Paprika' (1958) and two very useful shorter roses,
'Tip Top' (1963) and 'Topsi' (1971).

    Well aware as I am that my achievements so far as a rose breeder will
never put me anywhere but near the bottom of any league table of breeders,
I hesitantly mention my own small contributions to the vast array of
Floribundas available today. Now and then, sandwiched in between the pre-
occupation of building a collection of historical and classical roses, running
a business and, I suppose, in deference to my learning the trade with
Edward LeGrice, I have, from time to time, dabbled in the fascinating, time-
consuming pastime of hybridizing. I still do occasionally, but now as tutor
to my children, who – who knows? – may one day do better than Dad. We
have abandoned any search for Floribundas or indeed Hybrid Teas to
explore other avenues, but in days now past I concentrated especially on the
cluster-flowered varieties.

I confess that 'Penelope Plummer' should never have been introduced. I had tested it well, I thought, but it developed a mild proneness to black spot which had not been noticed in its trials. Not having been in business long, I suppose I was anxious to make my mark. I shudder now at my naivety for I named it after the then reigning Miss World, thinking that such a name would bring stardom to the rose and recognition to its breeder. Sadly, no, the most I got was a picture of Miss World and myself together in our local weekly newspaper and a ragging from my friends.

The launch in 1975 of my next Floribunda was stage-managed much more efficiently, for it was sponsored by the insurance company Norwich Union. Colin Page, the company's Publicity Manager, and his colleagues were very good to me, for I was hard up at the time and without their sponsorship it would not have been easy to carry on in business, let alone continue the expensive luxury of breeding roses. For the rose this may not have been quite so good, for excellent and well-intentioned though the company was, its name did not lend itself well to a rose. 'Norwich Union' is an excellent, short-growing yellow bedding rose with a good scent. It has never been widely grown in Britain and – except for Australia and New Zealand, where I understand it is quite popular – is probably unheard of elsewhere. Other Floribundas of mine are 'Norwich Castle' (1979), which has been likened to the colour of best bitter beer, and the tall 'Everest Double Fragrance' (1979). This rose has one of the strongest scents of any

'Norwich Castle' is a free-flowering rose of upright growth

The shapely 'Lady Romsey' from Peter Beales

Floribunda I know though its colour, which changes from coral to soft blush-pink as it ages, does not endear it to some but pleases me enormously. My latest, 'Lady Romsey' (1985), is a short creamy-white with a pink blush and fine dark green foliage. I like this little rose, but as with all roses others unbiased will decide its destiny.

Shrub Roses and Procumbents

Although differences in dimension are built into most plant families, no other has such wide diversity of size as that of genus *Rosa*. By providing variation within a species, nature dictates just how far man can go in capturing advantage from any given attribute. As the majority of species within the genus are tallish and shrubby and the majority of colourful hybrids are short and shrubby, there can be no more lucrative area for a hybridizer to explore in order, perhaps, to break new ground than among the middle size-ranges; that is to say shrub roses, broad or tall or both. Of course, the laws of heredity are such that dominance and recessive factors will frequently intervene, but this only adds variety and interest to the job and will keep the hybridizer's feet firmly on the greenhouse floor.

Present-day landscaping trends and those for the foreseeable future demand the use of easily maintained shrubby plants. No other group or family of plants can possibly fulfil this role more successfully than roses – more specifically, shrub roses – while, at the same time, providing a succession of flowers. Several modern rose breeders saw this trend long before me and already there is a wide range of roses for this purpose. I suspect several more exciting new ones are on the way.

As with some other groups, the early development of hybrid shrub roses was more by chance than design, so I will not dwell on those from the nineteenth century except to say that before the introduction of the Tea–Scented and Chinese hybrids from the East, most of the European and Middle Eastern hybrids were, by today's criteria, shrub roses. There were one or two exceptions, such as the Dwarf Centifolias for example, but by and large the old Centifolia Damasks and Albas were tall, lax and shrubby. The Gallicas, generally speaking, were shorter but still could only be classified as shrubs in today's sense.

How is a shrub rose defined? These days, it is more a case of definition by usage rather than by description for, of course, all roses are shrubs; some of the larger ones, admittedly, could be called trees but most of us think of trees, even small trees, as being much bigger than roses. In the past – and even now from time to time – roses were regularly referred to as trees. This is a hark back to the days when the average garden variety was far bigger than it is today. My own definition is very much in usage terms: bush roses are those that should not normally reach more than 4 ft (1.2 m) high when fully grown and which, by their tidy habit of growth, are generally used for bedding, group planting or as border plants. Such roses invariably have a long flowering season. Shrub roses are those that are as a rule taller than 4 ft (1.2 m) when mature and which can be used individually for specimen planting or grown as shrubs in a shrubbery. Shrubs can flower once, can repeat or be continuous. By virtue of a preference for light pruning, most of the Bourbons and Hybrid Perpetuals from the last century are best termed shrub roses. Although generally much shorter, the Portlands are seldom used for bedding purposes either and they too should be considered shrubs.

Most rose breeders of this century have concentrated on working with Hybrid Teas and Floribundas. Although several good shrubs emerged from their work from time to time, any deliberate and planned breeding has been left to no more than a handful of dedicated men. One such man was Lord Penzance, who worked with Sweetbriars and bred no less than sixteen of them in the 1890s, but tempted though I am to discuss these I will move straight on to those who have worked with shrub roses this century. The first and perhaps most important was Joseph Pemberton, a clergyman turned nurseryman, who, by the time he introduced his first roses in 1913, was sixty-one years of age and well respected as an authority on his subject,

Shrub roses make fine subjects when mixed together in a border

acknowledged by the award of the first Dean Hole medal for outstanding service to the rose and his election to the high office of President of the National Rose Society. He was also a keen exhibitor at rose shows, so it is somewhat surprising that he chose to work with shrub roses when he started hybridizing and not the fashionable Hybrid Teas with which he was so accustomed to winning many prizes. We should be very grateful that he chose what was then a rather unorthodox programme of breeding, for it brought forth not just many good shrub roses but a complete, unique new group, the Hybrid Musks.

It was obvious from the start that Pemberton's roses were different, but for want of another classification they were introduced to begin with as Hybrid Teas. His first roses came on the market in 1913; they were 'Moonlight' with semi-double white flowers and 'Danaë' with smallish flowers of soft primrose-yellow. Both had flowers borne in clusters on long branches from shrubby plants. What is more, they both flowered throughout the summer and were scented. To create these and many of his subsequent introductions, Pemberton used a bushy, long-stemmed cluster rose called 'Trier', bred and introduced by Lambert of Germany in 1904. He could see at a glance that the habits of this variety were not too far removed from the Polyanthas, although much taller. He probably knew that 'Trier' was a seedling from a French rose called 'Aglaia', a climbing Polyantha of 1896, the parents of which were *Rosa multiflora* and 'Rêve d'Or', a Noisette from as far back as 1869. There is no reason to doubt this pedigree, for at certain times of the year considerable family resemblances, especially in foliage, can be seen between great-grandparent 'Rêve d'Or' and some of Pemberton's Musks. Obviously, too, it was from this lineage that his roses inherited their musk-like scent. Whoever christened Pemberton's roses could well have called them Hybrid Multifloras, but since they and their scent can be traced directly back through the Noisettes to *Rosa moschata*, Hybrid Musks is quite a suitable and appropriate collective name. Most of the shrub roses to come from the Pemberton stud between 1913 and his death in 1926 still adorn our gardens unsurpassed today. In chronological order, the best are 'Pax' (1918), 'Prosperity' (1919), 'Vanity' (1920), much taller and more angular in growth than the rest, 'Francesca' (1922), 'Penelope' (1924) and the versatile 'Cornelia' (1925). Some authorities attribute 'Buff Beauty', introduced thirteen years after his death, to Pemberton. I have faded recollections of a conversation with Edward LeGrice about this rose; it took place many years ago and had I realized its importance I would have listened more closely. I feel sure it affirmed Pemberton as the raiser of 'Buff Beauty', but I cannot be certain. LeGrice, of course, would have known Pemberton well.

After Pemberton's death, one of his gardeners by the name of J. A. Bentall started growing and breeding roses on his own accord, and very successfully, for in 1932 he introduced 'The Fairy' and five years later, in 1937, 'Ballerina'. Without wishing to take anything from Bentall's achievements, it

'Danaë', introduced by Joseph Pemberton in 1913

'Francesca', one of the Pemberton roses that eventually came to be known as the Hybrid Musks

'Vanity' is a vigorous Hybrid Musk from Pemberton

would seem that Joseph Pemberton had been not just an accomplished rose breeder but also a very good tutor.

The other Briton to work primarily with shrub roses is David Austin, but his work has all been done during the last thirty years. Nevertheless, the first of Austin's roses has made a real impact on the rose world. It is the tall, sprawly, almost climbing rose called 'Constance Spry' (1961), the first rose raised in modern times with enough charm, personality and fragrance to compete on almost level terms with the old classic roses from the past. But Austin was not satisfied. Although 'Constance Spry' showed him and, indeed, the rest of the world that a market existed for what might loosely be called reproduction roses, it flowers for only a short season and therefore is of limited appeal. After this rose, he set about a planned programme of crossing and recrossing old roses such as Damasks and Gallicas with modern Hybrid Teas and Floribundas. Progress was slow at first, but gradually he realized that his theories were beginning to yield results. Although his next rose, 'Chianti' (1967), was not remontant, most of those that followed in steadily increasing numbers were, if not fully continuous, certainly repeat-flowering. He calls his creations as a group 'New English Roses' and there is little doubt that many are here to stay. Most are scented and of accommodating size, hence their popularity for smaller gardens where long flowering is an important factor. Of those introduced in the 1970s, I very

'The Fairy', bred by J. A. Bentall who worked with Joseph Pemberton for many years

'Constance Spry', the first modern rose that could compete with the old classic roses, has myrrh-scented blooms much like the tall 'Charles Austin' (1973) and 'Chaucer' (1970). So many have been produced in the 1980s that it is quite impossible for me to pass judgement on the merits of all of them. Two in particular, however, 'Mary Rose' and 'Graham Thomas', both brought out in 1983, have taken my eye as being both beautiful and healthy; and, coming right up to date, 'William Shakespeare' (1987) promises well. Providing he does not overcrowd the market with too many of these roses they have a big future, and Austin should get the recognition he deserves for his work.

A few very good shrub roses have come from other British breeders this century. Two of real merit and note are the bright scarlet 'Geranium' (1938), a *Rosa moyesii* seedling from the Royal Horticultural Society, Wisley Gardens, and 'Helen Knight' (1964), a *Rosa ecae* seedling from Frank Knight of the same gardens. Another interesting *Rosa ecae* hybrid is 'Golden Chersonese' (1967), raised by E. F. Allen; both are spring-flowering, deep yellow singles. Another good yellow single of this type is 'Cantabrigiensis' which came forth as a chance seedling, probably from *Rosa hugonis*, at Cambridge University Botanic Gardens, most likely in 1931. Over the past ten years or so, several British breeders have had a measure of success with the introduction of some very useful Procumbent roses. Jack Harkness, for example, has bred a number from 'The Fairy'; they have rather pretty names like 'Fairyland' (1980) and 'Fairy Damsel' (1981). An out of the ordinary, offbeat colour from Harkness is the bluish-maroon Procumbent 'Cardinal Hume' (1984).

'Graham Thomas', a fine, vigorous, scented modern shrub from David Austin

'Golden Chersonese', a *Rosa ecae* hybrid, flowers profusely early in the season

The founders of the Floribunda roses, Poulsens of Denmark, have also been working on Procumbent varieties in recent years. Notable among their newer introductions are 'Pink Bells', 'Red Bells' and 'White Bells', all in 1983 and all ground-hugging varieties with healthy, dense foliage. Pat Dickson has produced, among others, a very good yellow spreader called 'Tall Story' (1984) which is, apparently, excellent for cutting. Using *Rosa wichuraiana* as a parent, Dennison Morey of the United States has added to the Procumbents with 'Temple Bells' (1971), sometimes described as a climbing Miniature. Contributions to shrub roses from Meillands of France have been more recent, most notably their introduction of some very good spreaders, outstanding among which are 'Bonica '82' (1981), 'Swany' (1978) and 'Fiona' (1982).

Not many shrub roses have come to Europe from across the Atlantic. Of those that have, only a few are widely grown. Excellent among them is the *Rosa pimpinellifolia* hybrid 'Golden Wings' (1956) from Roy Shepherd which has enjoyed ever-increasing popularity over the years. One I like is 'Lafter' (1948), this time from Brownell, which should be much more widely grown. Another shrub rose from the United States which ought to get more attention is 'Eos' (1950) from Ruys. A sumptuous rose which cannot decide whether or not to be a climber but nevertheless makes an excellent shrub is 'Aloha' (1949) from Boerner. A hybrid Rugosa rose from Canada, 'Agnes',

Top left: 'Bonica '82', a Procumbent rose from
Meillands of France
Bottom left: Rosa stellata mirifica, the 'Sacramento
Rose', originated in Mexico
Top right: 'Max Graf', brought to Europe from
North America
Bottom right: 'Golden Wings', an outstanding hybrid
of *Rosa pimpinellifolia*

is exceptionally hardy; it was raised in 1900 but not introduced until 1922. It
is one of the few yellow Rugosas and for this reason will always be in
demand. Two other Canadian varieties that do well in Britain are 'Eddie's
Crimson' (1956) and 'Eddie's Jewel' (1962). Both are hybrids of *Rosa moyesii*.

There can be no doubt that one of the most important roses ever sent to
Europe from America is the trailing shrub 'Max Graf' (1919), discovered
and named by James H. Bowditch of Connecticut. As it was a foundling
some disagreement initially arose over its parentage, but now it is generally
accepted to be a cross between *Rosa wichuraiana* and *Rosa rugosa* or the other
way around, perhaps. 'Max Graf' seldom sets any seed, but there could be
no better place for a pod to form than in Germany under the eyes of Herr
Wilhelm Kordes. Lesser rosemen might have raised their eyebrows at such a
sight but no more than that. Kordes, of course, raised the seed and produced a new species which was later named *Rosa kordesii*. The flowers of his
new species were of no great significance; its main attribute was hardiness
and again a less interested person might have ignored it as a fluke – but not

Above: Rose kordesii, a recent species bred by Kordes of West Germany from 'Max Graf', has proved valuable for its hardy offspring. *Below:* 'Fritz Nobis', a healthy, vigorous shrub

Wilhelm. He found it to be quite fertile and eventually bred some very hardy and useful climbing roses from it. In pursuit of hardiness for German winters, other interesting lines of breeding were followed by Kordes which threw up some very good shrub roses: 'Fritz Nobis' (1940), for example, came from the hybrid Sweetbriar 'Magnifica'; his 'Spring' or 'Frühling' roses came from *Rosa pimpinellifolia* and 'Scarlet Fire' ('Scharlachglut') from *Rosa gallica*. Reimer Kordes has recently set to work developing some ground-cover roses, of which two in particular, 'Grouse' and 'Partridge' (1984), are excellent. Two other shrub roses of note from Germany are Peter Lambert's Rugosa 'Schneezwerg' (1912) and 'Mozart' (1937), a 'Ballerina'-like rose that deserves to be better known.

A shrub rose that cannot go unmentioned is 'Nevada' (1927) from Pedro Dot of Spain. It makes a superb flowering shrub and is probably a *Rosa pimpinellifolia* hybrid. A pink form was discovered by Graham Thomas at Hillings Nurseries in 1959 and named 'Marguerite Hilling'. An omission so far is mention of the delightful 'Omar Khayyam', a Damask seedling from Edward Fitzgerald's grave in Suffolk, having been grown there from a seed collected from the great poet's tomb in Nashipur. The seed was sown in 1893 but the rose was not propagated and offered for sale until several years later.

The Japanese may not have made too many inroads into the ranks of Hybrid Teas and Floribundas west or, indeed, east of Tokyo, but the same cannot be said of their shrubby spreading varieties. A notable one is the pinkish-white 'Nozomi', a rose from Toru Onodera, an amateur breeder, which came to Britain in 1968 and is now seen almost everywhere where a dense, shrubby, ground-cover variety is called for; its many plum-coloured shoots and density of foliage compensate for its limited flowering season. Another densely foliated, shrubby spreader from Japan, this time with light green foliage, is 'Ferdy' (1984), raised by Suzuki. This too is non-recurrent.

Although most of nature's own roses found their way into our gardens in the last century, a few excellent species or near species have been discovered or raised during the past eighty years or so. These are too numerous to discuss in any great detail, but one or two must receive at least a small mention. *Rosa farreri persetosa*, for example – dubbed the 'Threepenny Bit Rose' – makes a fascinating and most useful shrub. It came from seeds sent from China by the plant-hunter Farrer in 1914. Another, *Rosa stellata mirifica* or the 'Sacramento Rose', is not easy to grow but well worth a try; it comes from northern Mexico and was introduced in 1916. One of the loveliest of species is *Rosa primula* or the 'Incense Rose', a medium-sized shrub with a large density of thorns; its waxy foliage, especially when crushed, gives off a strong aroma reminiscent of incense. The delicate single flowers are soft primrose-yellow. 'Micrugosa' (*Rosa × micrugosa*) is a very hardy and little-used shrub with a long flowering season; its soft pink flowers are single, of a satiny texture and sweetly scented. There is also a white form which I like even better.

While talking of first crosses, I must mention a very fine recent addition

to these roses sent to me in 1984 by Mrs Hazel Le Rougetel of Liphook, Hampshire. It is a cross between *Rosa rugosa* and *Rosa nitida*; not only does it have a long season but its flowers are followed by a good crop of attractive hips. A special feature is its rich and colourful autumn foliage. It was introduced in 1988 with the name 'Corylus'. Most of the best Rugosa hybrids were raised towards the end of the nineteenth century, but a few excellent ones have emerged spasmodically since. The most notable are the spreading 'Fru Dagmar Hastrup' (1914), 'Hansa' (1905) and 'Scabrosa', a foundling of the 1950s. Incidentally, Fru is correct, not Frau, because she is Danish not German.

So far, I have introduced three shrub roses of my own: 'James Mason' (1982), 'Sadler's Wells' (1983) and 'William and Mary' (1988). The first is a dark red, summer-flowering hybrid Gallica named after the actor of that name. I had mentioned to his wife Clarissa at a rose show that her husband really should have a rose named after him since she already had one named after her. I sent them a photograph, they liked it, and I duly went ahead with registration and despatched several plants to their home in Switzerland. They flowered in June the following year and James wrote to me saying how much he had enjoyed its first flowering. One month later he died, very suddenly. James Mason loved roses, as does his widow. He was a fine actor with a fine, out of the ordinary voice, so it is befitting that he should have chosen an out of the ordinary rose to be named after him. Sadly, so out of the ordinary that it will never be as widely grown as it should be.

'Micrugosa Alba' has a pleasingly long flowering season and good foliage

I well recall the launching of my second shrub rose. It was named to commemorate the tercentenary of the Sadler's Wells ballet company in 1983 and their publicity department had arranged for Lesley Collier, the ballerina, to visit our stand at the Chelsea Flower Show for a presentation of a bouquet. It was planned that I should meet her outside the main gate of the show on Chelsea Embankment to escort her to the rose. Having never met before, neither of us would recognize the other, but I felt sure that even in a crowd I would know a ballerina when I saw one. Just in case, we were each to wear a rose. I turned up at the Embankment gate in good time and waited. The pavement was crowded but not so much as to prevent recognition – or so I thought. Then came an announcement over the public address system: 'Would all members and visitors kindly leave the showground in an orderly way immediately.' The announcer did not say why such an evacuation was necessary, but in fact a terrorist organization had warned the police that a bomb was concealed somewhere among the flowers. Within minutes the whole of Chelsea Embankment was crowded with thousands of people standing shoulder to shoulder, and worse – many wearing buttonholes. My chances of spotting a ballerina were nil.

Eventually, after about an hour, the all clear came. As expected, it had been a hoax. The crowd jostled back in through the gates, and I accosted several likely looking ballerinas but none was Miss Collier. At last, feeling very confused, I followed the line of stragglers into the showground and

Autumn foliage is an attractive feature of many roses, as with 'Corylus', a cross between *Rosa rugosa* and *Rosa nitida* from Hazel Le Rougetel

'Sadler's Wells', a modern Hybrid Musk shrub that flowers throughout the season

made my way back to our stand where I was met by an agitated reporter ask-ing.where I had been. Miss Collier, one of the first through the gate at the all clear, had done her stuff, posed for her picture with the rose and was then happily looking round the rest of the show. I never did meet her.

My third shrub rose in 1988 was also to commemorate a tercentenary. The years 1688 and 1689 are important years in British history, for it was then that William of Orange, and Mary, his Queen, arrived from Holland to supplant Mary's father, the unpleasant James II. To great public rejoicing, they became joint monarchs and ushered in a period of peace and prosper-ity throughout the kingdom. To commemorate this event and as a small part of the tercentenary celebrations, I was invited to name a rose 'William and Mary'. To do justice to such an important historical event it was felt that the rose selected should not only be a reliable garden plant but should also reflect the type of rose that could well have been growing in the gardens of England and Holland at the time. Thus we chose a blowsy, pinkish-crimson seedling, reminiscent of the roses to be seen in many an old master of the Baroque period. Its size will restrict its use in smaller gardens, except as a pot plant or small climber, and its weakness by today's standards is a short flowering season. I wish it was slightly less vigorous, but I have never consid-ered that length of flowering should necessarily rank higher than beauty in one's judgement of a rose, and with such a name, true historical reflections are not such a bad thing.

'James Mason' is a scented shrub and flowers profusely in early summer

Miniature and Patio Roses

Throughout my horticultural career and often to my regret, I have found myself avoiding plants that appear to be remotely fiddly to handle; and shying away, too, from any form of gardening that is not compatible with the wielding of a spade. Since, by definition, only roses that are smaller than others in every respect can qualify for classification as Miniatures, it would be wrong of me to pretend to know everything about this group. This is not to say that over the years I have not come to know quite a few of these little charmers, nor that these particular roses have always escaped my bedtime reading. Like all other types of small things, plants or otherwise, the more one gets to know them the more fascinating they become:

No one is quite sure from where the first true Miniature came. Several theories exist, some with credibility and considerable circumstantial evidence, but like so much of the scantily documented history of the rose one has to suspect a certain amount of factual licence. That so many hybrids, especially the early ones, have close *Rosa chinensis* characteristics makes the supposition that it came from China the most plausible.

Rosa chinensis is a far from stable species, and even within its several garden types considerable variation in growth is not uncommon; 'Mutabilis', for example, is quite unpredictable. Seeds sent to me from China some years ago as the long-lost *Rosa chinensis* (still not authenticated – see my previous book, *Classic Roses*), and all from the same plant, have yielded offspring of considerable variation, not only in habit of growth and size but also in colour and petal numbers. Of course, reproduction from seed, even of a species, does not take into account the activities of some Chinese-speaking bee. It may be a whimsical thought, but could it have been an early ancestor of that self-same bee that, perchance, way back in time, pollinated *Rosa chinensis* to spark a fusion of genes that led to a dwarf clone of this species? A clone which was eventually to find its way, by who knows what circuitous route, into the hands of breeders to become the progenitor of the Miniatures. Even though it does not exist today, *Rosa chinensis minima* would have been the obvious name and, therefore, we can accept that it came via Mauritius, having been found there by one Robert Sweet in about 1810, as was reported by the well-known and highly respected botanist Lindsey in 1920.

While in Bermuda recently, knowing the chameleon-like growth habits of Chinas, I kept my eyes open for any sign of a dwarf China among their 'mystery' roses. Bermuda has the perfect climate for rose longevity and I knew that many Chinas and Teas had found their way to the island at a time when *Rosa chinensis minima* would have been around. I knew, too, that

Above: Rosa chinensis: this particular form was sent to the author from China in 1983 *Right:* 'Cramoisi Supérieur' is known on Bermuda as 'Agrippina' and is the most common rose on the island

members of the Bermuda Rose Society since its formation in 1954 were preserving all the many naturalized and garden roses they could find.

For those who do not know of the Bermuda mystery roses, perhaps I can be allowed, yet again, to digress. I went there to attend a conference and had very little time for rose-hunting, but those I saw or was shown were fascinating. I was brought down to earth with a bump, in fact, for the roses in Bermuda are different and many I had never seen before. For a week, the island was teeming with rose people and there was much discussion. Who knows what subtle variations occur in roses that grow and flower all the year round and have never experienced frost? Can we compare such roses to those that take a rest for six months each winter in less temperate climates? Of the roses I recognized, their 'Cramoisi Supérieur', known in Bermuda as 'Agrippina', is certainly the same as the European although more vigorous. I noticed subtle differences in 'Archduke Charles', the European having fewer petals, but our 'Safrano' has more than theirs. 'Slater's Crimson', which, sadly, I have now lost, I recall having more petals than the one I saw on Bermuda. The flowers of my 'Sanguinea' are identical to those of their plant, but whereas their variety grows to more than 5 ft (1.5 m) mine struggles to attain even 2 ft (60 cm). Their 'Anna Olivier' is exactly the same as mine, but I believe we both have it wrongly identified. With the help of Bill and Lorna Mercer I was able to sort out a mix-up in my nursery between 'Maman Cochet' and 'White Maman Cochet'. Also, thanks to the Mercers, I came back very confused as to the true identities of 'Homère' and 'Mme de Tartas'.

By way of a positive identification of a mystery rose, the nearest I dare go is to say that the Bermudan 'Miss Atwood', although taller, closely resembles my 'Arethusa'. Interesting though a correct identification would be, I suspect that many Bermudan roses will remain mysteries, and anyone who dares to name them on the evidence of roses currently available for comparison would be very brave indeed. And, until positive proof is found, they should certainly retain their charming Bermudan names – 'Smith's Parish', 'Trinity', 'St Davids' or 'Brightside Cream' – and be known under those names not just in Bermuda but throughout the world. Furthermore, any suggestion as to probable names should be based on good, sound evidence, not on tenuous descriptions from books and catalogues except where such evidence forms part of more positive proof in the form of a proven, authenticated rose.

If I could be sure that all the names by which we now know our old roses are those designated by their raisers then I would, perhaps, take a different view. I concluded several years ago that it is impossible to be sure whether or not every rose in present-day catalogues that pre-dates 1920 is true to the raiser's name; and this bothered me. Now I ask myself: providing it is the same rose that others are offering under that name and, above all, providing it has been proved to be a garden variety, does the name matter? Roses are

Left: 'Safrano', whose petal count varies in different parts of the world
Below left: 'Miss Attwood', a Bermudan 'mystery' rose
Below right: 'Little Flirt' (whose flowers are some 1.5 in (3 cm) in diameter) was raised by Ralph Moore

not signed like works of art, so what matters most surely is that we have the rose, interesting though speculation and research might be.

Naturally I am fully conscious of the importance of correct names, but for want of a name too many good roses from the past have now been lost to our gardens for ever. For our roses' sake, let us not get bogged down by nomenclature and authenticity. I have several good but so far nameless roses sent to me over the years by keen rosarians which are destined never to go beyond our nursery gates. I call them 'was-not' roses – 'wait and see – name official tomorrow'. I would love to share some of them with the world, but purists would consider it a sin to rename them, even though it is most unlikely that their true identities will ever be known. Congratulations, Bermuda Rose Society, for naming your 'was-nots': the rose world is the richer for your doing so.

Getting back to Miniatures, these little roses enjoyed a longish spell of popularity as pot plants during the first part of the nineteenth century. In Victorian times other types became popular at their expense, and this, coupled with a rise in demand for other kinds of pot plants, caused Miniatures virtually to disappear from catalogues and florists. In 1918, however, so the story goes, a Swiss army officer named Roulet found in Switzerland a dwarf rose that he had never set eyes on before. A few years later, his discovery was introduced to the world as *Rosa rouletii*. Although designated a species it was really a hybrid, and after a short spell of popularity as a pot plant in its own right it inevitably fell into the hands of a hybridizer who put it to work as breeding stock. Others may have used it too, but the distinction of breeding the first popular hybrid Miniature goes to the Dutchman de Vink. He crossed 'Rouletii' with the Dwarf Polyantha 'Gloria Mundi' to bring forth 'Peon', a small Miniature whose red flowers each have a white eye. The polka-dot effect of each cluster was eye-catching and sales of the little rose in Holland, as a pot plant, soon proved its worth. De Vink then went on to produce a succession of good Miniatures.

Just before the Second World War a few examples of 'Peon' found their way to North America. When it arrived a man named Robert Pyle of Pennsylvania got permission to change its name to 'Tom Thumb', whereupon it found a ready sale. Furthermore, no doubt to Tom Thumb's great delight, he was put to stud and admirably proved his worth by producing a succession of colourful progeny. After the war Miniatures, as pot plants, caught on in a big way, first in America and then throughout the world. Names were no small factor in this success story, for such roses lent themselves admirably to pretty names like de Vink's 'Cinderella' (1953) and 'Humpty Dumpty' (1952). The lovely 'Cinderella' is still popular to this day, its charm inbred, for although 'Peon', its pollen parent, is hardly beautiful in the refined sense, its seed parent, 'Cécile Brünner', most certainly is.

While de Vink and Pyle were taking advantage of the consumer boom of the 1950s by breeding, promoting and selling their varieties, other breeders had not been idle; in fact, as time was to prove, others had not only been

Although a Miniature, 'Dresden Doll' (here photographed 1½ times actual size) has flowers in the old-fashioned style and is well mossed

working with 'Rouletii' since the 1930s but were also having even greater success. One of these men was an American, the other a Spaniard. The American was Ralph Moore from the state were so many good roses have been bred, California. Moore, it seems, found 'Rouletii' a reluctant parent, skipped the first generation and worked initially with 'Peon', crossing and recrossing it with other roses and, in particular, with seedlings of his own, many of complex genealogy. Moore has found Miniatures fascinating to work with and has devoted a distinguished career to breeding them in profusion; he is still very active. So far, he has given us such excellent varieties as 'Easter Morning' (1960), 'Baby Darling' (1964) and 'Rise 'n' Shine' (1977). He has also introduced several unusual ones, for by going back in time with his breeding stock he has found that he can induce some of the older roses to release some of their personality into the constitution of his Miniatures. 'Dresden Doll' (1975) and 'Mood Music' (1977), for example, are just two Miniatures with flowers in the old-fashioned style and as much moss on their buds and stems as the old Moss roses themselves.

The Spaniard, Pedro Dot, has been mentioned elsewhere in connection with his Hybrid Teas, and like Ralph Moore he soon came to realize that breeding Miniatures could be rewarding. He too discovered that, since the dwarfing characteristic of Miniatures was inbuilt and dominant, he could cross them with almost any type of rose and still retain the dwarfing habit. He used Hybrid Teas, in particular, to very good effect. It was Dot who first introduced yellow into Miniatures with 'Baby Gold Star' (1940). Whether 'Baby Gold Star' was responsible I do not know, but, like the early yellow Hybrid Teas, the first few yellow Miniatures were dogged with that horrible affliction, black spot. Another good yellow Miniature from Dot is the shapely 'Rosina' (1951), still a firm favourite today, but my favourite of all is his 'Perla de Montserrat' (1945), a soft pinkish colour with superbly shaped flowers in the mould of one of its parents, 'Cécile Brünner'.

Although the breeders so far mentioned have made by far the biggest contribution to the development of Miniature and shorter-growing roses, their range has been extended from time to time by several worthy contributions from others, among them de Ruiter, McGredy, Paolino, Harkness, Kordes, Saville and Laver. As we would expect, Meillands of France have not been slow in their appreciation and exploitation of dwarfing genes and, as a result, have bred and introduced some outstanding varieties. Two I particularly like are 'Darling Flame' (1971) and 'Colibri' (1979), both bright in colour and rather taller than average Miniatures.

This brings us to the new range of roses now finding their way into most catalogues – the Patio roses. 'Patio' as applied to roses is not yet an official term and is not a term that endears itself to a grower of old-fashioned roses such as myself. Its merit as a name, if it has one, is that it describes usage, but while a real patio may well be the 'in thing' to have in certain sections of society, such a name for a group of roses implies restrictions of use quite out of proportion to the not inconsiderable merits of these roses. It is strange that misleading terminology such as 'Patio' or 'Ground-Cover', for example, should be so readily accepted today, for surely such names are as misleading as 'Grandiflora' was in the 1960s?

It is easy to be critical of nomenclature and classification, and I know that much discussion is going on within the World Federation of Rose Societies about this subject with the ultimate aim of standardized classifications. But the aim is surely simplicity, with built-in references to both habit of flowering and limitations of use. To combine these two criteria in any classification we need look no further than our existing types of roses, and perhaps a good thesaurus. 'Floribunda' may well not be the nicest word, but it is descriptive, already in general use and more all-embracing than 'cluster', so it should be kept for the multiflowered types. Tempting though it is to retain 'Hybrid Tea', this has to go since all Large-Flowered roses are not necessarily that type of rose; 'Large-Flowered' is clumsy, so what is wrong with 'Grandiflora'? 'Ground-Cover' is misleading and, frankly, sometimes dishonest – so why not 'Procumbent'? 'Climbers' are climbers so they stay as they are, but perhaps also embracing ramblers. It seems to me that usage is almost always implicitly expressed by height or stature, the variations of which are adequately provided for in our language. Furthermore, there is usually a correlation between size of flower and stature, so any exception to the norm in this respect can be taken care of by the detailed catalogue

'Apricot Sunblaze' (whose flowers are some 1.5 in (3 cm) in diameter) from Meillands of France

description in the same way that colour or scent is at present. 'Miniature' implies diminutive. Short, medium and tall speak for themselves. Thus Floribundas would be either miniature, short, medium, tall or procumbent – likewise Grandifloras. Climbers would be simply Floribunda-type or Grandiflora-type. Such terms could be all-embracing and even cover the older roses, except that out of deference and respect for the past those from before 1900 could retain their present designations. The commercial arguments in favour of such new classifications as 'Patio' are not really valid; they complicate things for customers, who, if they want a certain type of rose, will have it and will seek it out more easily from simplicity than complicity, and more roses, rather then fewer, could be sold. A lot of nonsense, I hear you nurserymen say. I'm inclined to agree. But surely no more nonsensical than the classifications we have at present? (Current classifications in common use are found under the various separate headings in the Dictionary section.)

I have digressed yet again, so now back to what are known as 'Patios'. They are taller than Miniatures but not necessarily shorter than the short Floribundas; it is their denser habit and more numerous, smaller leaves that isolate them. They can be slightly spreading but not too much so, otherwise they become ground-cover roses, although some are broader than tall. Their flowers are always smaller than those of the shorter Floribundas; and in spite of what I have said about their group name, I can see why they are considered different from other roses and why they are here to stay. The trouble is that as they become more numerous, as they surely will to judge from the number of breeders now sending them into the marketplace, it will become more difficult to define the borderline between Patios and other roses. Their usage, as I have said, is wider than their collective name implies.

Meillands have been notably active in this field and those of their free-flowering, bright and colourful 'Sunblaze' range are outstanding, as is the excellent yellow 'Gold Bunny' (1981). Following a similar line to Meillands, both McGredy and Dickson have brought out some delightful Patios. I like McGredy's 'Regensberg' (1980) and 'Penelope Keith' (1984). Of Dickson's varieties both 'Gentle Touch', which speaks for itself as 'Rose of the Year' in Britain in 1986, and the charmingly named 'Peek a Boo' (1981) have made many friends since their introduction. Harkness has contributed a very good variety, 'Anna Ford', and what he calls his 'China' rose, 'Clarissa' (1983), named for Mrs James Mason. In recent years others have come from all parts of the globe, but I have not seen them all and where raisers have not defined them as Patio roses it is probably safer to confine my observations to those already mentioned.

'Gentle Touch', a Compact Floribunda with large clusters of flowers on a widish bush

Climbing Roses, Ramblers and Scramblers

Although climbers and ramblers have been used in our gardens ever since roses have been grown, it was not until the close of the last century and the early years of our own – when a wider colour range was introduced – that their true value was appreciated. Those were the days of Gertrude Jekyll and it was largely from her flair and imagination that gardeners of the day learned how to get the best from them. Indeed, her appreciation of the value of climbers and ramblers still has a great influence on the way we grow and use them today.

The history of these roses began with that of all roses, way back in the mists of time; and despite having much in common, the diversity of character between climbers and ramblers is considerable. The obvious common factor between the two groups is, of course, their vigour. The less obvious, at least to newcomers to roses, is their ancestry. Most of our present-day garden hybrids owe their genealogy to just a handful of the many wild climbing species so far discovered growing in various parts of the world, mostly China. Just as with our bush and shrub roses, the biggest single influence on their development has been *Rosa chinensis*: each time a new cross is made, it is the inherent dominance of this species that dictates the result. The other wild roses to play their part are *Rosa moschata*, *Rosa multiflora*, *Rosa gigantea* and, to a lesser extent though no less important, *Rosa wichuraiana*. Here and there another gene or two, from brief encounters with other types, show their influence, but until some enlightened young hybridizer sets about exploiting the vast range of possibilities within the ranks of climbers, only those few species will dictate their future.

Once again, it was John Champneys' seedling from his cross of 'Old Blush' with *Rosa moschata* that led the way. For it was the Noisettes, when fused with *Rosa gigantea* through the Teas, that brought forth many of the lovely old climbers of the nineteenth century. Many of the Noisettes are still with us today, such as the beautiful and bountiful 'Mme Alfred Carrière' (1879), together with several of the Noisette-Teas such as the classic and ubiquitous 'Gloire de Dijon' (1853). As the nineteenth century progressed, more and more climbers appeared and by 1900 the choice of varieties was extensive. By then two clearly distinct types had evolved, one with largish flowers produced on laterals from sturdy, upright growth known as climbers and another with clusters of smaller flowers with a more relaxed growing behaviour, generally called ramblers.

As a generalization, most of the first group, the climbers, had sprung either as hybrids from the Teas and Noisettes or as sports from the old Hybrid Perpetuals and early Hybrid Teas. Outstanding among the larger-flowered hybrids produced in this century as climbers in their own right are 'Cupid' (1915) from B. R. Cant, one of the most beautiful single roses I know, Mallerin's 'Guinée' (1938), an outstanding red, and Dot's 'Mme Grégoire Staechelin' (1927), the pick of the pinks. Of the slightly more off-beat colours I love the charming, almost single 'Meg' (1954) from Gosset and the dazzling 'Réveil Dijonnais' (1931) from Buatois of France.

Now and then, without warning, an apparently quite contented bush rose will sprout a climbing shoot: if such shoots are propagated vegetatively, more often than not they retain this new-found vigour in their offspring and it is by this means that many of our present-day climbers have come into being. Hybrid Tea sports to have proved excellent value over the years are Kordes' 'Crimson Glory' which first climbed in 1946, the delicious 'Mme Butterfly' (1926) and 'Shot Silk', the climbing form of which occurred in Australia in 1931. A few Floribundas have also produced climbing sports; among these 'Allgold' (1961) and 'Iceberg' (1968) are both outstanding.

I have already expressed the opinion that a short flowering season too often comes between a rose and success, but I fully realize that continuity of flower is of considerable importance in a small garden. There are one or two excellent varieties from the past quite capable of flowering all summer, among them the lovely 'Zéphirine Drouhin' (1868). Others, such as 'Gloire de Dijon', produce their first flush and take a rest, giving a repeat if slightly subdued performance in the autumn. For those with more modern tastes, however, several very good climbers have been introduced in recent years

Two Climbers: 'Mme Alfred Carrière', bred more than a century ago, and *right:* 'Clair Matin', an excellent modern variety

that can be relied upon to flower from June to October. To call them climbers is perhaps misleading, for they do not send up climbing shoots in the way of the once-flowering varieties but produce flowers on the end of each vigorous shoot instead. They are best supported in some way, perhaps on walls, trellises or pillars. It was Wilhelm Kordes who first got to work on this type of rose by breeding 'Hamburger Phoenix' (1954), 'Leverkusen' (1954) and 'Parkdirektor Riggers' (1957) from his *Rosa kordesii* (see page 68). Some excellent long-flowering climbers came from France in the 1950s and '60s. I consider the splendid 'Clair Matin' (1960) from Meilland to be one of the finest, but perhaps the most familiar is the bright red 'Danse de Feu' (1953) sent out by Mallerin, better known in America as 'Spectacular'. Mentioning America, no one can fail to notice Lammert's 'Golden Showers' (1956), for it is perhaps the most widely grown of all yellow climbers. Boerner's climbers are not so well known in Britain, but of those that are, 'Parade' is superb.

Of British raisers, McGredy has been by far the most productive. Among his varieties are 'Handel' (1956), 'Casino' (1963), 'Schoolgirl' (1964) and 'Bantry Bay' (1967). One of the best of the whites is the free-flowerer 'White Cockade' (1969) from Cocker, but without doubt the two best sellers today are Harkness's shapely 'Compassion' (1973) and Gregory's prolific 'Pink Perpétue' (1965). Apart from those from Kordes, it is interesting that by far the majority of this type of climber raised around the world since the war have come, directly or indirectly, from that superb rose for all seasons, 'New Dawn'.

Ramblers were undoubtedly the result of planned breeding by a few very worthy hybridists, most important of whom were Manda of America and

'Meg', an outstanding repeat-flowering modern climber with large scented flowers and healthy foliage

Barbier of France. It was Manda, just before the turn of the century, who first crossed *Rosa wichuraiana*, or possibly *Rosa luciae* (see Graham Stuart Thomas, *Climbing Roses Old and New*), with a large-flowered hybrid to produce the first of what are now loosely termed Wichuraiana ramblers. His first introduction was 'May Queen' in 1898. Barbier, pursuing similar lines of breeding, gave us the lovely 'Albéric Barbier' in 1900 followed by a succession of other equally good ramblers. His last of significance was 'Albertine' in 1921. A few other breeders followed the lead given by these two men and ramblers have now become commonplace in most gardens as a result.

Another breeder to have success with ramblers was the American Van Fleet, his major contribution coming in the form of 'Dr W. Van Fleet' (1910). It was this rose that sported in 1930 to become continuous-flowering and give us the lovely 'New Dawn'.

The other types of ramblers are those that owe much of their pedigree, or at least that part which provides the cluster flowers, to *Rosa multiflora*. Again, breeders crossed this species with large-flowered types to good avail and several are still quite widely grown today. Although *Rosa multiflora* was

'Casino'

'Albéric Barbier'

'Danse de Feu'

'New Dawn'

'Ghislaine de Féligonde', a Multiflora rambler that flowers all through the summer

tried as a parent as early as 1835 by a man named Wills to produce 'Mme d'Arblay', it was Schmitt of France who introduced the first two varieties of significance in 'Thalia' (1895) and 'Aglaia' (1896). As already mentioned elsewhere, the latter was used to good effect by Pemberton in breeding the first of his Hybrid Musks. Numerous breeders worked with *Rosa multiflora* from the late nineteenth century to the 1930s, their efforts being helped considerably when 'Crimson Rambler', of unknown parentage but with obvious Multiflora leanings, arrived from Japan in 1893. This rose was also known as 'Turner's Crimson' and 'The Engineer's Rose'. The first to use it successfully was B. R. Cant of England who produced 'Blush Rambler' in 1903; Walsh of America bred 'Hiawatha' from it in 1904 and Paul of England 'Tea Rambler' in the same year; but most importantly of all Schmidt of Germany used it as a parent for the bluest of all ramblers, 'Veilchenblau', in 1909. Almost all of the early Multiflora ramblers had quite a short flowering season, but later one or two eventually came along that flowered all summer through. Outstanding among these are 'Ghislaine de Féligonde', raised by Turbat of France in 1916, and 'Phyllis Bide' by Bide in 1923, both well ahead of their time and fitting comfortably into gardens today.

We cannot mention Multiflora ramblers without word of some of the very vigorous varieties from amid their ranks, for it is from among these that we can find some of our best and most stunning tree climbers. Top of my list

Raised in 1907, 'Seagull' is one of the best climbers for growing into trees

for this job is 'Rambling Rector'; it is far older than any of the others and its parentage is unknown, but there can be little doubt that its origins are rooted in *Rosa multiflora*. It is a popular rose, because of its name, and so it should be, for it is, without doubt in my eyes, the best of the middle-sized scramblers for festooning trees and covering eyesores. 'Rambling Rector's' main rival for excellence as a tree climber is 'Seagull' (1907) with 'The Garland' a very close third although, unlike the other two, the latter probably has *Rosa moschata* in its make-up. A more vigorous tree scrambler is the more recent 'Bobbie James' (1961) from Sunningdale Nurseries, which, although of unknown parentage, also probably owes something to *Rosa multiflora*. This rose is capable of reaching the top of the tallest tree. Although a number of the vigorous tree climbers have come to us from the distant past, I feel it quite valid to include them; for they perform a valuable service in modern garden landscapes. The best is, of course, that incredible hulk 'Kiftsgate', a refined – if that is the word – form of *Rosa filipes* discovered at Kiftsgate Court and introduced in 1954 by that dedicated rosarian Hilda Murrell of Shrewsbury.

Other climbers and ramblers from the more distant past, but pertinent in the context of modern gardening, are numerous and I must just mention a few – the thornless, dark-foliaged Boursaults, for example, which include the classic 'Mme Sancy de Parabère' of 1874. Another most useful group of hybrids are those of *Rosa sempervirens*. They were once known as Evergreens. My favourites are 'Adélaide d'Orléans' (1826) and 'Félicité et Perpétue' (1827). While writing of Evergreens, I must bring in 'Mermaid' (1918) from William Paul, a rose with vicious thorns, shiny foliage and beautiful single primrose-yellow flowers. Each time I admire a well-grown plant of this rose here in England and sing its praises to its owner, I do so with tongue in cheek for it brings back memories of a 'Mermaid' encountered in Australia in 1986. It was not only the biggest plant of this variety I had ever seen but probably the biggest ever rose tree. I was taken to see it by its owner, David Ruston, to conclude a tour of what must rank as, if not the best, then by far the most interesting rose garden I have ever visited. I had not realized the importance of this garden until my arrival in Adelaide, and since it was at Renmark over 200 miles to the northeast I had thought that a visit would be far too time-consuming to fit in during a stay of only two weeks. When I saw some of David Ruston's roses decorating the conference hall, however, I knew I would have to find the time to go. We left for Renmark in the Ruston van immediately after the conference. I shall be forever grateful to David – tired though he was after his heavy stint as chairman of the conference – for taking me by the scenic route, fifty or so miles further through South Australia than he need have done.

At Mount Pleasant we came, by chance, upon a small, overgrown garden full of huge, unpruned roses. As rosemen often do when they find a rose garden, we stopped, knocked on the door and asked the surprised owner if we could look around. Permission granted, David was saddened by so many

Top left: 'Bobbie James' can grow to a great height *Top right:* 'Mermaid', although raised in 1918, is still one of the best of the shade-tolerant climbers *Bottom:* 'Dr Huey', an understock used extensively in the United States

'Indica Major' suckers, but not I, for although this rose is commonly used as an understock in Australia it is seldom seen in England. Among the suckers, and rising above them, was the biggest plant of 'Sutter's Gold' either of us had ever seen. I lost count at seventy blooms on one side of the plant only. Its owner was a young lady, who, after getting over the sight of two grown men drooling over her roses, explained apologetically that her roses had not been pruned since her father had died ten years earlier. Before leaving, we extracted a promise from her that she would never, ever buy secateurs.

I had seen some very good roses around Adelaide, in particular a

'Mutabilis' some 8 ft (2.5 m) high and 10 ft (3 m) wide and a wealth of superb specimens at Deane Ross's display garden at Willunga, but I was quite unprepared for what I was to see in the Ruston gardens. Long before I awoke, David had been out to turn on the irrigation, for without water from the Murray River Renmark's fertile soil would be far too dry and parched to grow anything but native scrub. David Ruston, like myself, makes his living from roses, but he is also a superb gardener and an avid collector. His display gardens extend over several acres and include a wide variety of plants other than roses, including many interesting natives. I will forever remember that hot day in November when I found myself let loose among one of the biggest informal collections in the world. I came upon 'Maman Cochet' roses growing 10 ft (3 m) into a citrus and 'Devoniensis' 20 ft (6 m) up a gum tree. I found myself reacquainted with roses that were no more than memories from a far-off youth, for this garden is rich in roses from the 1950s. I must have missed dozens, but I came upon such Hybrid Teas as 'Charlotte Armstrong', 'Monique', 'Dr Debat' and 'Symphony', and upon the Floribundas 'Fashion', 'Donald Prior' and 'Goldilocks'. It was here that I met, for the first time, some of Thomas's Bloomfield roses of the 1920s. These are not hardy enough for England, so I was pleased to find them, in particular several fine specimens of 'Bloomfield Courage' and a superb 'Bloomfield Dainty' on a pillar. The gardens are surrounded by a tall, wire-mesh, kangaroo- and stock-proof fence which is festooned with climbers and it was among these that I found that huge plant of 'Mermaid'.

An unpruned 'Sutter's Gold', seen in a garden in South Australia

Top: The Lily Pool in David Ruston's rose gardens at Renmark, South Australia. The large dark rose in the background is a magnificent specimen of 'Bloomfield Courage'
Bottom: David Ruston dwarfed by his untamable 'Mermaid'

What of the Future?

In speculating upon what may lie in store for the rose, I first contemplated the changes that have occurred in my own lifetime. I was privileged to be born and bred in the countryside and have never had any reason to regret that fact. I say 'lifetime', for, although I did not become a rose grower until the age of sixteen, I was well aware of nature's wild roses long before that age; the roses of slow meanderings through country lanes returning from school on hot, balmy days in June. It was wartime and hedges were thriving in glorious neglect, so between daydreams I espied Dog Roses at their very best, for where hedges grow so Dog Roses flourish. Later, when hips were ripe and orange in the autumn, I collected them at half-a-crown a stone for the war effort, and, I presume, the manufacture of rosehip syrup. To come back to the point, I learned to notice subtle variations in the colour, shape and growth habits of those wild species and, from time to time, came upon a white one, different not only in colour of flower but in colour of stem, shape of leaf and habit of growth. Later I learned that this was the Field Rose, *Rosa arvensis*, and that the Dog Rose was *Rosa canina*. Those hedges have long since gone but a lonely plant of *Rosa arvensis* still lives on in a small stretch so far spared from the plough.

A simple story of a child walking home from school – what has this to do with roses of the future? Everything, for it takes us back to nature's own roses to which every new variety ever introduced owes its genealogy. The two species I encountered as a child do not, in themselves, form the ancestral beginnings of any particularly auspicious new rose, although *Rosa canina* can stake a claim as progenitor of that beautiful group, the Albas, and *Rosa arvensis* was responsible for starting off those interesting ramblers, the Ayrshires. Both Albas and Ayrshires are from the past and, in recent years, have been largely neglected by breeders, but they illustrate clearly the chain reactions that occur when genes of species and hybrids are mixed, perhaps by chance but now deliberately. The evolutionary path of the rose is full of side tracks, many of them culs-de-sac, but each diversion or new direction has led eventually to a development that has widened the road and signposted directions to the future. Every new direction has led to more complex, if not better, roses, and with the benefit of hindsight we have now reached a point in the history of the rose where its make-up and complexities are such that almost any change of direction will lead to the unknown.

What is there still left to do and what do we need most? The assumption that any change of direction would be random is based on history, for it

Rosa arvensis, the Field Rose, which gave rise to the Ayrshire ramblers

Left: The Dog Rose *Rosa canina*, a delightful
wild species
Above: 'Blue Moon', a question of taste

assumes that hybridity is now so mixed that hybridizers will, as those in the
past have done, simply play a hunch. This may not be so, however, for nowadays much more is known about genetics. We now have a good knowledge
of compatibility through chromosome counts, for example, and with
genetic engineering moving forward in leaps and bounds, who knows what
this might mean for the breeding of the humble rose? Perish the thought.
Ten years ago micropropagation was of unlikely benefit to rose producers,
so we thought, but this practice is now widespread and taken seriously – if
not for granted – especially in mass-producing Patio roses.

So, what is likely to come by way of new types in the future? There is no
doubt, whatever their collective name, that Patio roses are here to stay and
more will be raised. A big advantage to roses of this type is its healthy constitution, and with health the main aim of breeders in these days of black spot,
there can be little doubt that we should look forward to better disease
resistance in our roses of the future. Closely allied to the Patios are the
ground-coverers, or Procumbents. These too, by and large, are healthy and
have found a ready market, so more and more will come forth as there is still
plenty of scope, especially in size of flower and perfume. Looking further
ahead, I foresee improvements coming to the flexible ramblers, for example, where there is much potential for prolonging their flowering season and
improving their colour range, especially among the more vigorous tree
scramblers. Evergreen roses, autumn colour of foliage, improvements to
size and shape of hip, and greater hardiness are all possibilities within the
vast gene bank of existing hybrids and species. What about colour, a black or
a blue rose, or both? Without doubt, more and more unusual shades will
emerge, but it is unlikely that any will be closer to black or blue than those
we have at present unless a new species is discovered in some remote,

unexplored region with blue-making genes in its ovaries. Can you imagine a bright blue rose?

What about other areas of change? On the production side I foresee, not too far hence, more and more roses on their own roots, more effective fungicides, more container-grown roses for planting all the year round and – in this market-orientated era – more and more sponsorship for new varieties. As for classification? Discussion and argument will continue, simplified denominations will be recommended but no one will take any notice and new group names will be invented – what's a name anyway? Roses are here to stay.

PART II
Modern Roses in the Landscape

Some thoughts on where, why and how to
use them, or not to use them

Roses as Bedding Plants and for Massed Display

Apart from half-hardy annuals, there are few plants better suited to massed display than shorter-growing bush roses. They have a distinct advantage over annuals in that, once planted and with proper care and attention, they will remain *in situ* for many years. As I have mentioned, breeders of roses have not been slow to appreciate the value of massed bedding, and any good modern catalogue will give a choice of almost any colour in almost any height.

By far and away the best roses for bedding are Floribundas. They start flowering in late June and continue in flower until the first frost of November. As they come in all sizes, however, they are most effective when only one variety is grown en masse; and this applies not just in parks and large gardens but in small gardens, too. No matter how great the temptation to choose a wide variety of colours, mixed roses in beds, especially Floribundas, are never as effective as a single colour. This rule can perhaps be relaxed slightly if more than one variety of a particular colour range is used; but however hard one tries, it is very difficult to get an even height throughout any wide-ranging mixture. If a wide colour range is desired, the best effects are achieved by planting in groups of three or four.

The larger-flowered roses such as Hybrid Teas are not grown for massed display very often now, though several varieties enjoy just as long a flowering season as any Floribunda and provide the extra advantage of scent, which is still barely perceptible in so many Floribundas. Recent developments in other types now widen the choice for massing in beds and borders. Although short and compact, Patio roses lend themselves perfectly to group

Creamy apricot 'Chanelle', and *right*, 'Beautiful Britain', one of the brightest bedding floribundas

planting, especially in paved areas and formal, modern settings. For very large plantings where big expanses of one colour are required, there can be no better choice than some of the newer Procumbent roses, for not only do they provide continuity of flower but their planting density is also lower and their maintenance easier. To help promote their own roses of this type, Meillands advise local authorities and landscapers to use tractor-drawn flayers to prune them! Hardly advice to be heeded by experienced gardeners, but Meillands' recommendations are not given lightly and I understand they have used this method to prune the roses in their trial beds and display gardens for several years.

N.B. Roses suitable for bedding or for planting in groups are marked (B) in the Dictionary section.

Modern Roses with Companion Plants

In Victorian times roses were seen as somehow different from other plants and were almost always grown in fairly formal gardens set aside especially for them. This was the practice not only in larger gardens; smaller gardens, too, had their own patch for roses, which were seldom mixed with other horticultural hoi polloi. There is still no more pleasant sight than to see roses growing together, either in their own part of a garden or as a whole rose garden forming a collection. Minds have broadened since the turn of the century and roses are now used far more often in conjunction with other plants, a practice I wholeheartedly support and dealt with extensively in my previous book, *Classic Roses*. Bearing in mind, however, that *Classic Roses* largely ignored modern types such as Floribundas and Hybrid Teas, it is worth briefly discussing their role alongside other plants.

By far and away the most common use of Floribundas and Hybrid Teas is for bedding, but both can happily fit into mixed planting schemes. As individuals they are excellent in herbaceous borders, simply dotted here and there among shorter perennials of sympathetic colours or, conversely, adding a bright splash of contrasting colour to a group of quieter foliage plants. Standards and half standards are, I think, more at home when used functionally as relief plants in herbaceous borders, where they rise above the foliage, than they are standing like soldiers in ranks, alone with their own kind. Roses of all dimensions can be found that will fit into mixed shrubberies, although except for the very tallest, some Hybrid Teas can look incongruous. Floribundas, especially in groups of three, will admirably provide that little extra colour and length of season without looking out of place.

The best mixers of all, however, are modern shrub roses, for they not only have all the characteristics of Floribundas but also the added dimension of height. Some of the more bushy ones fit comfortably among shrubs as individual plants, but others give the best effect planted in groups. Of all roses adaptable to mixed shrubberies, the species and Rugosas are the most widely used today, for not only do they provide flowers but in many cases also autumn colour and hips – valuable assets to any modern landscaper. It baffles me, though, why modern shrub roses are not used more extensively in mixed shrub plantings. Perhaps they are thought of too much as roses rather than as shrubs? Surely any shrub which flowers as roses do, summer through, would be a natural choice if it were not a rose. When I talk to

Cleverly mixed roses and shrubs

A herbaceous border with roses in the gardens of the Royal National Rose Society, St Albans, Hertfordshire

landscapers about this they usually cite high maintenance factors as the reason for their neglect – how do they know if they never try? My shrub roses need no more maintenance than most other shrubs; and even if it is true that such roses are more expensive to maintain, I can think of several dull shrubberies where it would have been cost-effective to have included them. And, speaking of cost-effectiveness, most modern climbing roses are grown on walls, trellises or pillars, so what could be more efficient than to plant other climbers such as clematis, honeysuckle and jasmine to intermingle with them? Such mixtures take full advantage of their site and add extra colour and foliage to the roses.

But to return to mixed borders. Procumbent roses are the modern landscaper's dream and, in fairness, gardeners have not been slow to appreciate their potential; even so, they are still too often segregated on plots of their own rather than integrated with the shrubbery. Groups of three or five, allowed to grow naturally into spreading clumps, are ideal among slightly taller shrubs, even conifers. Indeed, with their habit of growth, the quieter colours of such roses make them as compatible with conifers as heathers and spreading cotoneasters.

N.B. Wide-growing or ground-cover roses are marked (GC) in the Dictionary section.

The Use of Modern Climbers and Ramblers

It is interesting, in view of the not inconsiderable number of modern climbers introduced over recent years, how many climbers and ramblers from earlier times are still used today, despite their relatively short flowering season. It prompts one to wonder what the great Gertrude Jekyll would have made of modern-day climbers, for she relied heavily on cascading, garlanding and festooning. Had she had the range of today's long-flowering climbers at her command, would she have ignored their existence? I doubt it. She would have realized, ahead of her time, that all that was new was not necessarily bad and would have harnessed the extensive capabilities of the modern climbing rose, painting it into her landscape just as she did delphiniums and foxgloves.

Just as I feel sure Miss Jekyll would have enjoyed our modern varieties, I am equally sure that we should not let the utilitarian qualities of such plants dominate our thinking to the exclusion of her type of roses today. For there is a place for both in our late-twentieth-century gardens. Flipping through my old copy of Jekyll and Mawley's book *Roses for English Gardens* makes me realize just how underused climbing roses now are. Why? Is it that they need attention from time to time, that they need expensive supports, that they have thorns that might grab us as we pass, that they spoil our modern sandfaced bricks or, simply, that we do not know how to use them with no modern Gertrude Jekyll to show us how? It is likely a combination of all these things, but most of all the first, for climbing roses need attention and that costs time and money.

One reminder of bygone days which is certainly not out of fashion,

Well-grown Floribundas and climbers at the Deane Ross rose gardens, South Australia

A fence covered in climbing roses at the Ruston rose gardens, South Australia

'Maigold', one of the earliest-flowering climbers

to judge by the number sold, is the tree climber. Many vigorous roses are capable of this and although most of the best are in shades of white and cream, there is usually one tailor-made to fit any size of tree.

The rustic trellis and pergola are now out of vogue, but this is not necessarily a bad thing, for many were ugly structures needing an army of 'Kiftsgates' to conceal them. The iron arch is different, however, for it is less obtrusive and can support the heaviest of climbers with ease, each eventually holding up the other. The trouble is that so many modern continuous-flowering climbers are upright in stance and not flexible enough to look comfortable on an arch in the way of, say, 'Félicité et Perpétue' or 'Adélaide d'Orléans'. This does not mean that modern roses fail to respond to a little persuasion. Given time and patience, 'New Dawn', for example (perhaps no longer thought of as a modern), and some of her offspring such as 'Pink Perpétue', can be bent and twisted to good effect. It is their upright stance that lends modern climbers so readily to walls and other solid structures like interwoven panels, for against such supports they need less attention than their more eager, older counterparts. Many of the modern climbing sports are also far too stiff and upright for use on anything other than a fairly strong structure; the more such roses can be bent, twisted and trained, the more productive they are. Not that ramblers, in contrast, need much bending or twisting; in addition to their conventional roles, they make reasonable ground-cover plants if given their head, especially on high banks or mounds of earth.

N.B. Roses suitable for use as climbing or pillar roses are marked (CL) in the Dictionary section; vigorous kinds suitable for growing up into trees are marked (T).

Roses as Hedges

There are few natural hedging plants, but nature offers gardeners many subjects adaptable to this purpose. Roses fit comfortably among them.

Roses not only make good hedges by themselves but can also do wonders in softening the sometimes harsh outlines of modern man-made fences. No matter what size or from what material the fence is made, there is always a rose that will willingly perform such a task without much effort. Some of the modern shrub roses are ideal, especially those of upright stance such as 'Cocktail', 'Joseph's Coat', 'Nymphenburg', 'Fountain', 'Karl Forster', 'Lafter' and 'Vanguard'. All are continuous or repeat-flowering and will grow to 6 ft (1.8 m) or more.

Obliging in hiding, disguising or adding colour to the shorter man-made fence are many of the taller, upright-growing Floribundas. 'Iceberg', 'Everest Double Fragrance', 'Chinatown', 'Escapade', 'Scarlet Queen Elizabeth' and 'Mountbatten' are a few that spring readily to mind. Like the modern shrubs, they need pruning annually in spring and dead-heading and occasional spraying in summer; beyond that, they require little or no attention nor will they intrude too much into adjacent borders, drives or paths. If uniformity is required, plant all of the same variety. For informal, free-standing rose hedges some of the older once-flowering roses are worth consideration. Many thrive on neglect and form rugged, impenetrable screens; I have described some of them in *Classic Roses*.

Modern roses usually flower throughout the summer. This necessitates pruning and, in consequence, they do not lend themselves too readily to informality. Some of the Hybrid Musks are quite relaxed in growth, however, and will provide some informality, particularly when different varieties are mixed and planted close enough to embrace; 'Buff Beauty', 'Cornelia', 'Penelope', 'Pax' and 'Prosperity' are all ideal. The Rugosas make some of the best hedges and they, too, can be informal when allowed to run free, especially those that bear hips such as 'Scabrosa', *Rosa rugosa*, *Rosa rugosa alba* and the shorter-growing 'Fru Dagmar Hastrup'. The double forms of Rugosa such as 'Roseraie de l'Hay', 'Blanc Double de Coubert' and the splendid 'Hansa' do not produce many hips, so with a combination of dead-heading and pruning they can be formed into quite dense, formal hedges. Rugosas provide superb autumn colours as a bonus. Many of the more

'Roseraie de l'Hay', a double Rugosa, makes a fine hedge and shows wonderful autumn colour *(right)*

hybrid ones such as the 'Grootendorst' range, 'Nyveldt's White' and 'Sarah Van Fleet' also make very good hedges. Beware of cheap hedging roses advertised as 'the perfect hedge' – they seldom live up to the superlatives applied to them and will need constant attention throughout their life to keep them looking anything but an overgrown mess.

Although they are useful for concealing fences, many modern shrub roses make good hedgerows in their own right. This is not to say that such roses are suitable as boundary hedges on their own, but in conjunction with wire mesh they are superb. They also make excellent free-standing ornamental hedges within the garden. The list is almost endless: 'Alexander', 'Elmshorn', 'Erfurt', 'Fritz Nobis', 'Fred Loads', 'Kassel', 'Sadler's Wells' and 'Wilhelm' are only a few. For the shorter hedge it is almost impossible to exclude any of the Floribundas. Across the colour range the following, in addition to those mentioned earlier, are ideal: 'Beautiful Britain', 'City of Leeds', 'Frensham', 'Korresia', 'Living Fire', 'Margaret Merril', 'Nathalie Nypels', 'Southampton' and, of course, 'Queen Elizabeth'. To a lesser extent some Hybrid Teas also make reliable, trouble-free hedges, such as those of the 'Peace' family and the lovely, single 'Dainty Bess', as well as 'Silver Jubilee', 'Sandringham Centenary' and 'Uncle Walter'.

Dwarf Polyantha roses were used to great effect as dividing hedges during the 1920s and '30s, a fashion I would love to see resurrected. They have a good range of colour, are dense in habit, quite unobtrusive when not in flower and demand the minimum of attention.

As for the cultivation of a good rose hedge, this simply means plenty of organic material in the soil to start it off, pruning as and when appropriate to keep the hedge in shape, spraying and feeding as with other roses and the removal of unsightly dead-heads when necessary. The one golden rule is to prune hard in the first year of planting to encourage all the first year's growth to come from the base of the plant.

N.B. Roses that make fine hedging plants are marked (H) in the Dictionary section.

Both 'Buff Beauty' (*above*) and 'Iceberg' (*right*) are
excellent for growing in ornamental containers

Modern Roses in Containers

Pots, urns, boxes and tubs come in a variety of shapes and sizes, and to avoid
repeating myself too often I will refer to them all as pots. Since Victorian
times this method of growing roses has gone slowly out of fashion. The
decline is fairly predictable because until the turn of the century there were
far more conservatories and far more Tea roses to grow in them. Terraces,
too, were more common, especially in bigger gardens, and they made ideal
standing areas in summer for pot-grown roses after the first flush of flower
under glass. Gardens are much smaller today, so in a way it is surprising that
more roses are not grown in pots, particularly as the range of varieties suitable for the purpose is infinitely greater than it was a century ago. This is not
to say that only certain roses can be grown in pots, for given the right size of
container almost any rose can be made to feel comfortable in one, even
climbers 10 ft (3 m) tall – I know a superb, seven-year-old 'Coral Dawn'. The
secret, apart from size and capacity, is in the soil. If the right compost is used
and good drainage provided, roses grown in pots will live and thrive for
years. More detail on soils and so forth will come later in the cultivation
section (see pages 117–30).

While all roses will grow in pots, some are better at it than others. Miniatures, for example, do well, especially those propagated by grafting, as such
plants are bigger and more vigorous than those grown on their own roots.

'Swany', a Procumbent rose of merit in the author's display garden

Dwarf Polyanthas also thrive and look quite at home, as do many Floribundas, particularly shorter ones like 'Lady Romsey' and 'Meteor'. Hybrid Teas will, of course, grow quite successfully but may not be such good value, for they tend to have fewer blooms. Of all the shorter-growing roses, though, the newer Patio varieties lend themselves best to this purpose and the posture of such varieties as 'Sunblaze' and 'Gentle Touch' is well suited to modern stoneware. Of the larger roses, the taller Floribundas do well; 'Queen Elizabeth' and 'Iceberg', for example, make excellent pot plants as do some of the wide range of bushy shrubs – 'Ballerina' and 'Yesterday' spring readily to mind. Most suitable of all are some of the Procumbents, especially when they can be given their head in large containers and cascade over the edge of the pot. 'Nozomi' is ideal and enjoys the extra mollycoddling it gets by being grown in this way, but sadly its flowering season is rather short and others, such as 'Fairyland', 'Fairy Damsel' and 'Smarty', are better. In larger pots it is possible to use the very prostrate varieties such as 'Snow Carpet' as undergrowth to larger, more upright roses such as 'Iceberg'. Tall standards often look ridiculous in pots, but half and quarter standards can be effective, particularly when underplanted with smaller roses.

Except for the Teas and Dwarf Polyanthas I have so far mentioned only modern roses, but many good roses from the past and not a few species thrive in the restricted environment of pots, especially the Portlands such as

'Comte de Chambord', 'Rose de Rescht' and 'Jacques Cartier', the Chinas 'Cécile Brünner' and 'Perle d'Or', and the dwarf-like Centifolias 'Rose de Meaux' and 'Pompon de Bourgogne' – I could go on. As for species I have a *Rosa stellata mirifica* in a small pot, about eight years old, thoroughly enjoying the experience.

For those who have never tried growing roses in pots, it is well worth the effort; indeed in small gardens roses may not be possible in any other way. I can vouch for the fact that it is not difficult, for we have several hundred at our nursery, some over ten years old. They almost thrive on neglect and, each year, find themselves on display at the Chelsea Flower Show.

N.B. Roses suitable for growing in containers are marked ▽ in the Dictionary section.

Roses under Glass

Throughout the world many millions of roses are grown commercially under glass. Where climates are unpredictable this is the sure way of producing roses for the cut-flower market, at least in centres of high population such as Europe and North America where demand is high. To produce cut flowers on this large scale, growers plant their roses direct into greenhouse soil. Such methods are not possible for most amateurs since they usually have to make do with far less space; so, the most common practice is to grow them in pots. To get roses very early in spring heaters have to be used, but this is an expensive luxury and it is quite possible to bring roses into flower four to five weeks earlier than those outdoors by growing them in cold greenhouses or conservatories.

Forced roses can be very rewarding and, properly tended, can be equal to, if not better than, blooms grown outdoors. As mentioned elsewhere, many of the old Tea-Scented and China roses were grown in this way in days gone by. Varieties like 'Catherine Mermet', 'Le Vésuve' and 'Perle d'Or' positively enjoy the experience. I have tried several such roses over the years and can well see why so many Victorian gentlemen sported buttonholes out of season. For those with more modern leanings, all the Hybrid Teas have Tea rose in their veins to some degree and will respond to the extra loving care they receive under glass with blooms of excellent quality. I have tried only a few, but two varieties that always do well for me are 'Whisky Mac' and 'Pascali'. To get the best quality flowers, plants need to be disbudded so that only the blooms on the central apex are allowed to mature. I seldom do this, however, preferring my roses to look their most natural. If the aim is to produce cut flowers, then it is better to use varieties that have been specifically bred for forcing, such as 'Baccara', 'Sonia' ('Sweet Promise') and 'Belinda'. If quantity rather than quality of flowers is the target then 'Garnette' is a must, for this red rose produces clusters that last for well over a week when cut; a

Rosa banksiae lutea, seen here in Trevor Griffiths' nursery in New Zealand, will add shade and colour to a greenhouse *Right:* 'Catherine Mermet', a good forcing rose

pink form of the same type is 'Carol Amling'. Some of the older Hybrid Teas make superb forcing roses too, and unlike so many modern forcing varieties not a few are superbly scented. 'Ophelia' and her two sports 'Mme Butterfly' and 'Lady Sylvia' are excellent under glass, as is, if you can still get it, the beautiful yellow Hybrid Tea of 1963, 'Dr A. J. Verhage'.

From time to time under glass, shading is necessary to protect the blooms from intense sunlight. In larger greenhouses, it is nice to use a climbing rose to help provide this. Choose a suitable variety with ample foliage, plant it at the edge of the greenhouse border nearest to the glass and train it to scramble up on the inside of the glass by stretching strands of wire 6 in (15 cm) from the glass at about 12 in (30 cm) apart along the length of the greenhouse. When the rose is fully grown it will provide dappled shade for the plants beneath. A rose ideal for this purpose is the vigorous, half-hardy, soft yellow *Rosa banksiae lutea*; under glass it will flower in early April and give little or no trouble with disease, and, being evergreen, it will not shed its leaves.

N.B. Roses suitable for forcing or for growing under glass are marked (Gh) in the Dictionary section.

Roses for Cutting and Arranging

All the flower arrangers I know enjoy working with roses, though most will admit to a nervousness when using them because of their relatively short life when cut. I have never quite made up my mind whether or not I totally approve of cutting roses, a hark back, I think, to the days when it was quite in order for my grandmother to have flowers in the house, provided they came from someone else's garden. There are no such rules in our house, however, so I suppose I belong to the cutting brigade.

Flower arranging is an art, and is all about proportion and balance. In its simplest form, one bloom placed in a vase by one person can look good, but by another, ridiculous. In its complex form, like painting, the same dozen roses can look either a daub or a masterpiece, depending upon the eye and hands of whoever arranged them. At flower shows I always visit the Floral Art section but so far have seldom agreed with a judge's verdict. This makes it all the more fascinating. The ladies of flower clubs must have temperaments of steel. Some years ago, a very persuasive lady telephoned me to ask for help. 'I need a thousand blooms,' she said, 'for a festival of Rossini Music and Song.' Marj Barton will know who I mean. Until the day I arrived in Sunderland I cursed myself for not saying No; the logistics were ridiculous – cut 1000 blooms one day, up at the crack of dawn, travel for seven hours the next. But when I arrived at Bishopswearmouth church I knew it was all worthwhile. I was besieged by, embraced and thoroughly spoilt by an army of 'Geordie' lady flower arrangers who produced some real works of art with my roses in that church. Later, when the soprano hit top C, petals fluttered to the floor to add an extra sense of unreality to my first encounter with the friendly Northeast.

Selecting roses for cutting is, in itself, an acquired skill. Cut them too tight and they never open, too open and they last only fleetingly. The best stage is when the sepals have started to fold back and the furled petals are showing colour. Timing is important. Early morning or late evening are best, but at whatever time flowers are cut they should always be placed in water up to their necks and stood in a cool place for two or three hours before they are arranged. A couple of spoonfuls of sugar or even a pint of lemonade to about a gallon of water will help them to stay fresh for a few hours longer. Before placing the flowers in water it is best to remove the two bottom leaves – no more – and scrape the thorns from the bottom 3 in (7.5 cm). Some people crush the base of each stem but I usually make a cut about half-an-inch (1 cm) long upwards into it. This exposes a bigger area of inner tissue and enables the flower to take up more water. Cut roses will often wilt in warm, dry conditions, and lightly syringing the leaves with cold water will help to revive them. I am told by the experts that plunging the bottom inch of stem into boiling water for about a minute and then quickly back into cold water will sometimes revitalize wilting blooms.

At its best, flower arranging is a subtle art

Some people believe that harm can be done to rose bushes by the cutting of blooms, and certainly if too many are taken with long stems the plants do suffer slightly, but they should come to no real harm. Try to cut to an eye, though, so as not to leave an unsightly stump to die back on the bush.

Carnations are delightful flowers and they have longer-lasting qualities than roses, but I never wear them as buttonholes. I prefer roses and, to keep them fresh, I use one of the little water holders that fix to the back of the lapel. These can be bought from most good florists for a trifling sum.

N.B. Roses that make good cut flowers are marked ✂ in the Dictionary section.

Roses for Exhibition

The first ever National Rose Show in Britain was staged in Piccadilly, London, in 1858. It heralded the beginning of an important aspect of rose growing which has been popular ever since, giving growers the opportunity to pit their skills against one another by producing the shapeliest and biggest possible blooms and staging them at their best. Exhibitors need an immense amount of expertise, a thorough understanding of the subject and the patience of Job. It also helps to be a good loser, for judges have a habit of awarding first prize to the other chap's rose which, in no way, is ever as good as yours.

I should declare here that I have not entered roses for 'the best bloom in the show' for many years. At most shows, both national and provincial, nurserymen compete for the best overall display of roses, but the quality of their blooms, although very high on the judges' list, is just one criterion; the others are quantity, arrangement and educational interest. Nurserymen also compete for customers, which is a very good reason for beating the other chap at his own game.

Competitive exhibiting for the amateur is not without cost, so, having gone through catalogues and visited shows to select those varieties likely to win awards, the decision has to be made as to which ones to grow. Bear in mind that show schedules often have classes of from one to twelve blooms of the same variety, so purchases have to be made in sufficient quantity to allow for spares. Certain varieties constantly win prizes and they are the ones to choose; they will, almost certainly, be Hybrid Teas.

Having selected the varieties, it is then a case of getting down to growing them for this special purpose. First, you need a good, heavy loam with plenty of added organic matter, followed by regular feeding with rose fertilizers. Hard pruning is vital in the first year; remember, it is quality that counts, not quantity, so usually, depending upon the variety, only the best and strongest shoots should be allowed to develop. Healthy roses lead to big blooms, so spraying programmes must be religiously followed. Timing, too, is important and pruning dates should be adjusted to the date of the show. As the show gets nearer so protection of blooms becomes necessary; small umbrellas and windbreaks then come into play – on or off – according to the weather. Most Hybrid Teas, as a matter of course, produce several buds around the central apex bud. To encourage the bush to put all its efforts into one good bloom, all the smaller buds should be removed.

Well before the show, exhibitors should familiarize themselves with the expectations of the particular society staging the show and carefully read the schedule. Disqualification will follow for even the slightest infringement of the rules. In Britain a set of standard rules, covering both exhibitors and judges, has been drawn up by the Royal National Rose Society. Judges are usually experienced growers themselves. The winning bloom of each class will be the one, or group, that displays the best form, size, substance, freshness, purity of colour, refinement and trueness to type at the exact time it is judged. Different criteria apply to other types but Hybrid Teas are at their best when, at the time the judge examines them, they display all these attributes and are at a stage where the outer rows of petals are unfurled and well spaced, and the centre ones are still holding a conical shape. Other factors come into the reckoning, too, depending upon the class and the type of rose. These include quality, cleanliness of foliage, length and condition of stem, balance between size of flower and thickness of stem and so on.

Exhibitors are free to indulge in what is termed 'dressing'. This requires much skill and patience, and hours are spent preparing blooms with camel-hair brushes, tweezers, bent wire, cottonwool buds, toothpicks, etc. With these instruments every petal and petal fold is preened to form the favoured

Both 'Royal Highness' (*above*) and 'Red Devil' (*left*) are popular exhibition varieties

shape of the particular variety. All beauty treatment is done during the last hours before the blooms are left alone on the bench and to the mercy of the judges. Prior to this, from the moment the roses are selected and cut, the utmost care is taken to ensure that no harm comes to them. Special travelling boxes are often used, with each rose segregated in its own compartment. While in transit blooms showing any signs of opening too much are held together with soft wool or raffia and those of slightly uneven shape, or not yet sufficiently open, have little pellets inserted between the rows of petals to correct, if possible, these faults. The pellets are usually shaped to fit and can be made of polystyrene, cottonwool or tissue paper.

Most show schedules have dozens of classes for dozens of different types of roses. This necessarily brief account has not touched on such things as the spacing of blooms, the importance of correct length of stem, the different skills required in displaying Cluster-Flowered types and how the wiring of blooms is frowned upon by some but not others. Already I may have gone too far, for the skills of exhibiting are best explained by those who have proved themselves at the art. I can, perhaps, recommend a few roses that I have seen winning major prizes from time to time: they are 'Admiral Rodney', 'Amatsu-Otome', 'Big Chief', 'Lakeland', 'Montezuma', 'Perfecta', 'Red Devil' and 'Royal Highness'. There are lots of others, but attention must be paid to labelling. Judges like correct names, and if they fail to notice an incorrect one, a fellow exhibitor surely will.

N.B. Roses suitable for exhibiting are marked (E) in the Dictionary section.

Roses as Standards

I have declared elsewhere that growing roses as standards is not a favourite pastime of mine. I find them contrived and too regimental for my taste.

'Veilchenblau' growing as a standard in the Ruston rose gardens, South Australia

'Buff Beauty' as a standard in the Ruston rose gardens, South Australia

Nevertheless, in fairness, I accept that there is considerable scope for this type of rose in many modern gardens. On my travels, I have seen excellent standards or tree roses as they are called in some parts of the world. Two, in particular, stand out in my memory, both in Australia at the Ruston rose garden; each had trunks far thicker than we could ever expect in Europe and heads large enough to conceal their upright disposition. One was 'Buff Beauty', the other 'Veilchenblau'. Standards first came into fashion in the mid-1800s and many varieties were offered in catalogues in the days of William Paul. Nowadays far fewer varieties are available – not all roses enjoy having to draw their sap up long stems and others are easily blown out by wind.

Standards are produced by the budding of named varieties at preselected heights on to specially grown stems (for the technique of budding, see page 121). In Europe *Rosa rugosa* is by far the most popular for this purpose; another is a form of *Rosa canina* called 'Pfander'. In other parts of the world *Rosa multiflora* and climbing 'Dr Huey' are more widely used. Standards are usually 'worked' (that is, budded) at about 3 ft 6 in (1.05 m), half standards at 2 ft 9 in (82.5 cm) and weeping standards at 5 ft (1.5 m). A fairly recent development is the quarter standard which is budded at about 18 in (45cm) from the ground; Miniatures are often seen at this height and, as such, make good subjects for growing in pots. Another group now popular as standards are the long-flowering Procumbents. 'Nozomi', although once-flowering, is extremely good grown in this way, drooping, as it does, to

the ground from at least 5 ft (1.5 m). This variety seems to be incompatible with *Rosa rugosa* and, for no obvious reason, suddenly dies off. I am now trying it on 'Pfander' stems and those so far produced have proved rudely healthy.

The weepers are my favourites, flexible ramblers that cascade to the ground without too much help. Special wire frames can be employed to assist their downward growth and add extra strength, but I prefer to grow

Fragrant virtues: 'Sir Frederick Ashton' (*top*), one of the few white roses with scent; 'Lady Sylvia' (*bottom left*), popular for its scent for more than sixty years; and 'Kazanlik' (*bottom right*), grown for centuries in Bulgaria for attar of roses

them naturally. 'Albéric Barbier', 'Minnehaha' and 'Excelsa' are excellent. Some shrub roses also make good standards but these can easily get top heavy as they grow, so staking is important. In particular I like 'Ballerina', 'Yesterday' and, of course, the lovely 'Canary Bird' which, when placed at the top of a stem, makes an elegant semi-weeper.

Floribundas such as 'Iceberg', 'Evelyn Fison' and 'Arthur Bell' make superb plants as either full or half standards. Of the Hybrid Teas, the best are those that grow bushily with good foliage such as 'Silver Jubilee', 'Alec's Red' and 'Grandpa Dickson'. Orange is a popular colour, but in colder areas roses of this shade are best avoided since they tend to be less hardy than those of other colours. Standards are vulnerable to wind damage, so they should be secured to an adequate stake by, at least, two strong straps; and all weepers should be pruned very hard in their first season, for nothing looks more ungainly than a leggy standard.

Fragrance in Modern Roses

Noses are instinctively drawn to roses and it is always a great disappointment to find a beautiful bloom without perfume. An unfair criticism levelled at modern roses is lack of fragrance. Certainly there was a period in the 1950s and '60s when many varieties were introduced without much scent, but breeders soon realized the error of their ways and things are different now. These days very few Hybrid Teas are introduced that are not worth a second sniff. Floribundas still have some way to go but there are several fine exceptions; no gardener should lack choice if perfume is his or her priority.

The famous 'Frau Karl Druschki' was the first white rose to be condemned for lack of scent. Since then, several other white varieties have suffered the same fate, though two recent introductions, 'Margaret Merril' and 'Sir Frederick Ashton', are both well endowed. When talking of roses with perfume, it is impossible to exclude the sisters 'Ophelia', 'Mme Butterfly' and 'Lady Sylvia', for these three ladies owe much of their long-standing popularity to this virtue alone. And since the Second World War, 'Prima Ballerina', 'Fragrant Cloud' and 'Anna Pavlova' have won many friends as the result of that first sniff.

'Dusky Maiden' was the first Floribunda with perfume, and although still in a minority, several excellent and highly scented varieties have been raised since then; 'Arthur Bell', 'Fragrant Delight' and 'Margaret Merril', again, immediately spring to mind. Breeders are well aware that a good scented rose will always triumph over a good non-scented one of the same colour, so we need never fear that perfume will disappear from our favourite flower.

N.B. A fragrance rating is given to each rose in the Dictionary section.

PART III
The Cultivation of Roses

Choosing and Buying Roses

Unless you have a good all-round knowledge of roses to the point where you know the foibles and limitations of the varieties you wish to grow, choosing roses is not a straight-forward exercise. It is not like buying a manu-factured commodity. A spade is a spade and, as a general rule, will be as good as the price you wish to pay. While the adage 'you get what you pay for' can be applied to roses in the commodity sense, often depending on where you buy them, it does not necessarily follow that a more expensive variety in any one cata-logue will be any better than a less expensive one of the same colour. It could be worse, in fact, for the pricing of different varieties is not determined by their size or quality. It is usu-ally calculated by balancing the following fac-tors: the degree of difficulty in producing the rose, the length of time it has been on the mar-ket, the royalty the nurseryman has to pay to its raiser, its rarity and the likely demand in comparison to other varieties.

Roses can be purchased in three different ways. By far the most common way and undoubtedly the best is direct from the nurs-ery that has produced them, usually by mail order. Most such roses are termed 'bare root' or 'open ground' plants. In Britain the rose industry is. well served by the RGA (Rose Growers Association), an organization which is run by its members and is consumer-orien-tated, setting standards of quality and service to the public besides attending to the needs of its membership. There is no price fixing within the industry, so prices vary from nurs-ery to nursery and region to region, but by and large a rose purchased from a member of the Association should be at least up to the standard recommended as first quality by the British Standards Institution. Other countries have similar guidelines for growers. This does not mean that there are no good growers out-side the RGA, of course, but beware of cheap roses, for inferior stock sometimes finds its way on to the market through dealers who have never grown a rose themselves. Such roses may be sub-standard, wrongly labelled or both – you may be lucky but not often.

The second way to purchase roses is in containers. These are usually obtained from garden centres, although many specialist growers offer a selection of them – but they are seldom, if ever, sent by mail order. Those bought from garden centres will have been acquired for resale from a wholesale grower. Container-grown roses are becoming very popular – though the range of varieties on offer is often limited – because they have the one clear advantage that you can see what you are buying. They are usually sold in spring and summer when it is impossible to plant bare-root specimens. It is also possible to buy root-wrapped plants from garden centres, usually in the spring. These are bare-root plants placed in a polythene bag with damp peat to keep them reasonably fresh.

The third method of purchase is through a shop or store. Roses sold through these out-lets are usually packaged in polythene, often with an exaggerated colour picture of its con-tents displayed on the bag. If you intend to buy such roses, examine them carefully before doing so; and if they are at all dry or have less than two strong shoots at a mini-mum – think twice.

It is important to buy roses only of the highest quality, for if you start with good plants they give far better value for money over the years. There is no doubt, however, that roses are best bought freshly dug from a nurseryman who has grown them himself. He is usually confident of his product and will sel-dom decline to replace any that fail to grow

A commercial nursery: although now in bloom, plants will be lifted for sale in the autumn

during the first few weeks of the growing season after purchase.

As for selecting varieties, again there is no better place than a nursery to see roses growing, either in the fields or in a display garden. Some roses are more photogenic than others and printing processes vary too, so although most catalogues are written in a helpful way, try not to make your choice from pictures alone. Decide on your needs from written descriptions and speak to someone who knows. Most specialist rose growers are too concerned with their reputation to sell you something you don't want or a variety that is not up to your needs.

Flower shows provide good opportunities to see roses, but sometimes those on display have been produced under glass, especially for summer shows, so do not order without first speaking to the grower. Once you have made your choice, order early. Bare-root roses can be safely planted at any time during the dormant season, but if you wish to plant them in November you will need to order by midsummer at the latest. As most nurseries dig up and despatch their orders in rotation as received (and most good growers deal with thousands of orders in the lifting season), it is, therefore, impossible to send them all out at the same time. Another good reason for not ordering late is that if a variety is in short supply or in demand, you will be disappointed and it may well be too late to place an order elsewhere. This applies particularly to rare and unusual varieties and to those newly on offer. If you do have to place an order late in the season, prepare a small piece of ground by covering it with frost-proof material in readiness for your roses so that they can be heeled-in whatever the weather. Most nurseries will try to avoid sending roses during severe, frosty spells but sometimes, when the weather changes suddenly after despatch, they are caught out. If the ground is too hard for heeling-in when your roses arrive, plunge their roots (still in their bundle) into a bucket or box of peat or sand and leave them in the garage or a shed until the weather improves. Those that look a little dry on arrival should be completely buried for a couple of weeks; no harm will come to them and they will be as good as new when dug up.

N.B. An availability rating is given to each rose in the Dictionary section.

Commercial Production

Although no one is certain of the exact figure, between eighteen and twenty-five million rose bushes are produced annually in Great Britain – up to one bush for every three people in the population. Do a similar sum for the rest of the rose-loving world and the answer is – a very large number.

I decided to include a brief word about commercial production after a rather unpleasant experience with a customer who could not understand why it should take us two years to propagate a rare rose for her. Like all businesses, rose nurseries have to run at a profit so methods have changed somewhat since the beginning of this century, but the basic principles have remained unchanged since it was first discovered that two plants could be united by budding. In very recent times, in fact in the last ten years, other methods of production have been tried – micropropagation, for example, though it is by no means certain that the technique will ever become widespread, nor indeed whether all types of roses can be grown by this means. I shall confine my thoughts to a general outline of conventional practice and will deal with micropropagation on page 122.

Commercial rose growers need to own, or have access to, at least four times more land than is needed to grow a single crop. This is because rotation is important and also because roses take two full growing seasons to become saleable, so there will always be two crops of different ages growing at the same time. And, just as in the garden, roses never like growing on land that has previously had them without, at least, two years' rest in between.

Growers these days are well mechanized, for good land implements are important. Land is prepared by ploughing and surface cultivation well in advance; rootstocks are ordered from specialist growers many months beforehand, too. Stocks arrive in November and are kept, either heeled-in or in a cold store, until land and weather are suitable for planting. In Britain, this is usually in February or March. Stocks are planted by a tractor-drawn machine with four operators feeding

them in. The rows are usually from 30 to 36 in (75–90 cm) wide, with 6 in (15 cm) between the plants in each row. At these planting distances, the density is roughly 25,000 plants per acre. On a good day, a crew can plant about 25,000 stocks. When planting is finished, the sprayer moves in and sprays the soil with a pre-emergence herbicide. Fertilizers will have been applied well beforehand.

By mid-June the stocks are ready for budding (see page 121). Apart from lifting, this is the most expensive and time-consuming of all the tasks relating to the production of roses. Budding is a skill, the basics of which are not too difficult to learn providing the pupil is reasonably dexterous. Speed is acquired through practice and experience. It is very much a job for the young, for, although it is not physically demanding, it is not easy to work all day with the body bent double. The real secret of good budding is the speed at which it is carried out; the faster the budder works the more likely the buds are to 'take'. Budders usually work in pairs followed by a 'patcher' who places a small latex patch over the wound where the bud has been inserted. A good team of three will put on as many as six to seven thousand buds in a day. Budders are serviced by another team whose job is to cut the budwood from the correct varieties and dethorn them for ease of handling. Weather permitting, budding is usually finished by the end of July. It is never done in the rain. After July the buds will still 'take' but the percentage that live declines as the days get shorter. In peak season budders hope to get at least 90 per cent to take; 100 per cent is not uncommon on some varieties. Anything less than 85 per cent on modern varieties is considered poor, although with old-fashioned roses such a take would be considered good. Throughout the summer the stocks are kept clear of pests and diseases by regular spraying.

After budding, the next stage in the process is 'heading back', as it is known in Norfolk; in other parts of Britain it is called variously 'cutting down', 'heading off' or 'topping'. This takes place in the winter months, usually January or February depending on the weather, and involves the removal of all the top growth from the stock by cutting it off just above the point where the bud was inserted. Secateurs or long-handled pruners

1 A bud is removed from a stem or 'stick'. 2 The inner wood is carefully removed. 3 The bud is inserted into a prepared rootstock. 4 A protective latex patch is placed over the union

are used, though some large nurseries speed up the process with pneumatically operated secateurs. In early spring a balanced fertilizer is applied, together with further applications of pre-emergence herbicide. By May, the buds will have grown to about 3 or 4 in (7.5–10 cm). At this stage, some growers cut the young shoots back to just 1 in (2.5 cm) to encourage several shoots to grow from the union. By early June, the young maiden plants are about 6 in (15 cm) high and it is then that nurserymen pray for calm weather, for the plants are now very vulnerable and easily blown off at the union by wind; invariably there are a few windy days and losses can be heavy. By early July, the roses are in flower and in turn become the source of budding eyes for the next year's crop, and so on. As they grow, a careful watch is kept for suckers which appear from below the bud. These are removed as soon as they are spotted. A regular spraying programme is carried out against aphids, black spot, mildew and rust.

By October, the young plants will have rip-ened and lifting starts. This is usually done by a special tractor-drawn lifting plough which undercuts the plants, enabling them to be pulled easily from the ground with a gloved hand. On large, wholesale nurseries part of the crop is lifted and placed in cold stores where the roses come to no harm. On retail nurseries some growers do likewise; others simply lift the roses as they are needed for orders. Grading is important and by the time the roses have become saleable about 75 per cent of most varieties will be first quality; the remainder will have been lost through failure to take, by wind damage or inadequate size. It is impossible to forecast the demand for each variety two years ahead of sales, so few retail growers ever sell completely out of all varieties, although, of course, this is their aim. Roses, like most long-term crops, are both capital- and labour-intensive, and any form of bad husbandry can have dire consequences. Good training and skilled workers are there-fore essential.

Propagation

This section discusses briefly the various means by which roses are propagated. More details can be found in *Classic Roses*.

Budding

Budding is the form of propagation most commonly used by the commercial rose industry today. As the word implies, it is the removal of a bud – not a flower bud, but an axillary or growth bud – from the stem of one plant and the implantation of it into the stem or root of another. Providing the pupil is dexterous and has a supple body for bending, it takes only a few short lessons to teach the basic procedures. After that it becomes an acquired technique with proficiency coming from practice. Budding is the most economical means of producing roses because several new plants can be grown from just one branch of a bush. There are about six buds on an average shoot, so one well-grown bush with, say, five shoots can give rise to as many as thirty new plants.

Grafting

This form of propagation is seldom used today in the production of bush or climbing roses, but it is quite common as a method of producing Miniatures. As with budding it involves the removal of part of a shoot, known as the 'scion', of any variety one wishes to multiply and uniting it with the root, or 'stock', of another.

Miniature roses are normally grafted under glass in early spring, using semi-dormant material. With this technique, growers can obtain dozens of grafts from each stock plant and have the results of their work growing on into mature plants in just a few weeks. Despite their small size, or perhaps because of it, Miniatures grow quickly when grafted on to the roots of, say, *Rosa laxa*, and the resulting plants are sturdier and taller than those produced from cuttings.

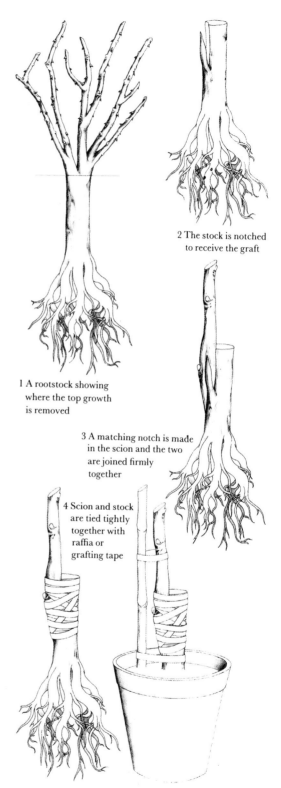

2 The stock is notched to receive the graft

1 A rootstock showing where the top growth is removed

3 A matching notch is made in the scion and the two are joined firmly together

4 Scion and stock are tied tightly together with raffia or grafting tape

5 After waxing to make the join watertight the plant is potted, staked and tied

Cuttings

Although roses other than Miniatures produced from traditional cuttings have not been a commercial proposition for growers in the past, this method is now more widely used to produce some varieties, especially the newer Patio and Procumbent varieties which seem to root easily and, when grown in pots, transplant very well. They never transplant well when raised as bare-root specimens. In time, when the consumer comes to appreciate the advantages of own-root roses and accepts them in smaller pots than he has previously been used to, many more will become available through both garden centres and nurseries. Most own-root roses are produced from relatively small, soft or semi-hardwood cuttings, rooted under glass in a mist propagation unit. In these conditions cuttings will root in a couple of weeks and, after potting and weaning, can be of saleable size in a matter of three or four months.

Winter-taken hardwood cuttings of some varieties also root well, but this is an uneconomical way to produce roses. Compared to budding, for example, one cutting equals up to six buds. For the amateur, hardwood cuttings are easiest and best; not a few varieties will root readily if taken in, say, October at about 6 in (15 cm) long, using ripened wood and plunged to half their length in sandy compost. Cuttings of a good thickness are taken in winter from suitable, vigorous stock plants of species such as *Rosa multiflora* and hybrids like 'Dr Huey' and 'Indica Major'. Until the technique of producing rootstocks from seed was developed in Europe, roses everywhere were produced by this means.

Softwood cuttings can be taken from early summer (mid June) onwards. The area of foliage is reduced to minimize transpiration and the cutting is placed in a pot of peat and sand, which must be kept moist, with a polythene bag over the top. When the cutting has made some growth the bag is removed and the young plant is hardened off before winter, when it can be potted on.

Micropropagation

Amateur rosarians are unlikely to practise this form of propagation, but since this book is concerned with twentieth-century roses and more and more of the roses bought in the future will be produced by this means, a few words should be included to give a brief outline of the process. The micropropagation of plants is a form of vegetative propagation carried out in sterile growing rooms or laboratories. Roses produced in this way are grown on their own roots, like cuttings. Before the technique was discovered, biologists and botanists believed that roots and shoots could be formed only from the actual growing parts of plants. Micropropagation is a type of tissue culture and involves the taking of a small piece of tissue, or even a single cell, from a growth point or axillary bud and stimulating this to produce more growth points which, in turn, produce more and so on. At first the shoots are without roots, so these are induced by adding naturally occurring, root-stimulating hormones to the medium in which they are grown. Once roots have formed, the tiny

CUTTINGS

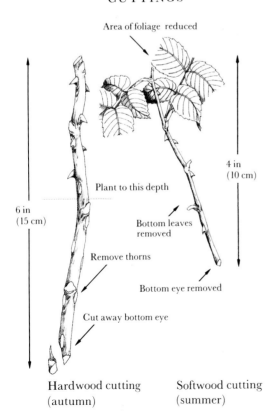

Area of foliage reduced

4 in
(10 cm)

6 in
(15 cm)

Plant to this depth

Bottom leaves removed

Remove thorns

Bottom eye removed

Cut away bottom eye

Hardwood cutting
(autumn)

Softwood cutting
(summer)

plants are grown on for a time and then carefully weaned into ordinary compost to take their place in the outside world.

There is still some way to go before this form of propagation becomes common practice in the commercial production of roses. The most difficult stage is the weaning of plants into ordinary soil, but research work is going on all the time and there is no doubt that ways and means will be found to make this easier.

Not all types of roses take readily to micropropagation. Hybrid Teas and Floribundas, by and large, do not grow as well on their own roots as they do when budded, and some shrub roses are even more reluctant. Many of the Miniatures and Procumbents seem to thrive, however, and it is these that are mostly produced by micropropagation at present. This is probably because plants formed in this way sprout many more shoots from the base in the first year than those produced by budding or from cuttings. One significant advantage of micropropagation is the speed of rooting; another is the large number of plants produced from just one small piece of tissue. By harnessing this technique, breeders can build up numbers and launch new varieties far more quickly than by conventional means, but this practice is by no means widespread.

Hybridizing

Hybridizers have been mentioned often in preceding sections, so a little space should be given to a brief explanation of the principles and mechanics of their work.

Hybridizing is the inducement of hybrids or crossbreeds by the deliberate crossing of two species or cultivars. Hybrids can also arise from the natural cross-pollination of two plants by insect activity. In days gone by, rose growers would collect the hips of roses grown in close proximity to others in the hope that nature had taken its course and produced hybrids. Nowadays hybridizing is more sophisticated and breeders create their hybrids by the deliberate cross-pollination of two preselected varieties. To be sure of success, cross-pollination is best carried out under glass, at least in Britain. In a greenhouse regime, roses are induced to flower earlier and this enables seeds to ripen fully, even in the most inclement summer.

In botanical terms, the flower of a rose is perfect; that is to say, both male and female organs are present in the same structure. To avoid self-fertilization, the male parts of the flower, the anthers, are removed before pollen is applied from another flower. This is termed 'emasculation'. During this operation care is required to avoid any damage to other parts of the seed pod or 'receptacle'. In order to remove the anthers, the petals must also be removed. The timing is fairly critical in that the flower should be fully developed and ready for fertilization and yet in a state when no self-pollination or chance cross-pollination could have occurred. This, in the case of a rose, is at a time when the petals are still furled around the reproductive organs, and just before the pollen is ripe.

Knowing full well that nothing is predictable when crossing two hybrids, hybridizers usually give careful consideration to the merits of possible offspring by looking at the pedigree of the roses they wish to cross. In this way they hope either to perpetuate a particular attribute or to avoid a serious fault. All possibilities are considered, such as colour, fragrance, habit of growth, foliage, hardiness and, above all else these days, resistance to diseases.

Having prepared the seed pod by emasculation, pollen from a selected pollen parent is applied to the stigma a day or so later when it has become receptive and slightly sticky. This stickiness normally manifests itself as a change of colour from, say, creamy-yellow to orange or gold. Pollen is applied with a camel-hair brush or direct from a fully open flower removed from the parent plant. Depending on the variety, pollen grains can be large, plentiful and very visible, or small, scarce and difficult to see with the naked eye. Most modern roses are fairly free with their pollen so that, depending on the method used to apply it, pollen from one male can fertilize several seed parents. After the pollen is applied, the cross is recorded on a label which is attached to the stalk below the pod. The standard method of recording crosses is with the seed parent's name written first. If cross-pollination is successful, the seed pod starts to

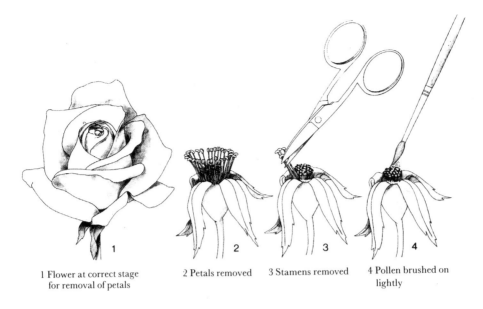

1 Flower at correct stage for removal of petals 2 Petals removed 3 Stamens removed 4 Pollen brushed on lightly

HYBRIDIZING

swell and ripen and after about six to eight weeks turns orange or red. At the end of the summer the hips are collected and the seeds removed. Each separate lot of seeds is best placed in a small polythene bag with their label, so that they can be handled easily.

It is important that rose seeds are exposed to fluctuating temperatures while dormant in the winter. In days not too long gone, they would be mixed with sand and placed outside to take all weathers, a process known as 'stratification'. To achieve the same effect these days, some breeders leave them in a freezer for a few weeks prior to sowing. Before sowing, germination can be improved if they are soaked for a time in a mild solution of gibberellic acid. Seeds are sown about half-an-inch (1.25 cm) deep into good compost on a bench in a preheated greenhouse in February. Germination is erratic and usually starts in April when the soil temperature is at about 7–10 °C (45–50 °F). After germinating, the seedlings grow quite rapidly and some can be in flower as little as six weeks later. At this stage only the best and most promising are kept. These are potted on or budded outside in the nursery for further observation. At the seedling stage as few as 10 per cent are sufficiently different or promising enough to warrant further testing. After the first year of trial out of doors, less than 1 per cent of those orig-inally selected will be considered good enough for further or prolonged trials.

Planting Bare-Root Roses

Bare-root roses can be planted at any time during the dormant season, which in the northern hemisphere usually means between the last week in October and the end of March. They should not, however, be planted during heavy frost.

Roses prefer good, deep, heavy loam, but with a little help they will grow in most soils. Do not despair if your soil is light and sandy or even chalky, for a careful choice of type and variety should still produce fine blooms. A good rule of thumb is to choose vigorous roses for light soils; even if they do not attain catalogue specifications they will, at least, stand a better chance than the shorter, more fussy varieties. Providing your soil has a pH of between 6.5 and 7.5, is of reasonable depth and your roses are given some love and attention, they should succeed in almost any conditions.

When planting a new rose, it is important to incorporate as much organic material as possible in the soil that will be packed around its roots. Well-rotted farmyard manure is best, but if this is not readily available then a mixture of peat and bonemeal – one handful of bonemeal to a bucketful of peat – makes an adequate substitute. Whatever is used must, however, be well mixed with the soil before planting. The hole should be large enough to accommodate the rose without cramping its roots and should be deep enough to enable the union – the point where the roots and shoots join – to be placed about 1 in (2.5 cm) below ground level. When the soil is replaced around the root it should be trodden firmly enough to eliminate any air pockets, with the last spadeful being used to cover footprints and to provide a good tilth around the plant. A top dressing of bonemeal or proprietary rose fertilizer will help the rose get off to a good start.

Planting distances vary according to the type of rose, but most modern Hybrid Teas and Floribundas are best placed about 24 in (60 cm) apart. Shorter varieties will tolerate 18 in (45 cm), and some Compact Floribundas and Miniatures can be planted even closer than this. For other types such as shrubs, Procumbents and climbers, consult a good catalogue for their dimensions and plant accordingly. Do not spoil the effect by planting roses too far apart, especially the smaller kinds. They quite enjoy embracing one another.

Planting Container-Grown Roses

More often than not container-grown roses are purchased during the summer months, but it is quite in order to plant them at any time of the year. When removing the pot, usually of polythene, the soil packed around the roots must not be disturbed. The best method is to place the rose in the hole and then cut off the container, rather than shaking it out or tipping it upside down. Once the plant with its undisturbed ball of soil is in position, refill the hole with care. Since most composts used for container roses are peat-based, which is difficult to moisten, plunge the rose for half an hour or so into a bucket of water before planting out. As with bare-root roses, make sure that the union is 1 in (2.5 cm) below soil level;

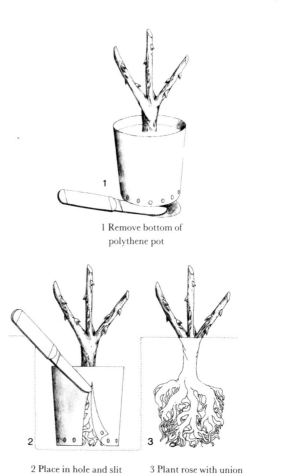

1 Remove bottom of polythene pot

2 Place in hole and slit side of pot – remove polythene

3 Plant rose with union 1 in (2.5 cm) below soil level

PLANTING CONTAINER-GROWN ROSES

this is very important as it reduces the possibility of suckers and stabilizes the bush against wind damage

Standard roses, either bare-root or container-grown, require a good stake to support them. This should always be in position before the tree is planted and should be driven at least 18 in (45 cm) into the soil to give adequate support, even deeper if the soil is sandy. One very important thing to remember is that roses have an aversion to soil which has previously grown their own kind. Never replant in exactly the same spot without first either changing the soil or giving it a rest from roses for at least two years. This problem can be tackled by sterilizing the soil chemically, but take very careful advice beforehand and exercise great caution over the application. Unless whole beds are treated, the chemical could harm adjacent plants.

Pruning

How and when to prune roses usually provokes friendly disagreement among rosarians, and in my experience almost all the arguments in favour of this method or that have some weight to them. In fact, pruning is far less complicated than many books and articles on the subject may suggest. The most important 'tools' a pruner needs are, first, common sense; secondly and most important, a feeling for the plant; thirdly, a strong pair of gloves to give confidence; and fourthly, good, sharp secateurs. Pruning is vital, for roses left unpruned, especially Hybrid Teas and Floribundas, quickly become spent and look tired, producing far fewer flowers and of diminishing quality as the years go by.

The chief and only golden rule that I apply to pruning is that it is vital in the first year after planting. Without fail, all newly planted roses should be pruned to approximately 3 in (7.5 cm) or 3–4 eyes from the bottom of each stem; this applies not only to bush roses but also to climbers, shrub roses and standards. The reason is to encourage all new growth to sprout from as near the base of the plant as possible and so to lay the foundation for well-balanced, sturdy growth in the future. There can be no doubt that timid pruning at this early stage leads to more disappointment with new roses than any other single malpractice. In the interest of satisfied customers, I would dearly love to send out all our modern roses ready pruned, but when we tried this some years ago, even with a note of explanation, we received too many complaints about quality and size to warrant perseverance.

In subsequent years pruning need not be so severe. It then becomes a question of judgement as to how many shoots to remove and by how much to reduce the length of the remaining ones. Remember, rose bushes will quickly become leggy and bare-bottomed if given half a chance. As a general guide, shoots of Hybrid Teas and Floribundas thinner than a pencil are unlikely to produce flowers of any decent size, so they should be cut back harder than thicker shoots. Bear in mind that all things are comparative, so the thickness of wood will depend upon the overall size of the plant. All dead wood should be removed and the aim should be to keep the centre of the plant as open as possible. I do not place as much importance on a slanting cut as some people do, but where possible the cut should be made just above a bud, preferably a healthy bud, facing outwards from the plant. As time goes on you will learn by your mistakes – but if in doubt, hard pruning is better than no pruning at all. As for timing, there are advocates of autumn pruning, winter pruning and spring pruning, and to some extent the choice is governed by location and the severity of cold weather. Here in Norfolk, late February to early March is about the right time but a few weeks either side might be more appropriate in other temperate climates. Whatever time is chosen for the main pruning, always tidy up the plant by removing a few inches of shoots in late autumn. This will improve the appearance of the garden and help to reduce wind-rock during the winter.

Dead-heading should be practised throughout the summer. This is very important both for the wellbeing of the roses and the appearance of the garden. Dead-heads should be removed at the point of the first true growth bud with secateurs; do not just detach the flower from its stalk with your fingers. Another summer job is to keep an eye open for suckers, which are shoots that grow from

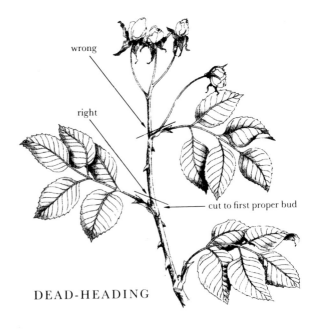

wrong

right

cut to first proper bud

DEAD-HEADING

An unpruned rose in early spring and *right:* the same rose correctly pruned – always cut above a healthy bud facing out from the plant, and to 3–4 eyes from the bottom of each stem

the stock below the union. They may not be recognized immediately by the inexperienced eye, but by the time they are 2–3 in (5–7.5 cm) long they will start to show differences from the main shoots of the bush and should be removed immediately. To do this, trace them back to their source. If your roses have been planted correctly, suckers will almost always appear from below ground, so it may be necessary to disturb soil to remove them without leaving a stump to grow yet more.

Standards should be pruned just as are bush roses of the same variety and suckers that sprout from the stem removed immediately. Climbing roses flower on wood produced earlier in the season and the more spurs that can be encouraged the better, as they are usually a source of flowers. Long, climbing shoots should be tied as horizontally as persuasion allows and bent in as many directions as possible without breaking. Where a climber is very vigorous, strong shoots should be reduced by about one-third of their length to encourage laterals.

Ramblers always flower on wood produced in the previous season, so it is often a good idea to prune them in the summer, after they have finished flowering. If this cannot be done and they have to be pruned later, aim to leave as many young shoots as possible, removing only older wood to keep the plant in shape. The same rule applies to weeping standards and most of the once-flowering Procumbent roses where density of growth is important. Any variety that flowers all summer through should be pruned in winter or spring. As for shrub roses, it will depend somewhat on type, but generally speaking the same rules apply as with modern bush roses: aim to keep the plant open and encourage plenty of strong shoots from the base. Some of the older, summer-flowering shrubs are often best left unpruned but this book is not really concerned with them (see *Classic Roses*).

Soils and Feeding

Roses prefer soil with a pH of about 6.5, in other words slightly acid of neutral, although they are not too fussy about alkalinity and many will tolerate up to pH 7.5. Should you suspect that your soil is lower or higher than these tolerance levels, then either have your soil tested or do so yourself with one of the inexpensive soil-testing kits available from most good garden centres.

If the rules of good husbandry have been followed, ample organic material will have been applied to the rose beds before planting. In future years a balanced fertilizer should be applied as a top dressing each spring. Even in the best regulated rose beds, however, the balance of nutrients sometimes becomes upset and as a result roses start to look peaky. Deficiency or excess of one or more minerals is a probable reason for unhappy roses. Lack of nitrogen shows up in small, discoloured leaves and a reluctance to grow. Excess nitrogen, a common fault from overfeeding, shows in lush, coarse foliage and shyness in producing flowers. Potash deficiency manifests itself in cloudy, dark, brittle foliage; phosphate deficiency in small, underdeveloped, purplish leaves. Ample potash is an essential part of the diet of roses and sufficient phosphate is frequently lacking in most soils, so it is difficult to overfeed with these two minerals.

Deficiency of one or more trace elements is the most common of the nutritional problems encountered by roses. Such deficiencies show up in leaves as chlorosis, a greenish-yellow discoloration. Yellow blotches here and there, especially on older leaves, could be caused by a shortage of magnesium, and when young foliage is pale green or yellow this often indicates a lack of iron. Epsom salts applied either as a foliar-feed or as a soil drench will correct magnesium deficiency, and iron deficiency can be corrected by using chelated iron. Trace elements, however, are often not taken up by plants because of an imbalance of other minerals in the soil; lime applied in early spring will help to release them, especially iron.

Nowadays proprietary rose fertilizers are formulated to provide a proper diet, so twice yearly applications of these should keep the plants in shape. If soil conditions are not right, of course, proper feeding will not help. Although roses are relatively deep-rooted, they need moisture to function just as other plants do. Spare a thought for roses in the next drought; nothing can be more frustrating than to gasp for a drink as a sprinkler misses by inches, when dousing the lush green grass of the lawn close by.

Compost for pot roses should be soil-based if possible. One-third sterilized soil, one-third peat and one-third sharpsand with grit, with balanced fertilizer and lime, is about the best formula. Add plenty of drainage material – pottery shards and so forth – to the bottom of the container before filling it.

N.B. Roses tolerant of poorer soils are marked (P) in the Dictionary section.

Pests of Roses

Aphids are the most common pest to attack roses, greenfly in particular. These little creatures multiply very rapidly in optimum weather conditions. The odd one or two are not particularly harmful but they seldom feed in pairs and, almost within hours, thousands can occupy young growing shoots and succulent flower buds. Any of the wide range of proprietary systemic insecticides are very effective against them.

The second most common pest is probably leaf-rolling sawfly, although unless of epidemic proportions its effect is more unsightly than harmful. In some years, usually after a mild, sunny spring, it can be a real problem. Sawflies especially like climbers and ramblers or roses growing close to walls, or in semi-shade. The adult fly travels from leaf to leaf laying eggs, at the same time injecting a substance which causes foliage to curl into a sort of tube, thus providing its offspring, a small grub, protection from predators. Regular spraying from early spring onwards with a systemic insecticide will help to control the adult flies, but control of the grubs themselves is more difficult due to the curled leaves. Mild infestations can be kept in check by squeezing the affected leaves between thumb and forefinger. Such treatment will not cure, but it will interfere with the life cycle of the insect and help to prevent worse infestations later in the year. For a serious outbreak, Derris seems to be the most effective of a range of chemicals to control grubs and caterpillars. Evidence of the latter's occasional presence are eaten-away leaves and tender young shoots.

Although less common, another little beast with a similar life cycle which from time to time renders roses unsightly is the slug sawfly. This feeds on the succulent parts of mature leaves, leaving behind just a skeleton of veins. Control is the same as for the leaf-rolling kind.

The evidence of another pest, red spider, is not immediately obvious, though signs of its presence usually mean that infestation is rife. The mites live on the undersides of leaves and individually are almost invisible. Affected leaves lose their colour, go limp and sometimes become cocooned in a ball of fine grey web. Except in hot, dry seasons red spiders seldom attack roses in the open. They are much more prevalent in greenhouses or on climbers and ramblers growing on hot, sheltered walls. Control is difficult, though special chemicals are available and can be effective if an infestation is noticed early enough.

Another group of minute creatures that enjoy the odd rose are thrips. These are a curse to exhibitors, for they nibble the edges of petals in hot, dry weather. Control them with the same systemic insecticides as those used for greenfly.

Except for offending the eye, the froghopper is not a serious pest. It spends its early life in a blob of spittle-like substance usually situated under buds at the top of young shoots. The best treatment is an extra-strong jet of liquid, to wash them off, when spraying against other pests and diseases. Finally there are two rural pests, rabbits and deer, which will nibble anything when hungry enough – and they love the flavour of roses. If they are known to be around, make sure the garden is fenced to exclude them. In winter rabbits can be a particular problem, stripping the bark from plants as high as they can reach, through sheer vandalism, it seems.

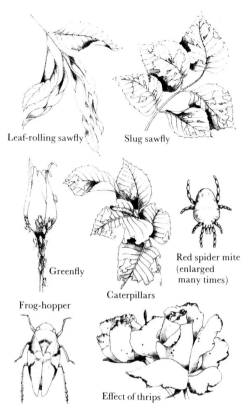

Leaf-rolling sawfly   Slug sawfly

Greenfly   Caterpillars   Red spider mite (enlarged many times)

Frog-hopper

Effect of thrips

PESTS OF ROSES

Diseases of Roses

Although the most common, mildew is probably the least harmful of the diseases that affect roses. If conditions are right, it can start very early in the growing season on some varieties. It first shows itself as small patches of grey mould on growing shoots, young leaves and small buds. These patches quickly spread and will soon cover all tender parts of the plant. Unless checked, mildew will suppress growth and look very unsightly. Fortunately, the disease is easily controlled by systemic fungicides – but the secret is to spray in anticipation rather than to cure.

Prevention is better than cure for black spot, too. As the name implies, its symptoms come in the form of black spots over the leaves. Given the chance, they spread rapidly until they completely cover the foliage, causing it to fall to the ground prematurely. Serious infections seldom set in before roses are in flower, though some varieties are susceptible to black spot and affected plants can be difficult to cure. At the first sign of trouble remove infected leaves and quickly burn them. Black spot is a fungal infection, and its spores are easily carried to the ground on fallen leaves, there to remain dormant in the soil through the winter before emerging again in the spring. It is wise, therefore, to spray plants and surrounding soil with a solution of Jeyes Fluid at pruning time.

Rust is by far the most pernicious and difficult to control of all the diseases of roses. It is also very surreptitious in that it develops on the undersides of leaves and so is usually well advanced in its life cycle by the time it is noticed. It starts with small orange or brown pustules which cluster together and spread to the upper surface of leaves and to stems and thorns, eventually turning black, reminiscent of soot. If a plant is badly infected it soon dies, if not from the disease itself then from an inability to resist winter frosts. At the first signs of the disease, remove and burn infected foliage and then spray the plant and its neighbours with a rust-control formula immediately. Some varieties are more susceptible to rust than others; avoid them, especially in gardens where the disease has proved a nuisance.

I know from bitter experience that the pests and diseases of roses can become almost a phobia to some people and nurserymen are frequently blamed for them, especially if plants show signs of trouble in their first year. I was once blamed for an epidemic of greenfly. Try to be realistic; roses have health problems just as we humans do. It is not your fault but is part of the balance of nature, and it is more the result of prevailing weather than any inadequacy of the grower. The best form of disease control is good husbandry. Healthy roses are less likely to suffer as badly from disease as those that are not doing so well. If a particular variety consistently gives trouble, banish it from the garden. It is not always easy to reject a friend just because of a few black spots, however, and if you plan a garden for disease resistance you may end up with a very dull garden indeed.

N.B. Roses susceptible to disease are marked in the Dictionary section as follows: BS✠ for black spot, R✠ for rust and M✠ for mildew.

Weed Control

The golden rule of weed control is to start off with clean soil. When digging and preparing a rose bed, therefore, make sure that the roots of all perennial weeds have been completely removed, for if they once become established they will be very difficult to eradicate. As with disease, prevention is far better than cure.

Except for those with time on their hands, hoeing has now become old fashioned. Gardeners today use two main methods to keep weeds at bay. The first is with chemicals, though herbicides can be dangerous both in application and in residual effect. Providing you have no aversion to the use of chemicals in the garden they can be very useful, however, but always follow the instructions on the packet exactly. Two types are generally available, selective contact and selective pre-emergence. These speak for themselves: the first kills existing weeds by contact; the second prevents their germination.

The other way of suppressing weeds is far less obnoxious. It is achieved by spreading a mulch of sterile material to a depth of 2–3 in (5–7.5 cm) over the soil. Coarse sedge peat can be used but this breaks down fairly quickly and will need replacing or replenishing each year. Bark chippings make by far the best mulch and are obtainable either from garden centres or direct from a sawmill, if you are lucky enough to live near to a forest. Sawdust, too, can be used but it will be toxic unless it is from mature wood and, being light, may also blow about in dry weather. No matter what is used as a mulch, it is advantageous to both the roses and the soil to till the soil beneath at least once a year, perhaps at pruning time. One of the disadvantages of chemicals and, to a lesser extent, of mulches is that they prohibit or restrict underplanting of rose beds with companion plants. If you can persevere for a year or two before applying either, therefore, other plants, such as bulbs, will have time to settle in.

PART IV
The Dictionary

Selections and Varieties

In choosing which varieties to include in the Dictionary I have analysed the most recent catalogues of specialist rose nurseries, not just from Britain but from the rest of the world. My final selection consists only of varieties and species that are currently available from nurseries and garden suppliers. I confess to a degree of favouritism in my choice of several roses, but of those selected, by far the majority should remain obtainable for not a few years to come.

In addition to trade catalogues, I have relied heavily on information gleaned from the following invaluable publications: *Find That Rose*, published annually by the British Rose Growers Association; *The Rose Directory*, published periodically by the Royal National Rose Society; *The Combined Rose List (Roses in Commerce and Cultivation)* compiled and published annually by Beverly R. Dobson, New York; and *Modern Roses 8 and 9* published by McFarland in conjunction with the American Rose Society.

The Descriptions

Most of the roses are described from personal experience. For those outside my sphere of knowledge which deserved inclusion, I have used the raiser's description or obtained information from reliable sources. Such roses are marked with a small asterisk beside the name.

Honours and Awards

Many roses have won awards of excellence at various trial grounds throughout the world. While I acknowledge such achievements and accept that such awards generally indicate a good variety, I do not accept that they necessarily reflect superiority, especially where awards are made on an annual basis and often after a relatively short period of, say, three years of trial. No specific honours are mentioned in the Dictionary, except where appropriate in passing.

Presentation

Letters and symbols are used throughout to indicate the special usages, aptitudes and foibles of roses. These are intended only as a guide for those who are not familiar with a particular variety; they merely indicate my own experience or, in some cases, the raiser's comments. Colour and degree of fragrance are, for example, from personal observation, likewise susceptibility to disease, which can depend upon factors outside the constitution of a particular variety, such as weather, soil conditions or, simply, bad husbandry. The raiser's name and the parentage and date of introduction of each variety are also included where known.

Synonyms

Where a synonym is in brackets it indicates the registered name of the rose for trademark purposes. Unbracketed synonyms are the names by which the rose may well be otherwise known.

Dimensions

Dimensions are expressed in both imperial and metric terms and assume the variety to be growing in normal garden soil and pruned regularly according to need.

Key to Letters and Symbols

(SP)	Spring-flowering only – usually from late May to early June in northern temperate climates		(SF)	Slight fragrance
			(MF)	Moderately fragrant
(S)	Summer-flowering only		(VF)	Very fragrant
(R)	Repeat-flowering from early summer		(B)	Good for bedding or for planting in groups
(C)	More or less continuous flowering throughout the summer from early summer on		(E)	Good for exhibition
(CL)	Suitable also for use as a climbing or pillar rose		▽	Suitable for growing in pots, tubs, urns and similar containers
(N)	Suitable for north walls (note: roses only tolerate such a situation)		BS	Susceptible to blackspot
			R	Susceptible to rust
(GC)	Procumbent or wide-growing, ground-cover varieties		M	Susceptible to mildew
(T)	Vigorous and suitable for growing up into trees		◍	Tolerant of shade
			☼	Prefers a sunny position
(P)	Tolerant of poorer soil		☺	Hates wet weather when in flower
(H)	Suitable for hedging		✂	Good as a cut flower
(Gh)	Good for forcing or for growing under glass		AW	Available widely at the time of writing
			AL	Availability limited to specialist suppliers

Hybrid Tea Roses (Large-Flowered Bush Roses)

The classification 'Hybrid Tea' may have been valid at one time – to describe hybrids from the Teas when they were first introduced – but it has no validity now, for most modern varieties have a far more mixed genealogy than the earlier ones.

In recent years Hybrid Teas have been reclassified simply as 'Large-Flowered' but this term has received scant attention from most nurserymen and, in many modern catalogues, they are still listed under their old name. Thousands have been raised and introduced since the first was named 'La France' in 1867 and many, probably deservedly, have quickly fallen by the wayside. In this Dictionary I have described 221. These include a number of up-to-date varieties and a few of my special favourites but, above all else, I hope my selection is a fair representation of the history of this much loved and auspicious group of roses.

Their uses are numerous. Many of the modern varieties are as floriferous as Floribundas and lend themselves readily to bedding and massed display. Many also grow happily among other plants; in a herbaceous border, for example, they can be very effective. Only a few are good as hedging plants, but most, if not all, will make themselves at home growing in urns or tubs. Almost without exception they are good for providing flowers for cutting and taking indoors. Some, in the right hands, will win prizes at shows; and quite a few more have prize-winning potential if forced under glass.

'Abbeyfield Rose' (Cocbrose)

Cocker UK 1985
'National Trust' × 'Silver Jubilee'
Free-flowering, with deep rosy pink blooms not over-full of petals but adequate to make this a shapely rose. Growth bushy with mid-green foliage.

[(C) (SF) (B) AL]   3' × 2'   90 × 60 cm

'Ace of Hearts', 'Asso di Cuori', 'Toque Rouge' (Korred)

Kordes GERMANY 1981
Parentage unknown
Shapely crimson to scarlet blooms with firm, crisp petals. They are slightly scented. Sturdy, upright growth with dark green, glossy foliage.

[(C) (MF) (B) AL]   3' × 2'   90 × 60 cm

'Admiral Rodney'

Trew UK 1973
Parentage unknown
Huge but shapely clear rose-pink flowers on a bushy, well-foliated plant. This variety is well loved by those keen on exhibiting but, sadly, lacks the vigour and floriferousness to make a good garden plant.

[(C) (MF) (E) ☺ B⬚ AL]   2' × 2'   60 × 60 cm

'Adolf Horstmann'

Kordes GERMANY 1971
'Colour Wonder' × 'Dr A. J. Verhage'
Deep yellow flowers flushed orange-pink which are large and shapely, especially so at the almost open stage. Upright and tidy growth with mid-green glossy foliage.

[(C) (SF) (E) AL]   3' × 2'   90 × 60 cm

'Alec's Red' and *below:* 'Alpine Sunset'

'Alec's Red' (Cored)

Cocker UK 1970
'Fragrant Cloud' × 'Dame de Coeur'
Crimson to cherry-red flowers are produced in abundance, the buds large and plump, almost black until they start to open. Strong necked, with dark green foliage and thorny stems. A good all-rounder.
[(C) (B) (VF) (P) AW] 2½' × 2' 75 × 60 cm

'Alexander' *see* Shrub Roses

'Alpine Sunset'

Cant UK 1974
'Dr A. J. Verhage' × 'Grandpa Dickson'
Soft peachy-yellow, large, full and shapely flowers are held on strong necks. Shortish, bushy but upright growth. Mid-green foliage.
[(C) (B) (E) (VF) AW] 2½' × 2' 75 × 60 cm

*'Amatsu-Otome'

Teranishi JAPAN 1960
'Chrysler Imperial' × 'Doreen'
Very large blooms of bright yellow flushed orange and coppery-red, held upright on leggy stems.

Foliage veined, mid-green, slightly glossy.
[(C) (E) BS◖⊞ AL] 4' × 3' 1.2 m × 90 cm

'Angèle Pernet'

Pernet-Ducher FRANCE 1924
'Bénédicte Sequin' × a Hybrid Tea
A beautiful rose of exquisite form and one of the most lovely to have come from the auspicious stable of Pernet-Ducher. Not an easy rose to grow and not the most free with its flowers, which are coppery-orange with no trace of garishness. Rich, dark, glossy foliage.
[(C) (MF) ▽ AL] 2' × 2' 60 × 60 cm

'Anna Pavlova'

Beales UK 1981

Parentage unknown

A beautiful, full, many petalled variety with a strong scent, each flower of blush-pink with deeper shadings held on a very strong neck. When fully open, some petals are fimbriated. Foliage large, rounded and rich dark green. In poorer soils this rose is best left unpruned.

[(C) (VF) (E) (Gh) ☺ ⁙ ▽ ✂ AL]
4' × 3'   1.2 m × 90 cm

'Anne Watkins'

Watkins UK 1962

'Ena Harkness' × 'Grandmère Jenny'

Creamy-pink blooms with peachy shadings and of exquisite, high-centred shape on a strong neck. Foliage dark green. Growth moderately vigorous with dark stems.

[(C) (MF) (Gh) ▽ ✂ AL]   2' × 2'   60 × 60 cm

'Apricot Silk'

Gregory UK 1965

Unknown × 'Souvenir de Jacques Verschuren'

A large and free rose with shapely orange-apricot to red flowers. Vigorous to a medium height but needs a good soil really to flourish.

[(C) (MF) (B) ▽ BS◧⁙ M◧⁙ AL]
2' × 2'   60 × 60 cm

'Arianna' (Meidali)

Meilland FRANCE 1968

'Charlotte Armstrong' × ('Peace' × 'Michèle Meilland')

Deep carmine blooms laced and suffused with coral; large, full and with crisp petals and high-centred until fully open. Dark green foliage. Vigorous and upright in habit.

[(C) (E) (B) (MF) (P) AL]   3' × 3'   90 × 90 cm

'Asso di Cuori' *see* 'Ace of Hearts'

'Baccara' (Meger)

Meilland FRANCE 1954

'Happiness' × 'Independence'

A vigorous, well-foliated, upright grower with strong, dark green stems and big thorns. The flowers are rich bright red when grown under glass where it flourishes; deeper red out of doors. Although now quite old, 'Baccara' is still unsurpassed as a long-stemmed florist's rose. No appreciable scent.

[(C) (Gh) ▽ ⁙ ✂ AL]   3' × 2'   90 × 60 cm

'Barbara Richards' (see text p. 136)

'Beauté'

'Barbara Richards'

Dickson UK 1930
Parentage unknown
An old Hybrid Tea not freely available but I could not resist including it. Shapely, fully double flowers of yellow flushed with pink, though too big for a rather weak neck. Very free-flowering. Bushy growth with good, dark foliage.

[(C) (VF) ▽ AL] 2′ × 2′ 60 × 60 cm

'Basildon Bond' (Harjosine)

Harkness UK 1980
('Sabine' × 'Circus') × ('Yellow Cushion' × 'Glory of Ceylon')
Freely produced large blooms reasonably well filled with apricot petals. Short and bushy in its habit of growth, and with good foliage.

[(C) (B) (MF) ▽ AL] 2′ × 2′ 60 × 60 cm

'Beauté'

Mallerin FRANCE 1953
'Mme Joseph Perraud' × a seedling
I hope this rose never goes out of fashion. Long, shapely buds open to delightfully semi-double flowers of rich apricot to orange. Not over-blessed with foliage and not the easiest rose to grow but well worth the effort. Upright in growth.

[(C) (SF) (B) ▽ ✂ AL] 2½′ × 2′ 75 × 60 cm

'Belle Blonde'

Meilland FRANCE 1955
'Peace' × 'Lorraine'
Freely produced, full and slightly globular blooms of clear yellow. Good leathery foliage in the fashion of its parent, 'Peace', but far less healthy. Growth bushy.

[(C) (SF) (B) ▽ BS AL] 2′ × 2′ 60 × 60 cm

'Benson & Hedges Gold' and *below:* 'Bettina'

'Benson & Hedges Gold' (Macgem)

McGredy NEW ZEALAND 1979
'Yellow Pages' × ('Arthur Bell' × 'Cynthia Brooke')
Deep golden-yellow blooms, large and full; quite shapely and free-flowering. Good, clean foliage. Growth bushy and vigorous.

[(C) (MF) (B) ▽ AW] 2½′ × 2′ 75 × 60 cm

'Bettina' (Mepal)

Meilland FRANCE 1953
'Peace' × ('Mme Joseph Perraud' × 'Demain')
A well-loved variety. Shapely buds of almost copper open to flattish, full blooms of soft orange-peach with deeper-coloured veins. Dark green foliage. Sadly, 'Bettina' is not fully hardy but is well worth growing in warmer climates.

[(C) (Gh) (SF) ▽ BS ⁘ AL]
2′ × 2′ 60 × 60 cm

'Betty Uprichard'

Dickson UK 1922
Parentage unknown
A fine old variety whose well-shaped, soft salmony-pink blooms have a deeper, cloudy reverse. It is very free-flowering. Growth habit upright and vigorous, with good, leathery foliage.

[(C) (VF) M⚡ ✂ AL]   3′ × 2′   90 × 60 cm

*'Big Chief', 'Portland Trailblazer'

Dickson UK 1975
'Ernest H. Morse' × 'Red Planet'
Very large, deep crimson blooms ideal for the exhibitor but not very suitable for the garden. Tall, leggy growth.

[(R) (SF) (E) (Gh) AW]   3½′ × 2′   1.05 m × 60 cm

*'Black Beauty'

Delbard FRANCE 1973
('Gloire de Rome' × 'Impeccable') × 'Papa Meilland'
Large, deep garnet-red blooms, quite fine. Its growth is bushy. Like many dark reds, this rose is not easy to grow.

[(C) (SF) ▽ AL]   2½′ × 2′   75 × 60 cm

'Blessings'

Gregory UK 1967
'Queen Elizabeth' × a seedling
A very free-flowering, shapely rose of soft salmon, producing ample foliage on dark stems. Its growth is fairly dense but upright. A good rose for massing in beds.

[(C) (MF) (B) (P) ✂ AW]   2½′ × 2′   75 × 60 cm

'Blue Moon', 'Blue Monday', 'Mainzer Fastnacht', 'Sissi' (Tannacht)

Tantau GERMANY 1964
'Sterling Silver' seedling × a seedling
Shapely buds open to large, full blooms of silvery-lilac, variable almost to lavender. Upright in growth with good foliage. 'Blue Moon' is certainly one of the best of the 'blues'.

[(C) (VF) (B) (E) ▽ ✂ AW]   2½′ × 2′   75 × 60 cm

'Blue Parfum' (Tanfifum)

Tantau GERMANY 1978
Parentage unknown
Mauve semi-double blooms with a soft grey-and-

'Blessings'

pink overlay. Growth upright. Needs loving care to give of its best.

[(C) (VF) (B) ▽ ☺ AL]   2½′ × 2′   75 × 60 cm

'Bobby Charlton'

Fryer UK 1974
'Royal Highness' × 'Prima Ballerina'
Its deep rose-pink blooms have a paler reverse and can be very large in good soils. Growth upright and vigorous, though inclined to legginess.

[(C) (VF) (E) ▽ AL]   3′ × 2′   90 × 60 cm

*'Bonnie Scotland'

Anderson UK 1976
'Wendy Cussons' × 'Percy Thrower'
Large, full, clear rose-pink and shapely flowers on an upright, medium-sized plant.

[(C) (SF) (B) AL]   2½′ × 2′   75 × 60 cm

'Bonsoir'

Dickson UK 1968
Seedling × a seedling
Peachy blooms with a pink overlay – large, shapely and full. Growth upright, but not very free-flowering. Good for exhibition.

[(R) (SF) (E) (Gh) ▽ ☺ AL]   2½′ × 2′   75 × 60 cm

'Buccaneer'

Swim USA 1952
'Golden Rapture' × ('Max Krause' × 'Captain Thomas')
A tall, upright rose classified as a Grandiflora in its home country. Although it is not often seen these days, I have included this rose partly from sentiment – I remember it well as a youth – and partly because it ranks as one of the best yellows. Long, pointed buds open to slightly shaggy, clear yellow

'Champs Elysées'

'Christian Dior'

blooms. Very free-flowering and healthy.

[(C) (P) (H) (MF) ✂ AL]   4′ × 2′   1.2 m × 60 cm

'Can Can' (Legglow)

LeGrice UK 1982
'Just Joey' × ('Superior' × 'Mischief')
Large, deep orange-red blooms are freely pro-
duced on a robust, bushy plant. Good foliage.

[(C) (MF) (B) AL]   2′ × 2′   60 × 60 cm

'Champion'

Fryer UK 1976
'Grandpa Dickson' × 'Whisky Mac'
Soft creamy-yellow blooms, flushed pink, which
are shapely, large and very full. Its growth is short
but bushy.

[(R) (MF) (E) ▽ B ⬚⋮ AW]   2′ × 2′   60 × 60 cm

'Champs-Elysées'

Meilland FRANCE 1957
'Monique' × 'Happiness'
Abundant, medium-sized, fully double and rich

'Chicago Peace'

'Chrysler Imperial'

'Comtesse Vandal' (see text p. 140)

crimson flowers come on an angular, bushy plant with good foliage. In view of the shortage of fine red bedding varieties, only its lack of scent can have condemned this excellent rose to the sidelines.

[(C) (P) (B) ♥ AL]   2′ × 2′   60 × 60 cm

'Cheshire Life'

Fryer UK 1972
'Prima Ballerina' × 'Princess Michiko'
Freely produced, moderately full, shapely blooms of rich vermilion. Upright with good foliage.

[(C) (SF) (B) AW]   2½′ × 2′   75 × 60 cm

'Chicago Peace'

Johnston USA 1962
Sport from 'Peace'
Identical to 'Peace' except for colour, which is shaded variably from rich yellow to primrose, heavily overlaid with copper and orange.

[(C) (P) (SF) (B) (H) (E) ✂ AW]
4′ × 3′   1.2 m × 90 cm

'Christian Dior' (Meilie)

Meilland FRANCE 1959
('Independence' × 'Happiness') × ('Peace' × 'Happiness')
Large, full, shapely, bright red blooms are held on a strong neck on a plant of upright growth. With a little extra attention, 'Christian Dior' can be superb. No scent.

[(C) (E) M⫚⫶ ☺ ✂ AL]   3′ × 2′   90 × 60 cm

'Chrysler Imperial'

Lammerts GERMANY 1952
'Charlotte Armstrong' × 'Mirandy'
Pointed buds open to large, full, somewhat muddled, deep velvety-red flowers. Its foliage is dark green, its growth bushy and vigorous. This rose has a fair scent.

[(C) (SF) (B) (E) AL]   2½′ × 2′   75 × 60 cm

'Cleo' (Beebop)

Bees UK 1981
'Perfecta' × 'Prima Ballerina'
Soft rosy-pink blooms, large and full. Bushy but upright in habit and free-flowering.

[(C) (SF) (B) (E) AL]   2½′ × 2′   75 × 60 cm

'Cocagold' see 'Golden Jubilee'

'Colorama', 'Dr R. Maag' (Meirigalu)

Meilland FRANCE 1968
'Suspense' × 'Confidence'
Bright red blooms with a yellow reverse, large and full. Growth upright but bushy. No scent.

[(C) (B) ♥ AL]   2½′ × 2′   75 × 60 cm

'Colour Wonder', 'Queen of Roses', 'Königin der Rosen', 'Reine des Roses' (Korbico)

Kordes GERMANY 1964
'Perfecta' × 'Super Star'
Very large, full blooms of orange and soft pink with

'Cynthia Brooke' and *below:* 'Dainty Bess'

a creamy reverse; very free-flowering too. Bushy, upright growth.

[(C) (SF) (B) (E) ▽ AW]   2½' × 2'   75 × 60 cm

'Comtesse Vandal'

Leenders NETHERLANDS 1932
('Ophelia' × 'Mrs Aaron Ward') × 'Souvenir de Claudius Pernet'
A very beautiful rose, especially to those who like their roses classically high-centred. Pointed, orange-toned buds open to pinky-apricot with deepening tones in the centre. A superb old variety, vigorous, bushy and well-foliaged.

[(C) (MF) (Gh) (B) (E) ▽ ✂ AL]
2½' × 2'   75 × 60 cm

'Congratulations', 'Sylvia' (Korlift)

Kordes GERMANY 1978
'Carina' × a seedling
A tall, healthy rose of upright growth. Clear rose-pink, shapely and fully double blooms, with good foliage.

[(C) (P) (SF) (E) AW]   4' × 2'   1.2 m × 60 cm

'Corso'

Cocker UK 1976
'Anne Cocker' × 'Dr A. J. Verhage'
Tall and upright, with large and full bright orange blooms on strong necks. This rose needs a little extra care to give of its best, which is superb. Good, glossy foliage.

[(C) (B) (E) (Gh) BS◖▦ M◖▦ AL]
4' × 2'   1.2 m × 60 cm

'Crimson Glory'

Kordes GERMANY 1935
'Catherine Kordes' seedling × 'W. E. Chaplin'
A fine old rose from the past, its large, globular, deep velvety-red blooms are superbly scented. They are, however, carried on a rather weak neck. Its foliage is dark green and a little sparse, with dark

and thorny stems on a bushy, angular plant.

[(C) (Gh) (B) ☺ AL]   2′ × 2′   60 × 60 cm

'Cynthia Brooke'

McGredy UK 1943
'Le Progrès' × ('Mme Mélanie Soupert' × 'Le Progrès')
Very large, fully double, globular flowers of deep burnished gold, brushed with salmon. An old variety which deserves more attention today. This rose has ample leathery foliage, is sparsely thorned, and is of stout and angular growth.

[(C) (VF) (B) (P) ▽ AL]   2½′ × 2′   75 × 60 cm

'Dainty Bess'

Archer UK 1925
'Ophelia' × 'K of K'
A superb, single, Hybrid Tea whose large, silvery-rose-pink flowers are produced in well-spaced clusters. The effect is considerably enhanced by rich, golden-brown stamens. Sweetly scented, with large, healthy foliage.

[(C) (P) (H) (MF) ▽ AL]   3′ × 2′   90 × 60 cm

'Dame Edith Helen'

Dickson UK 1926
Parentage unknown
Very large, many petalled, cupped flowers, sometimes opening quartered in the old-fashioned style, of rich, deep, silvery-pink. The blooms are held on a strong neck. Glossy, mid-green foliage and of upright but bushy growth.

[(R) (VF) ▽ ☺ AL]   3′ × 2′   90 × 60 cm

'Deep Secret', 'Mildred Scheel'

Tantau GERMANY 1977
Parentage unknown
The reasonably full, large, shapely, deep crimson flowers are held on a strong neck. Good glossy foliage on an upright plant.

[(C) (P) (VF) (B) ✕ AW]   2½′ × 2′   75 × 60 cm

'Diamond Jubilee'

Boerner USA 1947
'Maréchal Niel' × 'Feu Pernet-Ducher'
One of the classic Hybrid Teas. Shapely, buff-apricot blooms are produced freely on a strong, healthy plant with leathery, dark green foliage.

[(C) (P) (E) (B) ▽ (Gh) ✕ AL]   3′ × 2′   90 × 60 cm

'Doris Tysterman'

'Diorama'

de Ruiter NETHERLANDS 1965
'Peace' × 'Beauté'
Shapely and large blooms of yellow flushed red are carried on a bushy plant of medium height with good foliage.

[(C) (B) (P) ▽ ✕ AW]   3′ × 2′   90 × 60 cm

'Doreen'

Robinson UK 1951
'Lydia' × 'McGredy's Sunset'
The very deep yellow flowers of medium size, heavily veined and suffused with orange, open muddled and are freely produced on a short, bushy, dense plant. The foliage is coppery-green and the stems are very thorny.

[(C) (MF) (P) (B) AL]   1½′ × 2′   45 × 60 cm

'Doris Tysterman'

Tysterman UK 1975
'Peer Gynt' × a seedling
An upright grower with good bronzy-green foliage. Medium-sized, globular blooms of bright tangerine to orange, bronzing with age. Very free-flowering.

[(C) (P) (H) (Gh) (SF) ▽ ✕ AW]
3′ × 2′   90 × 60 cm

'Double Delight' (Andeli)

Swim & Ellis USA 1977
'Granada' × 'Garden Party'
Its blooms are large and reasonably full, creamy-white with pinkish-red brush strokes on the edge of the petals. A superb rose at its best but not easy to grow.

[(C) (Gh) (VF) ▽ ⁖ ☺ AW]   3′ × 2′   90 × 60 cm

'Dr A. J. Verhage', 'Golden Wave'

Verbeek NETHERLANDS 1963
'Tawny Gold' × ('Baccara' × a seedling)
Shapely flowers of yellow with deeper shadings, the petal edges paling attractively in sunlight to buffy-cream. A useful forcing variety with good foliage, perhaps better under glass than out of doors.

[(C) (Gh) (B) (P) ▽ ✂ AL]   2½' × 2'   75 × 60 cm

*'Dr John Snow'

Gandy UK 1979
'Helen Traubel' × a seedling
Large, full, creamy-white and scented flowers on a tall plant of upright growth with good foliage.

[(C) (B) (P) (VF) ✂ AL]   4' × 2'   1.2 m × 60 cm

*'Dr McAlpine' (Peafirst)

Pearce UK 1983
Parentage unknown
Large, fine blooms, shapely and deep rose-pink. Short, bushy, rather sprawling growth.

[(C) (VF) (B) AL]   1½' × 2'   45 × 60 cm

'Duke of Windsor', 'Herzog von Windsor'

Tantau GERMANY 1969
'Prima Ballerina' × a seedling
Shapely, pointed buds open quite formally to full, flattish, highly scented flowers held on a strong neck. A rose of stout, upright, thorny growth which needs extra attention to thrive.

[(C) (VF) (B) ▽ M◀▦ AW]   2½' × 2'   75 × 60 cm

'Dutch Gold'

Tysterman UK 1978
'Peer Gynt' × 'Whisky Mac'
Large, globular, clear yellow blooms with hints of orange. An upright and healthy rose.

[(C) (SF) (B) (E) (Gh) ✂ AW]   3' × 2'   90 × 60 cm

'Eden Rose'

Meilland FRANCE 1950
'Peace' × 'Signora'
Large and shapely, deep pink blooms with a paler silvery-pink reverse are held on a strong neck. Growth vigorous and robust, the stems stout and thorny with dark green foliage.

[(C) (P) (Gh) (MF) (E) AW]
3½' × 2'   1.05 m × 60 cm

'Electron' *see* 'Mullard Jubilee'

'Elina' *see* 'Peaudouce'

'Elizabeth Harkness'

'Ernest H. Morse'

'Eroica'

'Elizabeth Harkness'

Harkness UK 1969
'Red Dandy' × 'Piccadilly'
The large blooms are very full and shapely,
creamy-white to ivory flushed pink, a superb colour combination. Medium, bushy growth with
good foliage.

[(C) (P) (SF) (B) (E) AW]   2½' × 2'   75 × 60 cm

'Ena Harkness'

Norman UK 1946
'Crimson Glory' × 'Southport'
Bright velvety-crimson blooms, very shapely and
free-flowering though held on a weak neck. The
foliage is a little sparse with thorny stems.

[(C) (P) (Gh) (MF) (B) ☺ AL]   2' × 2'   60 × 60 cm

'Ernest H. Morse'

Kordes GERMANY 1964
Parentage unknown
Shapely, dark buds open to loosely formed, bright
crimson flowers held on a strong neck. The foliage
is dark green, the stems almost purple. Growth
upright.

[(C) (P) (Gh) (MF) (H) (B) ✂ AW]
3' × 2'   90 × 60 cm

'First Love' (see text p. 144)

'Eroica', 'Erotika'

Tantau GERMANY 1968
Parentage unknown
Surprisingly, for the 1960s, the name was changed
to 'Eroica' when it left Germany. Full, dark red
blooms on an upright plant with good, dark, glossy
foliage.

[(C) (VF) (B) AL]   3' × 2'   90 × 60 cm

'Erotika' *see* 'Eroica'

'Etoile de Hollande'

Verschuren NETHERLANDS 1919
'General MacArthur' × 'Hadley'

'Etoile de Hollande'

'Fragrant Cloud'

'Etoile de Hollande' is seldom seen today except as a climber, but merits inclusion as an important rose from the past. Very fragrant, cloudy red blooms with dark green foliage, and soft to the touch, on a plant of bushy, angular growth. A good forcer in its day.

[(C) (VF) (Gh) M⬤⬚ ✂ AL]   2′ × 2′   60 × 60 cm

'First Love', 'Premier Amour'

Swim USA 1951
'Charlotte Armstrong' × 'Show Girl'
Long, pointed buds open to loose, semi-double flowers of soft blush-pink with deeper shadings. The blooms are held on a strong neck on a narrow, upright plant. Very free-flowering, with good foliage.

[(C) (P) (Gh) (MF) ▽ ✂ AL]   3′ × 1½′   90 × 45 cm

'Flaming Peace' *see* 'Kronenbourg'

'Forgotten Dreams'

Bracegirdle UK 1981
'Fragrant Cloud' × 'Tenerife'
Its bright cardinal-red blooms open semi-double.

Foliage mid-green and semi-glossy on a plant of bushy, upright growth.

[(C) (B) (VF) AL]   3′ × 2′   90 × 60 cm

'Fragrant Cloud', 'Duftwolke', 'Nuage Parfumé' (Tanellis)

Tantau GERMANY 1968
Seedling × 'Prima Ballerina'
Its coral-red blooms are freely produced. They are highly scented and variable in colour: sometimes muddy, sometimes quite bright. Growth slightly open. Foliage dark.

[(C) (B) (VF) ▽ AW]   2½′ × 2′   75 × 60 cm

*'Fragrant Gold', 'Duftgold' (Tandugoft)

Tantau GERMANY 1982
Parentage unknown
Blooms deep yellow and semi-double when fully open. Upright growth. Good, glossy foliage.

[(C) (B) (VF) ▽ AW]   2½′ × 2′   75 × 60 cm

'Gay Gordons'

'Golden Melody' (see text p. 146)

'Frau Karl Druschki', 'White American Beauty', 'Reine des Neiges', 'Snow Queen'

Lambert GERMANY 1901
'Merveille de Lyon' × 'Mme Caroline Testout'
Really a Hybrid Perpetual but merits inclusion as one of the most famous early twentieth-century

roses. The large, fully double flowers are pure white. It is a strong, sturdy plant with healthy foliage, though its upright growth needs support in exposed gardens. Best pegged down in the old style. Sadly, totally lacking in scent.
[(R) (P) ☺ AL]   4' × 3'   1.2 m × 90 cm

'Fryjingo' *see* 'The Lady'

'Gail Borden'

Kordes GERMANY 1956
'Mrs A. Verschuren' × 'Viktoria Adelheid'
A large, many petalled, shapely rose, cupped when almost fully open. The rosy-pink blooms have a soft creamy-yellow reverse. Free-flowering, and very bushy with good foliage.
[(C) (P) (SF) (B) ▽ AW]   2½' × 2'   75 × 60 cm

'Gay Gordons'

Cocker UK 1969
'Belle Blonde' × 'Karl Herbst'
An aptly named rose whose orange and yellow blooms are suffused red, full, shapely and free-flowering. Growth bushy, with slightly glossy foliage and thorny stems.
[(C) (SF) (B) ▽ BS◁ AW]   2' × 2'   60 × 60 cm

'Gold Crown', 'Corona de Oro', 'Couronne d'Or', 'Goldkrone'

Kordes GERMANY 1960
'Peace' × 'Spek's Yellow'
A tall and upright, rather stiff and lanky plant. The deep yellow blooms, occasionally with outer petals splashed red, are large and full, sometimes quartered when fully open, and produced on long stems. The foliage is glossy and the stems are dark.
[(C) (P) (MF) ✂ AL]   3½' × 2'   1.05 m × 60 cm

'Golden Days' (Rugolda)

de Ruiter NETHERLANDS 1980
'Peer Gynt' × a seedling
Large, fully double, deep yellow flowers on a bushy plant with good, mid-green, slightly glossy foliage.
[(C) (SF) (B) AL]   2½' × 2'   75 × 60 cm

'Golden Jubilee' (Cocagold)

Cocker UK 1981
'Peer Gynt' × 'Gay Gordons'
Large, shapely, clear yellow blooms, brushed pink, a plant of upright growth with good, clean foliage.

'Grace de Monaco'

(Another 'Golden Jubilee' was introduced by Jacobus of the USA in 1948.)

[(C) (SF) (B) ▽ AL]   2½' × 2'   75 × 60 cm

'Golden Melody', 'Irene Churruca'

La Florida USA 1934
'Mme Butterfly' × ('Lady Hillingdon' × 'Souvenir de Claudius Pernet')
A beautiful rose, one of the best from the 1930s, with large, shapely, high-centred, moderately full blooms of soft yellowish-buff flushed pink with deeper centres. It has dark green foliage, with darker, almost maroon, stems and large, sparse thorns. A plant of angular growth whose hardiness is suspect.

[(C) (VF) (B) (E) ▽ ✂ AL]   2½' × 2'   75 × 60 cm

'Golden Sceptre' see 'Spek's Yellow'

'Golden Times'

Cocker UK 1970
'Fragrant Cloud' × 'Golden Splendour'
Clear lemon-yellow blooms, loosely formed when fully open. Upright and free-flowering with good foliage.

[(C) (SF) (B) AL]   2½' × 2'   75 × 60 cm

'Golden Wave' see 'Dr A. J. Verhage'

'Gold Star', 'Point du Jour' (Candide)

Cant UK 1983
'Yellow Pages' × 'Dr A. J. Verhage'
Medium to large, deep yellow blooms are freely produced on an upright, medium-sized plant. Good foliage.

[(C) (SF) (B) AL]   2½' × 2'   75 × 60 cm

'Grace de Monaco' (Meimit)

Meilland FRANCE 1956
'Peace' × 'Michèle Meilland'
The very large, globular blooms have satiny petals of silvery-pink. Its growth is dark and rather angular, the foliage dark green and leathery.

[(C) (VF) (B) ▽ ☺ AL]   2½' × 2'   75 × 60 cm

'Grandmère Jenny'

Meilland FRANCE 1950
'Peace' × ('Julien Potin' × 'Sensation')
The blooms are mostly soft yellow heavily brushed with pink, variable, sometimes deeper, flushed burnt orange. A shapely rose, a slimmer version of

'Grandmère Jenny' and *bottom:* 'Harry Wheatcroft'

'Peace' and beautiful when behaving itself. Upright growth with semi-glossy and leathery foliage.
[(C) (SF) (B) ▽ BS ◖▥ ✂ AL]
2½' × 2'   75 × 60 cm

'Grandpa Dickson', 'Irish Gold'

Dickson UK 1966
('Perfecta' × 'Governador Braga da Cruz') × 'Piccadilly'
Very large, graceful, shapely lemon yellow blooms, sometimes faintly brushed pink. Fully open, they are often splashed pink. Strong and upright growth with ample, mid-green foliage, and very thorny.
[(C) (SF) (B) (E) AW]   2½' × 2'   75 × 60 cm

'Harry Wheatcroft' (Caribia)

Wheatcroft UK 1972
Sport from 'Piccadilly'
The orange-red blooms are striped and splashed with yellow, flamboyant, deeper when fully open. Growth upright and strong, with plentiful and almost glossy foliage.
[(C) (SF) (B) ▽ R ◖▥ AL]   2½' × 2'   75 × 60 cm

'Hector Deane'

McGredy UK 1938
'McGredy's Scarlet' × 'Lesley Dudley'
A fine old variety with freely produced, high-centred, full flowers of orange and pink flushed and shaded deeper. Good, glossy foliage and of bushy growth.
[(C) (VF) (P) (B) ▽ AL]   2' × 2'   60 × 60 cm

'Helen Traubel'

Swim USA 1951
'Charlotte Armstrong' × 'Glowing Sunset'
A beautiful rose with long, pointed buds opening to pinkish-apricot. Rather a weak neck but many good points to make amends for this. Tall and upright, with large and darkish green foliage.
[(C) (H) (MF) (B) ☺ AL]   3½' × 2'   1.05 m × 60 cm

'Helmut Schmidt' *see* 'Simba'

*'Ingrid Bergman' (Poulman)

Poulsen DENMARK 1983
Seedling × a seedling
Fully double, dark red blooms on a free-flowering plant of upright growth with good, mid to dark green, semi-glossy foliage.
[(C) (SF) (B) ▽ AL]   2' × 2'   60 × 60 cm

'Intermezzo'

Dot SPAIN 1963
'Grey Pearl' × 'Lila Vidri'
The fully double, sometimes quartered, flowers of greyish-lavender with a pinkish sheen are produced in clusters, the buds rounded. A bushy plant, thorny and well endowed with glossy foliage.
[(C) (P) (MF) (B) ▽ AL]   1½' × 1½'   45 × 45 cm

'Irene Churruca' *see* 'Golden Melody'

'Irish Elegance'

Dickson UK 1905
Parentage unknown
A lovely single from the beginning of this century with large, orange-scarlet blooms shaded bronze, and of vigorous, upright growth and good foliage. Seldom seen now, but I could not resist including it as a representative of the early, single Hybrid Teas.
[(R) (MF) ▽ M ◖▥ AL]   2½' × 2'   75 × 60 cm

'Irish Gold' *see* 'Grandpa Dickson'

'Isobel Harkness'

Norman UK 1957
'Phyllis Gold' × 'McGredy's Yellow'
Very large blooms appear semi-double when fully
open and are bright yellow paling slightly with age.
Leathery, dark green foliage on a bushy plant.
[(C) (MF) (B) BS⬦⣿ ✂ AL]   2' × 2'   60 × 60 cm

'Jema'

Astor Perry USA 1982
'Helen Traubel' × 'Lolita'
Very full and shapely apricot blooms on a plant of
upright growth with light green foliage and lightly
coloured thorns.
[(C) (MF) (B) ✂ AL]   4' × 2'   1.2 m × 60 cm

'Jennifer Hart'

Swim USA 1982
'Pink Parfait' × 'Yuletide'
High-centred, very double, dark red blooms are
held on a strong neck with mid-green, semi-glossy
foliage.
[(C) (MF) (B) (Gh) ✂ AL]   3' × 2'   90 × 60 cm

'John Waterer'

McGredy UK 1970
'King of Hearts' × 'Hanne'
Large, full, high-centred, crimson blooms are
freely produced on an upright plant with good,
dark green foliage.
[(C) (P) (MF) (B) ▽ ✂ AL]   3' × 2'   90 × 60 cm

'Johnnie Walker' (Frygran)

Fryer UK 1982
'Sunblest' × ('Arthur Bell' × 'Belle Blonde')
Quite large apricot (whisky-coloured) blooms,
moderately full and semi-double when fully open.
Growth upright and bushy with mid-green matt
foliage.
[(C) (MF) (B) ▽ ✂ AW]   3½' × 2'   1.05 m × 60 cm

'Josephine Bruce'

Bees UK 1949
'Crimson Glory' × 'Madge Whipp'
At its best a superb and beautiful rose with shapely
velvet-crimson blooms. Sturdy, slightly angular
growth and matt greyish-green foliage.
[(C) (VF) (B) ▽ M⬦⣿ AW]   2' × 2'   60 × 60 cm

'King's Ransom' (see text p. 150)

'Joyce Northfield'

Northfield UK 1977
'Fred Gibson' × 'Vienna Charm'
Pointed buds open to large high-centred flowers of
deep orange. Dark foliage on a vigorous and
upright plant.
[(C) (P) (SF) (B) ✂ AL]   3' × 2'   90 × 60 cm

'Julia's Rose'

Tysterman UK 1976
'Blue Moon' × 'Dr A. J. Verhage'
The small but full, deep coppery-tan blooms are
blended with pink – this is an unusual rose. Its dark
foliage has reddish undertones and is borne on an
upright but not over-tall bush.
[(C) (SF) (B) ✂ AL]   2' × 2'   60 × 60 cm

'Just Joey'

Cant UK 1972
'Fragrant Cloud' × 'Dr A. J. Verhage'
A superb rose, its large, ragged-edged flowers are
coppery-orange with soft pink paling at the edges
when the flowers open. The foliage is dark green,
leathery and semi-glossy on a rather angular plant.
[(C) (MF) (B) ▽ AW]   2' × 2'   60 × 60 cm

'Kan-pai'

Suzuki JAPAN 1980
['Yu-ai' × ('Happiness' × 'American Beauty')] ×
'Pharaoh'
High-centred, deep red blooms on a strong neck.

Above: 'Kronenbourg' (see text p. 150)
Below: 'Lady Alice Stanley' (see text p. 150)

An upright grower with dark green foliage.

[(C) (P) (MF) (B) AL]   2½′ × 2′   75 × 60 cm

'Keepsake', 'Esmeralda' (Kormalda)

Kordes GERMANY 1981
Seedling × 'Red Planet'
A pleasing mixture of pinks from carmine to blush in very full, large blooms, the outer petals reflexed when partially open. Dark green foliage with stout stems bearing many large thorns. Its growth is upright but dense.

[(C) (P) (MF) (B) AL]   2½′ × 2′   75 × 60 cm

'King's Ransom'

Morey USA 1961
'Golden Masterpiece' × 'Lydia'
Shapely, full, high-centred, golden-yellow flowers are held on strong necks amid an abundance of glossy bright green foliage. Upright and amply thorned.

[(C) (Gh) (MF) (B) ▽ AW]   2½′ × 2′   75 × 60 cm

'Kordes' Perfecta' see 'Perfecta'

'Korzaun' see 'Royal William'

'Kronenbourg', 'Flaming Peace' (Macbo)

McGredy UK 1965
Sport from 'Peace'
The large, full blooms are a mixture of plum-red and buff with a soft yellow reverse. Identical to 'Peace' in all other respects.

[(C) (P) (H) (SF) (B) (E) ▽ AL]
4′ × 3′   1.2 m × 90 cm

*'Lady'

Weeks USA 1984
'Song of Paris' × 'Royal Highness'
Medium-sized flowers of mid-pink are freely produced on a compact plant with semi-glossy mid-green foliage.

[(C) (B) (SF) ▽ AL]   2′ × 2′   60 × 60 cm

'Lady Alice Stanley'

McGredy UK 1909
Parentage unknown
The full and very double flowers, made up of more than seventy densely packed petals, are flesh-pink with a deeper reverse. The foliage is rich green, the

growth angular and branching. This is a fine old variety.

[(B) (VF) ▽ (Gh) ☺ AL]   2′ × 2′   60 × 60 cm

'Lady Barnby'

Dickson UK 1930
Parentage unknown
Very large, double, high-centred bright pink blooms with leathery, rich green foliage. A short and bushy plant.

[(R) (B) (VF) (Gh) ▽ AL]   1½′ × 2′   45 × 60 cm

*'Lady Beauty'

Kono JAPAN 1984
'Lady' × 'Princess Takamatsu'
Its rounded buds open large and are pale pink flushed creamy-yellow, the reverse deeper. The foliage is plentiful, mid-green and glossy on an upright and vigorous bush.

[(P) (SF) (Gh) ▽ ✄ AL]   3′ × 2′   90 × 60 cm

'Lady Belper'

Verschuren NETHERLANDS 1948
'Mrs G. A. van Rossem' × a seedling
A shapely, slightly tubby, high-centred rose whose coppery-yellow blooms are heavily overlaid with burnt orange. Dark green, glossy foliage on a vigorous bush of medium growth.

[(C) (P) (B) (VF) ▽ AL]   2′ × 2′   60 × 60 cm

*'Lady Diana'

Hill USA 1983
'Sonia' × 'Caress'
A forcing variety with soft pink, high-centred blooms on a long stem and mid-green foliage. Tall.

[(C) (SF) (Gh) ▽ ✄ ⸫ AL]   4′ × 2′   1.2 m × 60 cm

'Lady Elgin' see 'Thaïs'

'Lady Rose' (Korlady)

Kordes GERMANY 1979
Seedling × 'Träumerei'
Long, pointed buds open to large, high-centred flowers of orange-salmon. Bushy with good, mid-green foliage.

[(C) (VF) (B) ▽ AL]   2½′ × 2′   75 × 60 cm

'Lady Sylvia'

Stevens UK 1926
Sport from 'Mme Butterfly'
A beautiful, shapely variety of upright growth with pale pink flowers and dark green, semi-glossy foliage. Still popular in spite of its age.

[(C)(P)(VF)(B)(Gh)▽✂AL] 2′×2′ 60×60 cm

'Lakeland'

Frver UK 1976
'Fragrant Cloud' × 'Queen Elizabeth'
Large, fully double flowers of light pink, and ample good foliage on an upright plant. A good rose for exhibiting.

[(C)(SF)(E)▽AL] 3′×2′ 90×60 cm

'Lady Belper'

'Lincoln Cathedral'

*'Las Vegas' (Korgane)

Kordes GERMANY 1981
'Ludwigshafen am Rhein' × 'Feuerzauber'
Large, high-centred, deep orange flowers with a paler reverse, and semi-glossy, mid-green foliage. Bushy and upright growth.
[(C) (P) (B) (MF) AL]   2½′ × 2′   75 × 60 cm

'Legglow' see 'Can Can'

*'Lincoln Cathedral' (Glanlin)

Langdale UK 1985
'Silver Jubilee' × 'Royal Dane'
The flowers are pink deepening to orange in the centre with a yellow reverse, shapely and quite large, and freely-produced. Glossy, mid-green foliage on a bushy and very thorny plant.
[(C) (P) (SF) (B) ▽ AL]   2½′ × 2′   75 × 60 cm

'Liselle' see 'Royal Romance'

'Lolita', 'Litakor' (Korlita)

Kordes GERMANY 1973
'Colour Wonder' × a seedling
Soft orange blooms on a tall, upright plant with

good foliage.
[(C) (B) (MF) ▽ AL]   3½′ × 2′   1.05 m × 60 cm

'L'Oréal Trophy see Shrub Roses

'Los Angeles'

Howard USA 1916
'Mme Segond Weber' × 'Lyon Rose'
A shapely rose, its pointed buds opening to fully double flowers of coral-pink with a deep gold base. Its growth is somewhat spreading with leathery, dark green foliage. Well ahead of its time when introduced and has since proved valuable at stud.
[(C) (P) (VF) (B) ▽ AL]   2′ × 2′   60 × 60 cm

*'Louisville Lady'

Weddle USA 1986
'Osiria' × a seedling
An exhibition-sized rose, pink with a silvery reverse, and with dark green, glossy foliage. Dense and upright growth.
[(C) (E) (VF) AL]   3′ × 2′   90 × 60 cm

'Lovely Lady', 'Dickson's Jubilee' (Ducjubell)

Dickson UK 1986
'Silver Jubilee' × ('Eurorose' × 'Anabell')
Mid-pink, fully double, shapely flowers on a bushy plant with glossy, mid-green foliage.
[(C) (B) (VF) AL]   2′ × 2′   60 × 60 cm

'Lover's Meeting'

Gandy UK 1980
Seedling × 'Egyptian Treasure'
High-centred, shapely blooms of bright vermilion-orange on an upright, tallish plant with bronzy green foliage.
[(C) (P) (VF) (B) ✕ AW]   3′ × 2′   90 × 60 cm

'Loving Memory', 'Burgund '81', 'Red Cedar' (Korgund '81)

Kordes GERMANY 1981
Seedling × a 'Red Planet' seedling
Large, fully double, high-centred, bright crimson blooms are borne on strong stems. Bushy and upright growth with glossy foliage.
[(C) (MF) (B) (E) (Gh) ✕ AW]
3½′ × 2′   1.05 m × 60 cm

'Luis Brinas'

Dot SPAIN 1934
'Mme Butterfly' × 'Federico Casas'
Cupped, pinkish-orange blooms are carried on strong stems. The foliage always appears to be slightly limp. A vigorous old variety well worth growing today.

[(R) (VF) (Gh) (B) ✄ AL]   3' × 2'   90 × 60 cm

'Lyon Rose'

Pernet-Ducher ·FRANCE 1907
'Mme Mélanie Soupert' × a 'Soleil d'Or' seedling
Coral-pink, yellow and red blooms, a colour combination that sounds more startling than it is, together with bushy growth and good foliage. An important old stud variety.

[(R) (VF) (Gh) ▽ AL]   2' × 2'   60 × 60 cm

'Maestro' (Mackinju)

McGredy NEW ZEALAND 1980
'Picasso' seedling × a seedling
Sizeable blooms of soft crimson brushed whitish-cream, their colour variable but always eye-catching. Dark green foliage on a prickly bush.

[(C) (SF) (B) ▽ AL]   2½' × 2'   75 × 60 cm

'Mala Rubinstein'

Dickson UK 1971
'Sea Pearl' × 'Fragrant Cloud'
Rich coral-pink, very full and shapely blooms, extremely free-flowering, with matt, dark green foliage on an upright and bushy plant.

[(C) (VF) (B) BS▥ AW]   2½' × 2'   75 × 60 cm

'Manuela'

Tantau GERMANY 1968
Parentage unknown
Large, shapely blooms of rich rosy-pink, glossy foliage and a bushy habit of growth.

[(C) (VF) (B) (E) ☺ AW]   2' × 2'   60 × 60 cm

*'Marijke Koopman'

Fryer UK 1979
Parentage unknown
Reasonably large blooms of soft satin-pink with a deeper centre and a yellow base, mid-green foliage and upright growth.

[(C) (P) (B) (SF) AL]   3' × 2'   90 × 60 cm

'Lovely Lady'

'Marion Harkness' (Harkantabil)

Harkness UK 1979
[('Manx Queen' × 'Prima Ballerina') × ('Chanelle' × 'Piccadilly')] × 'Piccadilly'
The shapely, deep yellow blooms are brushed orange, deepening with age. Upright, bushy growth, and well foliated.

[(C) (P) (SF) (B) ▽ AL]   2½' × 2'   75 × 60 cm

'Mary Donaldson', 'Lady Donaldson' (Canana)

Cant UK 1984
'English Miss' × a seedling
Large, full, salmon-pink flowers are produced on a strong, healthy, upright plant with plentiful, dark green, glossy foliage. (This rose is sometimes classified as a Floribunda.)

[(C) (P) (VF) (B) (E) ▽ AL]   2½' × 2'   75 × 60 cm

'McGredy's Yellow'

McGredy UK 1934
'Mrs Charles Lamplough' × ('The Queen Alexandra Rose' × 'J. B. Clark')
Superbly shaped, unfading primrose-yellow blooms on a sturdy plant with dark, bronzy and semi-glossy foliage. Bushy and vigorous. Unsurpassed today in its colour range.

[(C) (P) (SF) (B) ▽ ✄ AL]   2' × 2'   60 × 60 cm

'Message', 'White Knight' (Meban)

Meilland FRANCE 1955
('Virgo' × 'Peace') × 'Virgo'
A good old white variety, high-centred and full; not large but free-flowering. Foliage small and darkish on an upright, thorny plant.

[(C) (SF) (Gh) ▽ ✂ M◧▥ AL]   3′ × 2′   90 × 60 cm

'Michèle Meilland'

Meilland FRANCE 1945
'Joanna Hill' × 'Peace'
A classic from the past, its exquisitely formed creamy-buff blooms are shaded pink and salmon. Free-flowering on a bushy, upright plant with dark foliage and stems.

[(C) (MF) (B) (Gh) ▽ ✂ ⁙ AL]   2′ × 2′   60 × 60 cm

'Mischief' (Macmi)

McGredy UK 1961
'Peace' × 'Spartan'
A very free-flowering, rich salmon-pink rose, the colour deeper in the autumn. Bushy, free-branching yet of upright growth. Sadly, its ample, matt, dark green foliage is often marred by black spot.

[(C) (P) (B) ▽ BS◧▥ ✂ AL]   3′ × 2′   90 × 60 cm

'Miss Harp', 'Silhouette', 'Oregold', 'Anneliesse Rothenberger'

Tantau GERMANY 1975
'Piccadilly' × 'Colour Wonder'
Shapely, high-centred, deep yellow blooms on a robust, bushy plant with dark green, glossy foliage.

[(C) (B) (SF) ▽ AL]   3′ × 2′   90 × 60 cm

'Mister Lincoln'

Swim USA 1964
'Chrysler Imperial' × 'Charles Mallerin'
Its dark red flowers of good size and shape, and cupped when almost open, are held on a strong neck. Dark, leathery, matt foliage on an upright and vigorous plant.

[(C) (P) (VF) (B) (Gh) ✂ AW]   3′ × 2′   90 × 60 cm

'Mme Butterfly'

Hill USA 1918
Sport from 'Ophelia'
The soft blush-pink flowers, deeper in the centre with hints of yellow at the base, are beautiful when fully open and showing off golden anthers. The foliage is darkish green and semi-glossy. Growth upright. An exquisite all-rounder from the past.

[(C) (P) (VF) (B) (Gh) ▽ ✂ AL]   2′ × 2′   60 × 60 cm

'Mischief'

'Mme Louis Laperrière'

Laperrière FRANCE 1951
'Crimson Glory' × a seedling
Rich deep crimson flowers are produced in profusion on an upright yet bushy plant with dark green, matt foliage. A very good variety, especially for bedding.

[(C) (P) (VF) (B) ▽ AL]   2′ × 2′   60 × 60 cm

'Mojave'

Swim USA 1954
'Charlotte Armstrong' × 'Signora'
Heavily veined, apricot-orange flowers tinted russet-red are held prominently on a long, strong neck. The foliage is glossy and plentiful, the growth upright and vigorous.

[(C) (P) (MF) (B) (Gh) ▽ ❖ ✂ AL]
3′ × 2′   90 × 60 cm

'Monique'

Paolino FRANCE 1949
'Lady Sylvia' × a seedling
Shapely buds open to lovely, large, but well-proportioned flowers, cup-shaped with flattish tops, their colour an exquisite mixture of pinks. Matt, mid-green foliage and of upright and tidy growth.

[(C) (VF) (B) ▽ ✂ AL]   2½′ × 2′   75 × 60 cm

'Montezuma'

Swim USA 1955
'Fandango' × 'Floradora'
Plump, urn-shaped buds open to large, well-proportioned and high-centred blooms of salmony red. A vigorous rose with leathery, dark, semi-glossy foliage.

[(C) (P) (SF) (B) (Gh) ▽ ✂ AL]
2½′ × 2′   75 × 60 cm

*'Moriah' (Ganhol)

Holtzman ISRAEL 1983
'Fragrant Cloud' × a seedling
Large, shapely blooms of soft orange with a deeper reverse. Foliage good, matt and dark green. Growth bushy.

[(C) (VF) (B) ▽ ❖ ✂ AL]   2½′ × 2′   75 × 60 cm

'Mrs Oakley Fisher'

Cant UK 1921
Parentage unknown
Large clusters of evenly spaced, deep buff-yellow,

Top: 'Mme Butterfly' and *bottom:* 'Mme Louis Laperrière'

single flowers with pronounced amber stamens, and dark green, bronzy and semi-glossy foliage. The stems are plum-coloured and thorny. An eye-catcher from the past.

[(C) (P) (MF) (B) ▽ AL]   2′ × 2′   60 × 60 cm

'Mrs Sam McGredy'

McGredy UK 1929
('Donald Macdonald' × 'Golden Emblem') × (Seedling × 'The Queen Alexandra Rose')
Large, slightly shaggy blooms of burnt-salmon-orange with their reverse flushed red and their centre yellow, and bronzy and glossy foliage, the stems dark. Awkward, angular growth.

[(R) (P) (NF) (B) ▽ AL]   3′ × 2′   90 × 60 cm

'Mullard Jubilee', 'Electron'

McGredy UK 1970
'Paddy McGredy' × 'Prima Ballerina'
Large, deep rose-pink, high-centred flowers are freely produced on strong stems. The foliage is dark and plentiful on a plant of bushy growth.

[(C) (P) (MF) (B) ✂ AL]   2′ × 2′   60 × 60 cm

'My Choice'

LeGrice UK 1958
'Wellworth' × 'Ena Harkness'
Large, urn-shaped, high-centred blooms of dusky

salmon-pink with a soft yellowish-buff reverse. The foliage is matt greyish-green. Growth upright.

[(C) (P) (VF) (B) (E) AL]   2½' × 2'   75 × 60 cm

'National Trust', 'Bad Naukeim'

McGredy UK 1970
'Evelyn Fison' × 'King of Hearts'
A very free-flowering rose, with superbly shaped, high-centred flowers of bright red, larger if disbudded. Dark foliage on an upright and bushy plant.

[(C) (P) (SF) (B) ▽ AW]   2' × 2'   60 × 60 cm

*'Olympiad' (Macauck)

McGredy NEW ZEALAND 1984
'Red Planet' × 'Pharaoh'
Bright red, almost luminous, large and full blooms. Its growth is upright and bushy, with mid-green, matt foliage.

[(C) (SF) (E) (B) ✕ AL]   3' × 2'   90 × 60 cm

'Opéra'

Gaujard FRANCE 1950
'La Belle Irisée' × a seedling
Long buds open to fairly plump, cupped blooms of rich scarlet-red with a yellow base. The foliage is

'Monique' (see text p. 155)

leathery and mid to light green.

[(C) (P) (MF) (B) AL] 3′ × 2′ 90 × 60 cm

'Ophelia'

Paul UK 1912
Probably a seedling from 'Antoine Rivoire'
A classic, the superbly shaped soft pink blooms have a soft yellow base. Beautiful in bud and when fully open, they display golden stamens to advantage. Dark green foliage on a plant of upright growth. The progenitor of several sports of equal stature, in particular 'Mme Butterfly' and 'Lady Sylvia'.

[(C) (P) (VF) (B) (Gh) ▽ ✂ AL] 2′ × 2′ 60 × 60 cm

'Oregold' see 'Miss Harp'

'Orient Express'

Wheatcroft UK 1978
'Sunblest' × a seedling
Large and full, shapely blooms of coral-pink, with plentiful dark green-bronzy foliage. Growth vigorous and bushy.

[(C) (P) (H) (VF) (B) ▽ AL]
3½′ × 2′ 1.05 m × 60 cm

'Pacemaker' (Harnoble)

Harkness UK 1981
'Red Planet' × 'Wendy Cussons'
Clear, bright reddish-pink, high-centred blooms, and very free-flowering. Large, dark green foliage on a plant of upright and bushy growth.

[(C) (P) (H) (VF) (B) ▽ AL] 3′ × 2′ 90 × 60 cm

'Papa Meilland' (Meisar)

Meilland FRANCE 1963
'Chrysler Imperial' × 'Charles Mallerin'
Superb, deep velvety-crimson blooms with obvious veining. Mid to dark green, semi-glossy foliage on an upright plant with large thorns. Not an easy rose to grow but well worth the effort.

[(R) (VF) (M) BS – ⬛ AW] 3′ × 2′ 90 × 60 cm

'Pascali' (Lenip)

Lens BELGIUM 1963
'Queen Elizabeth' × 'White Butterfly'
Well-formed flowers of almost pure white with a creamy base, held erect. Foliage dark green and semi-matt. Upright growth.

[(C) (P) (Gh) (SF) (B) ▽ ✂ AW] 3′ × 2′ 90 × 60 cm

'Mrs Oakley Fisher' (see text p. 155)

'Paul Shirville', 'Heart Throb' (Harqueterwife)

Harkness UK 1983
'Compassion' × 'Mischief'
The blooms are blended soft salmon and peach, shapely and elegant in form. Slightly spreading in habit with large, dark green, almost glossy leaves.
[(C) (P) (VF) (B) ⬇ AW]   3′ × 2½′   90 × 75 cm

'Peace', 'Gioia', 'Gloria Dei', 'Mme A. Meilland'

Meilland FRANCE 1945
[('George Dickson' × 'Souvenir de Claudius Pernet') × ('Joanna Hill' × 'Charles P. Kilham')] × 'Margaret McGredy'
One of the best-loved of all roses, its large, globular buds opening to huge flowers of clear yellow edged rose-pink, sometimes deeper. Foliage firm and

very glossy. Growth vigorous and bushy. 'Peace' can sometimes be a little shy.
[(C) (P) (H) (SF) (E) ✂ AW]   . 4′ × 3′   1.2 m × 90 cm

*'Peaudouce', 'Elina' (Dicjana)

Dickson UK 1985
'Nana Mouskouri' × 'Lolita'
Very full, large, shapely blooms of ivory and soft yellow. Bushy and upright growth with ample foliage.
[(C) (P) (SF) (B) (E) AL]   2½′ × 2′   75 × 60 cm

'Peer Gynt' (Korol)

Kordes GERMANY 1968
'Colour Wonder' × 'Golden Giant'
Large, shapely flowers of rich clear yellow brushed red at the edge of the petals, and very full. Good, mid-green and semi-glossy foliage on a vigorous, bushy plant.
[(C) (P) (H) (SF) (B) ⬇ ✂ AW]
2½′ × 2′   75 × 60 cm

'Perfecta', 'Kordes' Perfecta' (Koralu)

Kordes GERMANY 1957
'Spek's Yellow' × 'Karl Herbst'
Very large, shapely blooms of soft cream heavily flushed deep pink and crimson with hints of yellow in the base. Free-flowering on an upright, thorny plant with dark, glossy and well-serrated foliage.
[(C) (P) (H) (MF) (B) ⬇ AW]   2½′ × 2′   75 × 60 cm

'Piccadilly'

McGredy UK 1960
'McGredy's Yellow' × 'Karl Herbst'
Shapely buds open to loosely formed blooms of scarlet and yellow, high-centred at the midway stage. Foliage dark and glossy. Stems very thorny. A dense, upright and very floriferous plant.
[(C) (P) (H) (SF) (B) ⬇ R◧ BS◧ AW]
2½′ × 2′   75 × 60 cm

'Picture'

McGredy UK 1932
Parentage unknown
A fine old rose. At the half-open stage, the clear pink flowers are beautifully scrolled; fully open, they are tidy and symmetrical. Foliage grey-green, matt. Growth short and bushy.
[(C) (P) (SF) (B) (Gh) ⬇ ✂ AL]
1½′ × 1½′   45 × 45 cm

Top: 'My Choice' (see text p. 155) and *bottom:* 'National Trust' (see text p. 156)

'Pink Favourite'

Von Abrams USA 1956
'Juno' × ('Georg Arends' × 'New Dawn')
A very free, large, cupped rose. Its pink flowers are produced on a bushy plant with glossy, mid to bright green foliage.

[(C) (SF) (B) (E) AL]   2½' × 2'   75 × 60 cm

'Pink Peace' (Meibil)

Meilland FRANCE 1959
('Peace' × 'Monique') × ('Peace' × 'Mrs John Laing')
Very large, globular blooms of bright, silvery deep pink with prominent veining. A vigorous, upright plant with mid-green, matt-finished foliage.

[(C) (P) (H) (VF) (E) R ☷ ☺ AW]
3½' × 2½'   1.05 m × 75 cm

'Pinta'

Beales UK 1973
'Ena Harkness' × 'Pascali'
Very free-flowering, with clusters of shapely, creamy-white flowers on a robust, slightly angular plant with dark green stems and mid-green, matt-finished foliage. A special feature is the distinct fragrance of eglantine.

[(C) (P) (H) (VF) (E) R ☷ ☺ ▽ AW]
3½' × 2½'   1.05 m × 75 cm

'Polar Star', 'Polarstern' (Tanlarpost)

Tantau GERMANY 1982
Parentage unknown
A free-flowering rose, its creamy-white, shapely blooms are held on a strong neck. Light green foliage and prickly stems.

[(C) (P) (B) AW]   3' × 2'   90 × 60 cm

'Polarstern' *see* 'Polar Star'

'Portland Trailblazer' *see* 'Big Chief'

'Pot o'Gold' (Dicdivine)

Dickson UK 1980
'Eurorose' × 'Whisky Mac'
Clear, bright yellow blooms touched gold, large and full. Foliage mid-green and heavily veined purple. Growth bushy but tidy, quite thorny.

[(C) (P) (H) (B) (VF) ▽ ✂ AW]
2½' × 2'   75 × 60 cm

Top: 'Perfecta' and *bottom:* 'Picture'

'Precious Platinum', 'Red Star', 'Opa Pötschke'

Dickson UK 1974
'Red Planet' × 'Franklin Englemann'
Bright red blooms with an almost luminous sheen, shapely and of good deportment. Glossy, leathery, mid-green foliage. Upright and bushy growth.

[(C) (P) (H) (B) (VF) (Gh) ▽ ✂ AW]
3' × 2'   90 × 60 cm

'President Herbert Hoover'

Coddington USA 1930
'Sensation' × 'Souvenir de Claudius Pernet'
Long, pointed flowers, orange-pink with a buffy-gold reverse, open flattish and are held on strong, long necks. The foliage is leathery and semi-matt. Growth vigorous and upright, almost lanky. An excellent old variety.

[(R) (H) (P) (VF) ✂ AL]   4' × 3'   1.2 m × 90 cm

'Prima Ballerina', 'Première Ballerine'

Tantau GERMANY 1957
Seedling × 'Peace'
The deep rose-pink, shapely and quite large flowers open blowsily. Foliage dark matt, with dark and

'Piccadilly' (see text p. 158) and *below:* 'Polar Star' (see text p. 159)

thorny stems. Growth upright and sturdy.

[(C) (VF) (B) M◁⋮⋮ AW]   2½' × 2'   75 × 60 cm

'Princess Margaret of England'

Meilland FRANCE 1968
'Queen Elizabeth' × ('Peace' × 'Michèle Meilland')
Bright rose-pink, full, shapely and large blooms.
Upright growth with leathery, matt foliage.

[(C) (SF) (B) ▽ AL]   2½' × 2'   75 × 60 cm

'Pristine' (Jacpico)

Warriner USA 1978
'White Masterpiece' × 'First Prize'
White flowers with a pink blush, quite large and
shapely. Dark green foliage on an upright, dense
but tidy plant.

[(C) (P) (H) (VF) (B) (Gh) ✄ AW]
3½' × 2'   1.05 m × 60 cm

Foliage semi-glossy, mid-green. Growth upright
and robust with strong, thorny stems.

[(C) (P) (SF) (E) ☺ ✄ AW]
3½' × 2'   1.05 m × 60 cm

'Red Planet'

Dickson UK 1970
'Red Devil' × a seedling
Large, fully double, bright crimson blooms. Foli-
age mid-green and glossy. Growth bushy but tidy.

[(C) (P) (VF) (B) AL]   3' × 2'   90 × 60 cm

'Red Devil', 'Coeur d'Amour' (Dicam)

Dickson UK 1970
'Silver Lining' × 'Prima Ballerina'
Very large, high-centred blooms of rosy-scarlet,
the reverse lighter, not over-freely produced.

'Pot o'Gold' (see text p. 159)

'Remember Me' (Cocdestin)

Cocker UK 1984
'Ann Letts' × ('Dainty Maid' × 'Pink Favourite')
A rich mixture of copper and orange shades, not
over-full but shapely blooms, and free-flowering.
Ample, smallish, dark green foliage. Bushy and
upright growth.

[(C) (P) (SF) (B) AW]   2½' × 2'   75 × 60 cm

'Rev. F. Page-Roberts'

Cant UK 1921
'Queen Mary' × a seedling
An old, flamboyant variety, still worthy of a place
in the garden. Fully double yellow blooms brushed
and shaded red. Foliage good, glossy. Growth
bushy and slightly angular.

[(R) (P) (VF) ▽ AL]   2' × 2'   60 × 60 cm

*'Roddy MacMillan' (Cocared)

Cocker UK 1982
('Fragrant Cloud' × 'Postillion') × 'Wisbech Gold'
Large, fully double blooms of rich apricot, and
shapely. Foliage mid-green and almost glossy.
Growth bushy.

[(C) (P) (MF) (B) ▽ AL]   2' × 2'   60 × 60 cm

'President Herbert Hoover' (see text p. 159)

'Rose Gaujard' (Gaumo)

Gaujard FRANCE 1957
'Peace' × 'Opéra' seedling
Not a colour that always appeals, but one of the
best all-round roses ever produced. Very large
cherry-red and silver blooms with a paler reverse,
sometimes opening split or quartered. Strong,
dark wood liberally clothed with dark green and
glossy foliage. Upright and rudely healthy.

[(P) (H) (SF) (B) (E) ☺ ✂ AW]
4' × 3'   1.2 m × 90 cm

'Prima Ballerina' (see text p. 159)

'Rosy Cheeks'

Anderson UK 1975
'Beauty of Festival' × 'Grandpa Dickson'
A big rose, slightly tubby in shape. Carmine to red blooms with a soft yellow reverse. Foliage dark green and matt. Growth bushy.
[(C) (P) (MF) (B) ▽ AL] 2½' × 2' 75 × 60 cm

'Royal Albert Hall'

Cocker UK 1972
'Fragrant Cloud' × 'Postillion'
An interesting, unusually coloured rose, deep wine-red with a soft primrose reverse. The fully double blooms open cupped and imbricated. Foliage small but plentiful, dark green. Growth upright and bushy.
[(C) (VF) (B) BS⬧⫶ R⬧⫶ AL] 2' × 2' 60 × 60 cm

'Royal Dane' *see* 'Troika'

'Royal Highness', 'Königliche Hoheit'

Swim USA 1962
'Virgo' × 'Peace'
A beautiful rose when at its best in fine weather, with long, pointed buds opening to large, full,

high-centred flowers of soft pearly-pink. Foliage lush dark green, the stems sturdy and upright.
[(C) (P) (MF) (B) (E) ☺ ✂ AW]
4' × 2' 1.2 m × 60 cm

'Royal Romance', 'Liselle' (Rulis)

de Ruiter NETHERLANDS 1980
'Whisky Mac' × 'Esther Ofarim'
Medium-sized, shapely flowers, a mixture of soft salmony-orange and peach. Foliage large, dark green and semi-glossy. Growth bushy and upright.
[(C) (B) ▽ AL] 2½' × 2' 75 × 60 cm

'Royal Smile'

Beales UK 1980
'Fragrant Cloud' × 'Pascali'
Creamy-white flowers with delicate soft pink shadings deepening towards the centre, and high-centred and shapely. A special feature is their strong perfume. The foliage is matt dark green and its growth bushy. Good in a warm climate.
[(C) (B) (Gh) (VF) ▽ R⬧⫶ ✧ ✂ AL]
2½' × 2' 75 × 60 cm

'Remember Me' (see text p. 161) and *below:* 'Royal Albert Hall'

'Royal Smile' and *below:* 'Royal William

'Royal William', 'Duftzauber '84' (Korzaun)

Kordes GERMANY 1984

'Feuerzauber' × a seedling

High-centred, deep red and shapely blooms are freely produced on an upright plant with dark green, semi-glossy foliage.

[(C) (B) (MF) ▽ ✂ AW]   2½' × 2'   75 × 60 cm

'Ruby Wedding'

Gregory UK 1979

'Mayflower' × unknown

Shapely, ruby-red flowers of medium size, with loosely arranged petals when fully open. Foliage mid-green. Growth bushy and tidy.

[(C) (Gh) (SF) (B) ▽ ✂ AL]   2' × 2'   60 × 60 cm

'Ruhm von Steinfurth', 'Red Druschki'

Weigand GERMANY 1920

'Frau Karl Druschki' × 'Ulrich Brunner Fils'

Although of Hybrid Perpetual parentage this rose is very Hybrid-Tea-like in both flowers and stature. Long, pointed buds open to beautiful, cupped, full blooms of considerable size, their ruby-red colour fading to cerise. Foliage large and matt with a grey lustre. Growth upright.

[(R) (P) (H) (VF) ▽ ✂ AL]   3' × 2'   90 × 60 cm

'Sandringham Centenary'

Tysterman UK 1981

'Queen Elizabeth' × 'Baccara'

Large, rich burnt-orange flowers paling slightly with age to salmon-pink, their colour particularly rich when almost fully open. Strong, vigorous and upright growth with plentiful, mid-green and semi-glossy foliage.

[(C) (P) (H) (Gh) (SF) ✂ AL]
4' × 2½'   1.2 m × 75 cm

'Shot Silk'

Dickson UK 1924
'Hugh Dickson' seedling × 'Sunstar'
Without doubt one of the best of the Dickson roses from before the Second World War. Globular, full, high-centred flowers of near salmon with a yellow base and a silky sheen. Luxuriant foliage, plentiful and glossy. Growth bushy, upright and shortish.

[(C) (P) (H) (Gh) (B) (MF) ▽ ✂ AL]
1½' × 1½'   45 × 45 cm

'Silver Jubilee'

Cocker UK 1978
[('Highlight' × 'Colour Wonder') × ('Parkdirektor Riggers' × 'Piccadilly')] × 'Mischief'
A shapely, very free-flowering rose of silvery-pink and apricot with a deeper reverse. The flowers are produced in clusters; disbudded, they become huge. Foliage glossy. Growth very bushy but upright, the stems amply endowed with thorns. One of the best roses ever raised.

[(C) (P) (MF) (H) (Gh) (B) (E) ▽ ✂ AW]
3½' × 2'   1.05 m × 60 cm

'Silver Lining'

Dickson UK 1958
'Karl Herbst' × 'Eden Rose'

Soft blush flowers with deeper pink highlights, and exquisitely shaped: bulbous but with high centres and held on strong necks. Foliage a little sparse, dull, matt green. Stems stout and thorny.

[(C) (P) (B) (SF) ▽ ✂ AL]   2' × 2'   60 × 60 cm

'Silver Wedding'

Gregory UK 1976
Parentage unknown
A superb, underrated rose, with shapely blooms of creamy-white. Foliage matt, mid-green. Growth medium bushy.

[(C) (SF) (B) (Gh) ▽ ✂ AL]   2½' × 2'   75 × 60 cm

'Ruhm von Steinfurth' (see text p. 163)

Top: 'Sandringham Centenary' (see text p. 163) and *bottom:* 'Shot Silk'

'Silver Lining' and *right:* 'Simba'

'Simba', 'Goldsmith', 'Helmut Schmidt' (Korbelma)

Kordes GERMANY 1981
'Korgold' × a seedling
Clear, bright yellow flowers, very large and fairly full of petals, held upright on a vigorous and bushy plant with good matt-green foliage.
[(C) (SF) (B) ▽ ✂ AL] 2½′ × 2′ 75 × 60 cm

'Sir Frederick Ashton'

Beales UK 1985
Sport from 'Anna Pavlova'
Very highly scented, large, full blooms of pure white with creamy centres. Foliage large, rounded and dark matt green. Stems strong from upright growth.
[(C) (VF) (E) (Gh) ☺ ❖ AL] 4′ × 3′ 1.2 m × 90 cm

'Sir Harry Pilkington', 'Melina' (Tanema)

Tantau GERMANY 1974
'Inge Horstmann' × 'Sophia Loren'
Large, shapely, bright red and very full blooms. Foliage dark. Growth bushy and upright.
[(C) (SF) (B) (E) AL] 2½′ × 2′ 75 × 60 cm

'Sonia', 'Sweet Promise', 'Sonia Meilland' (Meihelvet)

Meilland FRANCE 1974
'Zambra' × ('Baccara' × 'Message')
Soft silky-salmon blooms, superbly shaped, rounded but high-centred. A free-flowering rose and excellent under glass. Foliage mid-green and semi-matt. Growth dense but upright.
[(C) (SF) (B) (Gh) ▽ ☺ ✂ AW]
2½′ × 2′ 75 × 60 cm

'Spek's Yellow', 'Golden Sceptre'

Spek UK 1950
'Golden Rapture' × a seedling
Long, pointed buds open to loose, deep golden-yellow flowers on long stems, though this rose needs disbudding to produce sizeable blooms. Foliage rich light green. Growth rather sprawling. Good under glass.
[(C) (MF) (B) (Gh) ✂ AL] 3′ × 2′ 90 × 60 cm

'Stella'

Tantau GERMANY 1958
'Horstmann's Jubiläumsrose' × 'Peace'
A plump yet high-centred rose of soft pink flushed

deeper pink held on a strong neck, but not very free-flowering. Foliage dark green and leathery. Growth strong and bushy.

[(C) (SF) (B) ▽ BS◁▥ ✂AL]
2½' × 2'   75 × 60 cm

'Summer Sunshine', 'Soleil d'Eté'

Swim USA 1962
'Buccaneer' × 'Lemon Chiffon'
A tall, almost carefree rose bearing an abundance of loosely formed blooms from long, pointed buds. Foliage mid-green and leathery. Growth upright.

[(C) (P) (H) (Gh) (SF) ✂AL]   3' × 2'   90 × 60 cm

'Sunblest', 'Landora'

Tantau GERMANY 1970
Seedling × 'King's Ransom'
A very free-flowering bedding rose. The flowers from slim buds are rich yellow, fairly large and full, and are held on strong necks. Foliage mid-green, glossy. Growth bushy and upright.

[(C) (SF) (B) (Gh) ▽ ✂ AW]   3' × 2'   90 × 60 cm

'Sunny South'

Clark AUSTRALIA 1918
'Gustav Grünerwald' × 'Betty Berkeley'
Large, globular, highly scented flowers of mid-pink flushed carmine with a yellow base, and semi-double when fully open. Foliage plentiful and rich green. Growth bushy and vigorous. A beautiful rose superbly representative of Australia.

[(R) (VF) (B) (Gh) ▽ ✂AL]
3½' × 3½'   1.05 m × 1.05 m

Top left: 'Stella' (see text p. 165) and *top right:* 'Sunny South'

'Sunset Song' (Cocasun)

Cocker UK 1981
('Sabine' × 'Circus') × 'Sunblest'
With amber yellow blooms overlaid copper, this is a shapely, full rose of personality. Good, light green, glossy foliage. Upright, bushy growth.

[(C) (SF) (B) ▽ ✂ AW]   3' × 2'   90 × 60 cm

'Super Star', 'Tropicana' (Tanorstar)

Tantau GERMANY 1960
(Seedling × 'Peace') × (Seedling × 'Alpine Glow')
Large, full, high-centred blooms of bright coral-vermilion. Foliage matt-grey, with thorny stems. Growth angular.

[(C) (H) (MF) (B) ▽ M◁▥ ✂ AW]
3½' × 3'   1.05 m × 90 cm

'Super Sun'

Bentley UK 1967
Sport from 'Piccadilly'
Deep yellow flowers brushed and veined orange with a paler reverse, shapely and opening loosely formed. Foliage dark green and glossy, the stems very thorny. Growth dense and upright.

[(C) (P) (H) (SF) (B) ▽ BS◁▥ AL]
2½' × 2'   75 × 60 cm

'Susan Hampshire' (Meinatac)

Paolino FRANCE 1972
('Monique' × 'Symphonie') × 'Maria Callas'
A free-flowering rose with amply proportioned, full, high-centred, bright rose-pink flowers. Foliage mid-green and matt. Growth upright and dense.

[(C) (P) (H) (SF) (B) ▽ ✂ AW]
2½' × 2'   75 × 60 cm

'Super Sun' and *below:* 'Susan Hampshire'

'Sutter's Gold'

Swim USA 1950
'Charlotte Armstrong' × 'Signora'
Very free-flowering, the slim buds held on long, strong necks opening to loosely formed, attractive flowers of deep yellow brushed and shaded with orange and pink. Foliage mid-green and semi-glossy. Growth upright but bushy.
[(C) (P) (MF) (B) (Gh) ▽ ✂ AW]
3′ × 2′   90 × 60cm

'Sweetheart' (Cocapeer)

Cocker UK 1980
'Peer Gynt' × ('Fragrant Cloud' × 'Gay Gordons')
Large and full blooms of deep glowing pink. Foliage mid-green. Growth upright and tall.
[(C) (P) (SF) (B) ✂ AL]   3½′ × 2′   1.05 m × 60 cm

'Sweet Promise' *see* 'Sonia'

'Sylvia' *see* 'Congratulations'

'Talisman'

Montgomery USA 1929
'Ophelia' × 'Souvenir de Claudius Pernet'
Its fully double blooms open attractively flat-topped, not large but held on strong stems which

makes them ideal for cutting. Golden-yellow in colour though tinged orange-copper. Foliage light green and glossy. Growth upright. A good and much-loved older variety.
[(C) (MF) (P) (Gh) (B) ▽ ✂ AL]
3′ × 2′   90 × 60 cm

'Tallyho'

Swim USA 1948
'Charlotte Armstrong' × a seedling
Large, globular buds open to large, cupped flowers of very deep pink, almost maroon. Foliage leathery. Very dark wood on a bushy plant.

[(C) (P) (VF) (B) ☐ AL]   3' × 2'   90 × 60 cm

*'Tenerife'

Bracegirdle UK 1972
'Fragrant Cloud' × 'Piccadilly'
Large, very full flowers of orange-red with a peach-yellow reverse. Foliage glossy. Growth upright.

[(C) (P) (VF) (B) ☐ AL]   2½' × 2'   75 × 60 cm

'Texas Centennial'

Watkins USA 1935
Sport from 'President Herbert Hoover'
Long, pointed buds, held on long strong necks, open to flattish blooms of bright vermilion-red with a gold base. Foliage leathery and semi-matt. Growth vigorous, upright. A rose that can be used as a free-standing shrub.

[(R) (H) (P) (VF) ✂ AL]   4' × 3'   1.2 m × 90 cm

'Thaïs', 'Lady Elgin'

Meilland FRANCE 1954
'Mme Kriloff' × ('Peace' × 'Genève')
I could not resist including this old variety, despite its rarity. Rounded buds open to full, cupped flowers of apricot-buffish-yellow washed and veined orange. Foliage dark green and leathery. Growth upright.

[(C) (P) (VF) (E) ☐ ✂ AL]   3' × 2'   90 × 60 cm

*'The Coxswain' (Cocadilly)

Cocker UK 1985
('Super Star' × 'Ballet') × 'Silver Jubilee'
Blended shades of pink and cream. The large and full flowers are freely produced. Foliage mid-green and semi-glossy. Bushy, upright growth.

[(C) (P) (B) (H) (E) ☐ ✂ AL]   2½' × 2'   75 × 60 cm

'The Doctor'

Howard USA 1936
'Mrs J. D. Eisele' × 'Los Angeles'
A famous variety which, despite a martyrdom to black spot, should not be allowed to vanish into oblivion. It has large flowers of rich silver-pink with a satin sheen, shapely and high-centred at the mid-open stage. Foliage matt grey-green. Growth

'Texas Centennial'

'Uncle Bill'

vigorous and upright.

[(C) (VF) (B) (E) ⛉ B⟊⫶ ☺ ✄ AL]
2½′ × 2′   75 × 60 cm

'The Lady' (Fryjingo)

Fryer UK 1985
'Pink Parfait' × 'Redgold'
Very large, exhibition-sized blooms of honey
yellow brushed salmon. Semi-glossy and mid-
green foliage. Upright growth.

[(C) (P) (MF) (E) ⛉ ✄ AL]   2½′ × 2′   75 × 60 cm

*'Torvill & Dean' (Lantor)

Sealand UK 1984
'Grandpa Dickson' × 'Alexander'
Glowing, mid-pink blooms with a cream underlay
and base, large and shapely. Foliage mid-green
and semi-glossy. Growth habit upright.

[(C) (SF) (B) (E) ⛉ AL]   2½′ × 2′   75 × 60 cm

'Tranquillity', 'Handout' (Barout)

Barrett UK 1982
'Whisky Mac' × 'Pink Favourite'
Large, peachy-pink blooms flushed apricot and
yellow. Foliage dark green and glossy. Growth

upright and bushy.

[(C) (SF) (B) ⛉ AL]   2½′ × 2′   75 × 60 cm

'Troika', 'Royal Dane'

Poulsen DENMARK 1971
['Super Star' × ('Baccara' × 'Princesse Astrid')] ×
'Hanne'
The large, full, colourful blooms are a blend of
orange and pink. Foliage large, dark and glossy.
Growth bushy and upright.

[(C) (MF) (B) (H) ⛉ ✄ AW]   2½′ × 2′   75 × 60 cm

'Tropicana' *see* 'Super Star'

'Typhoon' (Taifun)

Kordes GERMANY 1972
'Dr A. J. Verhage' × 'Colour Wonder'
Medium-sized blooms, a blend of salmon and yellow. Foliage mid-green and semi-matt. Growth
upright.

[(C) (MS) (B) (H) ⛉ ✄ AL]   2½′ × 2′   75 × 60 cm

'Uncle Bill'

Beales UK 1984
Sport from 'Alec's Red' (discovered by Rev. W.
Temple-Bourne)

Soft, silky, mid-pink blooms are produced in abundance from large and plump buds. Half open, the flowers are high-centred. Foliage mid-green, matt, the stems thorny. Growth bushy and upright.

[(C) (VF) (B) (P) AL]   2½' × 2'   75 × 60 cm

'Velvet Hour'

LeGrice UK 1978
Parentage unknown
Freely produced, medium-sized, full, blood-red flowers on strong necks, with a very good scent. Foliage dark and semi-glossy. Growth upright.

[(C) (P) (H) (SF) (B) ▽ ☺ ✂ AL]
2½' × 2'   75 × 60 cm

'Vienna Charm', 'Charming Vienna', 'Wiener Charme', 'Charme de Vienne' (Korschaprat)

Kordes GERMANY 1963
'Chantré' × 'Golden Sun'
Large, pointed buds open to large, full blooms of coppery-orange, and well scented. Foliage dark and semi-glossy. Growth tallish, upright. Not totally hardy.

[(C) (H) (MF) (B) ▽ ✿ ✂ AL]
3½' × 2'   1.05 m × 60 cm

'Violinista Costa'

Camprubi SPAIN 1936
'Sensation' × 'Shot Silk'
Shapely flowers, freely produced, of deep orange-pink with deeper undertones and a yellow base, at times almost red. Foliage mid-green, glossy, the stems well armed with thorns. Growth angular.

[(C) (P) (H) (B) (SF) ▽ AL]   2½' × 2'   75 × 60 cm

'Virgo', 'Virgo Liberationem'

Mallerin FRANCE 1947
'Blanche Mallerin' × 'Neige Parfum'
Shapely, pointed buds open to loose blooms of good size on strong stems, white with a heavy base. Foliage mid-greyish-green and semi-matt. Growth slender and upright.

[(C) (MF) (B) (Gh) ▽ ✂ AL]   2½' × 2'   75 × 60 cm

'Wiener Charme' *see* 'Vienna Charm'

'Wendy Cussons'

Gregory UK 1963
Seedling from 'Independence'
Superbly shaped, high-centred blooms of deep cerise-red are freely produced on a strong, angular,

'Violinista Costa'

'Virgo' and *below:* 'Wendy Cussons'

'Whisky Mac' and *below:* 'White Wings'

rather awkward plant with dark matt-green foliage.
[(C) (P) (VF) (E) ☺ AW]   2′ × 2′   60 × 60 cm

'Whisky Mac' (Tanky)

Tantau GERMANY 1967
Parentage unknown
Shapely blooms of rich gold and amber with dark green, glossy foliage. Growth angular but upright. Not totally hardy.
[(C) (P) (VF) (B) (Gh) ▽ ✂ BS ◖⃚ R ◖⃚ AW]
2½′ × 2′   75 × 60 cm

'White Knight' *see* 'Message'

'White Wings'

Krebs USA 1947
'Dainty Bess' × a seedling
Long, pointed buds open to large, single, pure white flowers with pronounced chocolate-brown stamens. A beautiful rose when it finds the right situation. Foliage mid-green and matt. Growth bushy.
[(C) (MF) ▽ ⁙ AL]   3½′ × 2½′   1.05 m × 75 cm

'Wisbech Gold'

McGredy UK 1964
'Piccadilly' × 'Golden Star'
The large, shapely blooms are held upright on strong necks and are golden-yellow edged pink. Foliage dark green and glossy. Growth upright.
[(C) (P) (MF) (B) (Gh) ▽ ✂ AL]
2½′ × 2′   75 × 60 cm

*'With Love' (Andwit)

Anderson UK 1983
'Grandpa Dickson' × 'Daily Sketch'
Freely produced, medium blooms of clear yellow edged pink. Foliage mid-green and glossy. Growth upright.
[(C) (MF) (B) ▽ ✂ AL]   2½′ × 2′   75 × 60 cm

'Yorkshire Bank', 'True Love' (Rutrulo)

de Ruiter NETHERLANDS 1979
'Pascali' × 'Peer Gynt'
White blooms with hints of pink, free and large, and bright green, semi-glossy foliage. Growth bushy.
[(C) (P) (B) (MF) ▽ AL]   2′ × 2′   60 × 60 cm

Floribunda Roses (Cluster-Flowered Bush Roses)

The classification 'Floribunda' covers all bush roses, cluster-flowered roses other than Miniatures and the unofficial group known as 'Patio roses'. More recently, Floribundas have been reclassified as 'Cluster-Flowered'. As in the case of 'Large-Flowered', however, the term has not been fully accepted by commercial growers and, in most catalogues, the roses are still listed under the heading 'Floribundas'.

Many hundreds and probably thousands have been raised and introduced worldwide during the last fifty or so years and it would be impossible to include them all here. I have selected 167 which I believe to be a fair representation of the best available today, together with a few classics from the past. Although the latter are not readily available, they are important as outstanding examples of their type.

Floribundas have many uses, the most common of which is for bedding. Many make excellent hedging plants and most can be used for group planting in herbaceous borders or among other shrubs. Not a few, especially the shorter ones, make very good pot plants for urns, tubs and the like. Others, especially the taller ones, are ideal for providing cut flowers.

*'Abundance'

Gandy UK 1974
Seedling × 'Firecracker'
Clusters of fully double, mid-pink blooms on a sturdy and low-growing bush with dark, matt-green foliage.
[(C) (P) (H) (SF) (B) ▽ AL]   1½' × 1½'   45 × 45 cm

'Alison Wheatcroft'

Wheatcroft UK 1959
Sport from 'Circus'
Large clusters of shapely, cupped, fully double flowers, deep yellow and apricot flushed crimson. Foliage plentiful and glossy. Growth upright.
[(C) (P) (H) (SF) (B) AL]   2½' × 2'   75 × 60 cm

'Allgold'

LeGrice UK 1956
'Goldilocks' × 'Ellinor LeGrice'
An outstanding old variety, with loosely arranged clusters of clear golden-yellow, semi-double flowers. Its foliage is small, mid-green and glossy. Growth upright.
[(C) (P) (SF) (B) ▽ ✂ AW]   2' × 2'   60 × 60 cm

'Amanda' (Beesian)

Bees UK 1979
'Arthur Bell' × 'Zambra'
Globular buds open to clear yellow flowers which are fully double and produced in good, large clusters. Small, plentiful, light green foliage. Upright growth.
[(C) (SF) (B) AL]   2' × 2'   60 × 60 cm

'Amberlight'

LeGrice UK 1962
(Seedling × 'Lavender Pinocchio') × 'Marcel Bourgouin'
Fully double, rather muddled flowers are produced, well spaced in large clusters. Darkish green and semi-matt foliage. Growth bushy.
[(C) (MF) (H) (B) ☺ AL]   2½' × 2'   75 × 60 cm

Above: 'Alison Wheatcroft'
Below: 'Amber Queen' (see text p. 175)

'Anisley Dickson'

'Amber Queen' (Harroony)

Harkness UK 1984
'Southampton' × 'Typhoon'
Large, well-packed clusters of fully double blooms of amber-yellow. The foliage is large, maroonish, almost glossy. Growth bushy.
[(C) (MF) (B) (Gh) ▽ ✕ AW]   2' × 2'   60 × 60 cm

'Anisley Dickson', 'Dicky', 'München Kindl' (Dickimono)

Dickson UK 1983
'Coventry Cathedral' × 'Memento'
Deep salmon-pink, lighter on the reverse, large, fully double flowers in clusters. Foliage mid-green and glossy. Growth bushy.
[(C) (P) (SF) (B) ▽ AL]   2½' × 2'   75 × 60 cm

*'Anita'

Christensen USA 1982
'Rumba' × 'Marmalade'
A blend of assorted pinks, its clusters of large, fully double blooms are borne on an upright plant with good, glossy foliage and large, spiteful thorns.
[(C) (SF) (B) (H) AL]   2½' × 2'   75 × 60 cm

'Ann Aberconway'

Mattock UK 1976
'Arthur Bell' × a seedling
Largish, double-formed flowers of apricot-orange are borne in medium-sized clusters. Foliage dark and leathery. Growth upright.
[(C) (SF) (B) (H) AL]   2½' × 2'   75 × 60 cm

'Anna Wheatcroft'

Tantau GERMANY 1958
'Cinnabar' seedling × unknown
Very large, single blooms are produced in huge clusters of bright salmon, almost vermilion, with pronounced yellow stamens. Foliage dark, semi-glossy. Growth vigorous.
[(C) (SF) (B) (H) AL]   3' × 2'   90 × 60 cm

'Anne Cocker'

Cocker UK 1970
'Highlight' × 'Colour Wonder'
The very double, small, bright vermilion flowers are closely packed in large clusters, with light to mid-green, crisp and glossy foliage, and very prickly stems. Growth upright. Lasts a good time in water when cut.
[(C) (P) (B) (H) M❊∷ ✕ AW]
3½' × 2'   1.05 m × 60 cm

'Anne Harkness' (Harkaramel)

Harkness UK 1979
'Bobby Dazzler' × [('Manx Queen' × 'Prima Ballerina') × ('Chanelle' × 'Piccadilly')]
Moderately medium-sized, full blooms come in very large clusters, apricot-yellow with a deeper base. Semi-glossy foliage. Growth upright and tall.
[(C) (P) (SF) (B) (H) (Gh) ▽ ✕ AW]
3½' × 2'   1.05 m × 60 cm

'Apricot Nectar'

Boerner USA 1965
Seedling × 'Spartan'
The buff-yellow and apricot flowers are large and cupped, several in each cluster, and with good scent. Foliage dark and glossy. Growth bushy.
[(C) (VF) (B) (H) AW]   2' × 2'   60 × 60 cm

'Arcadian', 'New Year' (Macnewye)

McGredy NEW ZEALAND 1982
'Mary Sumner' × a seedling
Medium-sized, fully double flowers are borne in clusters, a blend of orange and gold. Foliage dark green and glossy. Growth upright.
[(C) (P) (SF) (B) (H) ▽ ✕ AL]   2½' × 2'   75 × 60 cm

*'Ards Beauty' (Dicjoy)

Dickson UK 1986
('Eurorose' × 'Whisky Mac') × 'Bright Smile'
Large, Hybrid-Tea-like flowers are produced in good-sized clusters, soft yellow and well scented. Foliage mid-green and glossy. Growth bushy.
[(C) (MF) (B) (H) AL]   2' × 2'   60 × 60 cm

'Ards Beauty'

'Arthur Bell'

McGredy UK 1965
'Cläre Grammerstorf' × 'Piccadilly'
Shapely buds open to well-formed, semi-double flowers of rich deep yellow, fading to lemon with age, in large clusters, though occasionally singly. The foliage is mid to light green and glossy. Growth densely upright.

[(C) (MF) (B) (H) ▽ ✂ AW]   2½' × 2'   75 × 60 cm

'August Seebauer', 'The Queen Mother'

Kordes GERMANY 1944
'Break o'Day' × 'Else Poulsen'
Large, double, clear pink and high-centred blooms

are carried in sizeable clusters. Foliage small but plentiful, mid-green and semi-glossy. Growth bushy and vigorous.

[(C) (P) (SF) (B) (H) ▽ AL]   2½' × 2'   75 × 60 cm

'Avignon'

Cant UK 1974
'Zambra' × 'Allgold'
Clear yellow, medium-sized and double flowers are borne in clusters. Foliage light green and glossy. Growth upright and vigorous.

[(C) (P) (SF) (B) (H) AL]   3½' × 2'   1.05 m × 60 cm

*'Avocet' (Harpluto)

Harkness UK 1984
'Dame of Sark' × a seedling
It produces very large clusters of semi-double blooms, orange faintly edged pink to copper. Foliage plentiful, dark green and glossy. Growth bushy.

[(C) (P) (SF) (B) (H) ▽ ✂ AL]   2½' × 2'   75 × 60 cm

'Baby Bio'

Smith UK 1977
'Golden Treasure' × a seedling
Very large clusters of double, deep yellow blooms

Top: 'Arthur Bell' and *bottom:* 'August Seebauer'

Above: 'Beautiful Britain' (see text p. 178)
Below: 'Bonfire Night' (see text p. 178)

are produced on a well-foliated, dark green, glossy, short and bushy plant. A most useful rose.

[(C) (SF) (B) (H) ▽ AW]   1½' × 1½'   45 × 45 cm

'Beautiful Britain' (Dicfire)

Dickson UK 1983
'Red Planet' × 'Eurorose'
With shapely blooms of rich orange-tomato-red, well spaced in large clusters. Foliage mid-green and semi-glossy. Growth bushy and upright. A good, bright variety.

[(C) (P) (SF) (B) (H) ▽ ✕ AW]
2½' × 2'   75 × 60 cm

*'Beauty Queen' (Canmiss)

Cant UK 1984
'English Miss' × a seedling
Its mid-pink blooms are well arranged in large clusters and are very double. Foliage dark green and glossy. Growth upright.

[(C) (MF) (B) (H) ▽ AL]   2½' × 2'   75 × 60 cm

'Bonfire Night'

McGredy UK 1971
'Tiki' × 'Variety Club'
Bears large clusters of semi-double, sizeable flowers of orange-scarlet and yellow. Foliage dark green, matt and well serrated. Growth bushy.

[(C) (SF) (B) (H) AL]   2½' × 2'   75 × 60 cm

*'Bright Smile' (Dicdanse)

Dickson UK 1980
'Eurorose' × a seedling
Flattish, convex blooms, semi-double and clear yellow, are borne in good-sized clusters. Foliage dense and mid-green with dark thorns. Bushy and upright growth.

[(C) (SF) (B) (H) AW]   2' × 2'   60 × 60 cm

'Brown Velvet', 'Colorbreak' (Macultra)

McGredy NEW ZEALAND 1982
'Mary Sumner' × 'Kapai'
Deep orangy blooms tinted brownish, and very double, are produced in large clusters – an unusual combination. Foliage dark green and glossy. Growth upright.

[(C) (SF) (B) (H) ▽ ✕ AL]   3' × 2'   90 × 60 cm

'Burma Star'

Cocker UK 1974
'Arthur Bell' × 'Manx Queen'
Largish, double, apricot-yellow flowers are carried in large clusters on a tall, well-foliated plant, the leaves large and glossy. Growth upright.

[(C) (P) (MF) (B) (H) AL]   3' × 2'   90 × 60 cm

'Cairngorm'

Cocker UK 1973
'Anne Cocker' × 'Arthur Bell'
Gold heavily overlaid with tangerine, fully double flowers are borne in large clusters. Foliage dark green and glossy. Growth upright.

[(C) (P) (SF) (B) (H) AL]   2½' × 2'   75 × 60 cm

'Centenaire de Lourdes', 'Delge', 'Mrs Jones'

Delbard-Chabert FRANCE 1958
('Frau Karl Druschki' × a seedling) × a seedling
Huge clusters of well-spaced flowers, each shapely both in bud and when fully open, of bright shrimp-pink. Foliage large, dark green and shiny. Growth bushy and upright. A little tender for cold districts, but a superb variety.

[(C) (P) (SF) (B) (H) AL]   3' × 2'   90 × 60 cm

*'Champagne Cocktail' (Horflash)

Horner UK 1985
'Old Master' × 'Southampton'
Medium-sized, double flowers of soft yellow splashed with pink, several blooms in a cluster. Foliage mid-green. Growth bushy.

[(C) (SF) (B) (H) AL]   2½' × 2'   75 × 60 cm

'Chanelle'

McGredy UK 1959
'Ma Perkins' × ('Fashion' × 'Mrs William Sprott')
Large clusters of semi-double, creamy-apricot flowers are carried on a vigorous plant with good, dark green, glossy foliage. Growth bushy.

[(C) (MF) (B) (H) AW]   2½' × 2'   75 × 60 cm

'Charleston' (Meiridge)

Meilland FRANCE 1963
'Masquerade' × ('Radar' × 'Caprice')
Clusters of semi-double blooms of soft yellow heavily flushed crimson, deepening with age. Foliage leathery. Growth bushy.

[(C) (SF) (B) (H) BS ▯⫶ AL]   2½' × 2'   75 × 60 cm

'City of Belfast' (see text p. 180) and *below:* 'Clydebank Centenary' (see text p. 180)

'Chinatown' (Ville de Chine)

Poulsen DENMARK 1963
'Columbine' × 'Cläre Grammerstorf'
The very large, fully double individual flowers of clear yellow are often flushed pink. These are displayed in medium-sized clusters amid lush, light green foliage. Growth upright and vigorous. 'Chinatown' could well be used as a free-standing shrub rose.

[(C) (P) (VF) (B) (H) AW]   4' × 3'   1.2 m × 90 cm

'Chorus' (Meijulito)

Meilland FRANCE 1975
'Tamango' × ('Sarabande' × 'Zambra')
Sizeable, double, bright red flowers are borne in large clusters. Foliage mid-green and glossy. Growth vigorous and upright.

[(C) (P) (SF) (B) (H) AL]   2½' × 2'   75 × 60 cm

'Chuckles'

Shepherd USA 1958
('Jean Lafitte' × 'New Dawn') × 'Orange Triumph'
Large, semi-double flowers of deep orange-pink with a central white eye are produced in large clusters on a bushy plant.

[(C) (SF) (B) (H) AL]   2' × 2'   60 × 60 cm

'Circus'

Swim USA 1956
'Fandango' × 'Pinocchio'
The large clusters of shapely, cupped, fully double flowers are yellow flushed orange, and the foliage is plentiful and glossy. Growth upright.

[(C) (P) (H) (SF) (B) AL]   2½' × 2'   75 × 60 cm

'City of Belfast' (Macci)

McGredy UK 1968
'Evelyn Fison' × ('Circus' × 'Korona')
The bright scarlet-red, very eye-catching blooms
are in large clusters. Foliage plentiful and glossy.
Growth bushy.
[(C) (P) (B) (H) AW]   2′ × 2′   60 × 60 cm

'City of Leeds'

McGredy UK 1965
'Evelyn Fison' × ('Spartan' × 'Red Favourite')
Large, semi-double, salmon-pink flowers are pro-
duced in large clusters. Foliage dark and leathery.
Growth upright and bushy.
[(C) (P) (B) (H) (SF) AL]   2½′ × 2′   75 × 60 cm

'City of Portsmouth'

Cant UK 1975
'Arthur Bell' × a seedling
Coppery-orange and yellow with pink highlights,
the flowers are large and are borne in sizeable clusters. Foliage bronzy-green. Growth vigorous and
upright.
[(C) (P) (B) (SF) (H) AL]   3′ × 2′   90 × 60 cm

*'Clydebank Centenary' (Cocdazzle)

Cocker UK 1987
Seedling × 'Darling Flame'
Well-formed Hybrid-Tea-like flowers of sparkling
orange-vermilion with a yellow reverse, and a rose
of good foliage and upright growth.
[(C) (B) (H) (SF) ▽ AL]   2½′ × 2′   75 × 60 cm

'Daily Sketch' (Macai)

McGredy UK 1961
'Ma Perkins' × 'Grand Gala'
Hybrid-Tea-shaped, fully double blooms of silver
edged pink are produced in clusters. Foliage dark
green and semi-glossy. Growth vigorous and
upright.
[(C) (P) (B) (SF) (H) AL]   2½′ × 2′   75 × 60 cm

'Dainty Maid'

LeGrice UK 1940
'D. T. Poulsen' × unknown
The beautiful, large, single flowers of silvery-pink
have a deeper reverse and pronounced yellow stamens, and are carried in large clusters. Foliage
dark green and leathery. Growth upright.
[(C) (P) (B) (H) AL]   3′ × 2′   90 × 60 cm

'Disco Dancer' and *below:* 'English Miss'

'Dame of Sark'

Harkness UK 1976
('Pink Parfait' × 'Masquerade') × 'Tablers' Choice'
A striking variety, a mixture of orange and yellow
with red marbling on fully double flowers in large
clusters. Foliage dark green. Growth bushy and
upright.
[(C) (P) (B) (H) ◑ AW]   2½′ × 2′   75 × 60 cm

'Dearest'

Dickson UK 1960
Seedling × 'Spartan'
Large, semi-double, salmon-pink blooms are
borne in sizeable clusters, and have a fine scent.

Foliage dark greyish-green and matt. Growth bushy.

[(C) (B) (H) (VF) ☺ AW]   2′ × 2′   60 × 60 cm

'Deb's Delight' (Legsweet)

LeGrice UK 1983
'Tip Top' × a seedling
A delightful blend of silvery-salmon and pink, fully double blooms in large clusters. Foliage mid-green and semi-glossy. Growth bushy and upright.

[(C) (B) (H) (MF) ▽ AL]   2′ × 2′   60 × 60 cm

'Dicky' *see* 'Anisley Dickson'

*'Disco Dancer' (Dicinfra)

Dickson UK 1984
'Coventry Cathedral' × 'Memento'
The very bright scarlet blooms have orange reflections, and are semi-double and produced in large clusters. Mid-green and glossy foliage. Bushy and vigorous.

[(C) (P) (B) (H) (SF) ▽ AW]   3′ × 2′   90 × 60 cm

'Dreamland', 'Traumland'

Tantau GERMANY 1958
'Cinnabar Improved' × 'Fashion'
Peachy-pink, fully double and shapely blooms, in large clusters. Foliage dark green and leathery. Growth short and bushy.

[(C) (P) (B) (H) (SF) ▽ AW]   1½′ × 1½′   45 × 45 cm

'Dusky Maiden'

LeGrice UK 1947
('Daily Mail Scented Rose' × 'Etoile de Hollande') × 'Else Poulsen'
Large, single, deep velvety-red blooms are borne in clusters on an upright, sturdy plant with dark green foliage. A superb old variety.

[(C) (P) (B) (H) (VF) ▽ ✄ AL]   2′ × 2′   60 × 60 cm

'Elizabeth of Glamis', 'Irish Beauty' (Macel)

McGredy UK 1964
'Spartan' × 'Highlight'
The superbly formed, well-scented double flowers of rich salmon-pink are produced in clusters. Foliage dark green, matt. Growth upright. Needs protection in cold districts.

[(C) (B) (H) (VF) ▽ BS◧ M◧ ✄ AW]
2½′ × 2′   75 × 60 cm

'Europeana'

'English Miss'

Cant UK 1977
'Dearest' × 'Sweet Repose'
Soft, blush-rose-pink, shapely, individual flowers in large, tight clusters. Foliage dark green overlaid purple. Growth bushy and upright.

[(C) (P) (B) (H) (SF) ▽ AW]   2′ × 2′   60 × 60 cm

'Escapade' (Harpade)

Harkness UK 1967
'Pink Parfait' × 'Baby Faurax'
Scented, semi-double blooms of rosy-violet with hints of lavender are borne in large clusters. Foliage light green and semi-glossy, on an upright and branching bush.

[(C) (P) (B) (H) (MF) ▽ ✄ AW]   3′ × 2′   90 × 60 cm

'Europeana'

de Ruiter NETHERLANDS 1963
'Ruth Leuwerik' × 'Rosemary Rose'
Beautifully formed, large, fully double, deep red flowers opening flat and quartered are produced in large, heavy clusters. Foliage very dark green heavily overlaid with maroon. Stems dark, with few thorns. Bushy and angular growth.

[(C) (B) (H) (SF) ▽ M◧ AL]   2′ × 2′   60 × 60 cm

'Evelyn Fison' and *below:* 'Everest Double Fragrance'

'Evelyn Fison', 'Irish Wonder' (Macev)

McGredy UK 1962
'Moulin Rouge' × 'Korona'
Large clusters of evenly spaced flowers, fully double and bright red. Foliage dark to mid-green. Growth bushy.

[(C) (P) (B) (H) (SF) ▽ AW]   2½′ × 2′   75 × 60 cm

'Evening Star'

Warriner USA 1974
'White Masterpiece' × 'Saratoga'
Large clusters of double flowers of pure white with lemon shadings, high-centred and shapely. Foliage dark green and leathery. Upright, bushy growth.

[(C) (P) (B) (H) (SF) ▽ AW]   2½′ × 2′   75 × 60 cm

'Everest Double Fragrance'

Beales UK 1979
'Dearest' × 'Elizabeth of Glamis'
The large, fully double and shapely blooms are borne in trusses, a soft powder-pink sometimes almost coral, and highly scented. Dark green, leathery and heavily veined foliage, and stout stems with prickles, on a plant of upright and vigorous growth.

[(C) (P) (B) (H) (VF) R⬚ ✕ AL]
4′ × 2′   1.2 m × 60 cm

'Eyepaint', 'Tapis Persan' (Maceye)

McGredy NEW ZEALAND 1975
Seedling × 'Picasso'
Medium-sized, single blooms of scarlet with a white eye, in large clusters. Foliage dark green, the leaves numerous but small. Growth bushy and tall.

[(C) (P) (B) (H) ▽ AL]   3′ × 2′   90 × 60 cm

Above: Fergie
Top right: 'Frenzy' (see text p. 184) and *bottom right:*
'Geraldine' (see text p. 184)

'Fashion'

Boerner USA 1949
'Pinocchio' × 'Crimson Glory'
Rich salmon to coral, shapely, high-centred flowers are carried in large clusters. Dark green, glossy
foliage and brownish wood, the growth bushy.

[(C) (B) (H) ▽ R⬤⬚ AL]   2′ × 2′   60 × 60 cm

*'Fergie' (Ganfer)

Gandy UK 1987
Parentage unknown
Eye-catching, Hybrid-Tea-like flowers of orange-
buff and ginger with a shell-pink edge to the petals.
Grey-green foliage on a plant of compact growth.

[(C) (B) ▽ AL]   1½′ × 1½′   45 × 45 cm

'Firecracker'

Boerner USA 1956
'Pinocchio' seedling × a 'Numa Fay' seedling
Large, semi-double flowers in sizeable clusters,
scarlet on yellow. Foliage light green and leathery.
Compact and upright growth.

[(C) (B) (H) (SF) ▽ AL]   2′ × 2′   60 × 60 cm

'Fragrant Delight'

Tysterman UK 1978
'Chanelle' × 'Whisky Mac'
Soft orange-salmon blooms, large and semi-
double, are produced in huge trusses on a
well-balanced plant with glossy reddish foliage.
Growth upright.

[(C) (B) (H) ▽ AW]   2½′ × 2′   75 × 60 cm

'Frensham'

Norman UK 1946
Floribunda seedling × 'Crimson Glory'
Shapely, pure crimson flowers are borne in clusters
on a vigorous, angular plant with bright green foliage and vicious thorns.

[(C) (P) (B) (H) M⬤⬚ AL]
4′ × 2½′   1.2 m × 75 cm

'Frenzy', 'Prince Igor' (Meihigor)

Meilland FRANCE 1970
('Sarabande' × 'Dany Robin') × 'Zambra'
Shapely little flowers of orange-red with a yellow
reverse, and abundant, darkish and matt-green
foliage. Bushy growth.

[(C) (P) (B) (H) (SF) ▽ AL]   2′ × 2′   60 × 60 cm

'Garnette'

Tantau GERMANY 1951
('Rosenelfe' × 'Eva') × 'Heros'
Never at its best out of doors but excellent under
glass, this is still used extensively as a florist's rose.
The flowers are cupped, double, garnet-red and
are borne in clusters. Foliage dark green. Growth
upright.

[(Gh) ▽ ✂ AL]   2′ × 2′   60 × 60 cm

*'Geraldine' (Peahaze)

Pearce UK 1984
Seedling × a seedling
A pleasing combination of oranges in clusters very
full of semi-double flowers. Foliage light green and
semi-glossy. Growth upright.

[(C) (B) (H) (SF) AW]   2½′ × 2′   75 × 60 cm

'Grüss an Aachen'

'Glenfiddich'

Cocker UK 1976
'Arthur Bell' × ('Sabine' × 'Circus')
Large, well-shaped, full flowers of rich amber-
yellow, in large clusters. Foliage dark green and
glossy on a plant of upright growth. Not hardy in
cold districts.

[(C) (B) (H) (SF) ▽ AW]   3′ × 2′   90 × 60 cm

'Gold Badge' *see* 'Gold Bunny'

'Gold Bunny', 'Gold Badge' (Meigronuri)

Paulino FRANCE 1978
'Poppy Flash' × ('Charlston' × 'Allgold')
Full, fairly large blooms of clear yellow are borne
in large clusters on a bushy plant with mid-green
foliage.

[(C) (B) (H) (SF) ▽ BS ◖▥ AL]
2′ × 2′   60 × 60 cm

'Golden Slippers'

Von Abrams USA 1961
'Goldilocks' × a seedling
Loosely formed, semi-double flowers of orange
and yellow are produced in large clusters on
an upright and bushy plant with glossy, leathery
foliage.

[(C) (B) (H) (SF) ▽ AL]   2′ × 2′   60 × 60 cm

'Greensleeves' (Harlenten)

Harkness UK 1980
('Rudolph Timm' × 'Arthur Bell') × [('Pascali' ×
'Elizabeth of Glamis') × ('Sabine' × 'Violette Dot')]
An unusual rose, its semi-double, chartreuse-
green flowers with a pink overlay are borne in large
clusters. Dark green, matt foliage on a plant of
upright growth.

[(C) (B) (H) (GH) ▽ ✂ AL]   2½′ × 2′   75 × 60 cm

'Grüss an Aachen'

Geduldig GERMANY 1909
'Frau Karl Druschki' × 'Franz Deegen'
A charmer from the past, its fully double, creamy-
white flowers have soft pink and peachy highlights
and are very freely produced in smallish clusters.
Foliage matt dark green. Growth bushy, upright.

[(C) (B) (H) (Gh) (SF) ▽ AL]
1½′ × 1½′   45 × 45 cm

'Horstmann's Rosenresli'

'Hannah Gordon' (Korweiso)

Kordes GERMANY 1983
Seedling × 'Bordure'
With large clusters of blooms, full and shapely, white to cream touched deep pink. Foliage of good size, mid-green and semi-glossy. Growth bushy and upright.

[(C) (P) (B) (H) (SF) ▽ AW]   3′ × 2′   90 × 60 cm

'Heaven Scent'

Poulsen DENMARK 1968
'Pernille Poulsen' × 'Isabel de Ortiz'
Soft salmon, fully double, large blooms are produced in large clusters. Good, mid-green foliage. Bushy growth.

[(C) (B) (H) (VF) ▽ ✂ AL]   2′ × 2′   60 × 60 cm

'Honeymoon', 'Honigmond'

Kordes GERMANY 1960
'Cläre Grammerstorf' × 'Spek's Yellow'
With large clusters of clear yellow blooms, fairly large with ruffled petals. Foliage exceptionally good, rich mid-green, semi-glossy and veined. Growth upright and dense.

[(C) (P) (B) (H) ▽ AL]   3′ × 2′   90 × 60 cm

'Honigmond' *see* 'Honeymoon'

'Horstmann's Rosenresli'

Kordes GERMANY 1955
'Rudolph Timm' × 'Lavender Pinocchio'
Pure white, fully double flowers in large clusters. Foliage mid-green, semi-glossy on a plant of bushy and upright growth. An excellent variety.

[(C) (P) (B) (H) (SF) ▽ AL]   2½′ × 2′   75 × 60 cm

'Iceberg', 'Schneewittchen', 'Fée des Neiges' (Korbin)

Kordes GERMANY 1958
'Robin Hood' × 'Virgo'
One of the best Floribundas ever raised, its shapely little buds open to loosely formed flowers of pure white which are carried in large trusses. Foliage light green and glossy, the stems light green. Growth upright and bushy.

[(C) (P) (B) (H) (Gh) (MF) ▽ ✂ AW]
3′ × 2′   90 × 60 cm

'Iced Ginger'

Dickson UK 1971
'Anne Watkins' × unknown
Pale pink to ivory flowers with a coppery reverse, large and full, in sizeable clusters. Foliage overlaid red and heavily veined on an upright plant.

[(C) (B) (H) (SF) ▽ ✂ AL]   3′ × 2′   90 × 60 cm

*'Inner Wheel' (Fryjasso)

Fryer UK 1984
'Pink Parfait' × 'Picasso'
Carmine-pink flowers edged rosy-pink, full, shapely and in large trusses with reddish, matt foliage. Growth bushy.

[(C) (B) (H) (SF) ▽ AL]   2½′ × 2′   75 × 60 cm

*'Intrigue', 'Lavaglut', 'Lavaglow' (Korlech)

Kordes GERMANY 1978
'Grüss an Bayern' × a seedling
Shapely, rounded flowers with slightly crumpled petals, very dark red, in large clusters. 'Intrigue' stands sun very well. Foliage dark green and glossy. Growth bushy. More than one variety has this name.

[(C) (B) (H) (SF) ▽ AW]   2½′ × 2′   75 × 60 cm

'Intrigue' (Jacum)

Warriner USA 1984
'White Masterpiece' × 'Heirloom'
Large double flowers of reddish-purple, foliage

dark green, semi-glossy. Growth bushy.

[(C) (B) (H) (VF) AL]   2½' × 2'   75 × 60 cm

*'Invincible', 'Fennica' (Runatru)

de Ruiter NETHERLANDS 1983
'Rubella' × 'National Trust'
Large clusters of semi-double, clear red blooms on a tidy and bushy plant with mid-green, glossy foliage.

[(C) (B) (H) (SF) ▽ AL]   2½' × 2'   75 × 60 cm

'Iceberg' (see text p. 185)

'Irene of Denmark', 'Irene von Dänemark'

Poulsen DENMARK 1948
'Orléans Rose' × ('Mme Plantier' × 'Edina')
Very double, shapely flowers of pure white with a creamy base which are cupped until fully open, then flat and well formed. Foliage mid-green and glossy. Growth upright and bushy.

[(C) (P) (B) (H) (MF) ▽ ✄ AL]
2½' × 2'   75 × 60 cm

'Irène Watts'

Guillot FRANCE 1896
Parentage unknown, of Chinese origin
Although it was raised in 1896, I could not resist including this charming little rose, for it is well placed even ninety years on and has superbly shaped, scented blooms of ivory with pinkish-orange shadings, especially deep in the centre. Foliage dark green, matt. Growth bushy and short.

[(C) (B) (H) (MF) (Gh) ▽ AL]
1½' × 1½' 45 × 45 cm

'Irish Mist', 'Irish Summer'

McGredy UK 1966
'Orangeade' × 'Mischief'
Large clusters of semi-double blooms of orange-salmon. Foliage dark green and semi-glossy. Growth bushy.

[(C) (B) (H) (SF) ▽ AL] 2½' × 2' 75 × 60 cm

'Jenny Wren'

Ratcliffe UK 1957
'Cécile Brünner' × 'Fashion'
Small, exquisite flowers of creamy-apricot, their reverse a soft salmon, are borne in large sprays in the fashion of 'Cécile Brünner'. Foliage dark and semi-glossy. Growth bushy.

[(C) (B) (Gh) ▽ ✄ AL] 2' × 2' 60 × 60 cm

'Jiminy Cricket'

Boerner USA 1954
'Goldilocks' × 'Geranium Red'
Shapely buds open to loosely formed blooms of pinkish-coral-orange in medium-sized clusters on a twiggy but dense plant with good, dark, glossy foliage.

[(C) (B) (H) ▽ AL] 2½' × 2' 75 × 60 cm

'Jocelyn'

LeGrice UK 1970
Parentage unknown
Fully double flowers of mahogany age to bluish-brown on a compact and bushy plant with dark green foliage.

[(C) (B) ▽ ✄ AL] 2' × 2' 60 × 60 cm

'Joyfulness', 'Frohsinn'

Tantau GERMANY 1963
'Horstmann's Jubiläumsrose' × 'Circus'
Large clusters of semi-double flowers of orange-

'Irene of Denmark' and *below:* 'Irène Watts'

red to salmon with some cream are carried on a bushy, upright plant with mid-green and glossy foliage.

[(C) (B) (H) (SF) AL] 2½' × 2' 75 × 60 cm

'Kim'

Harkness UK 1973
('Orange Sensation' × 'Allgold') × 'Elizabeth of Glamis'
A delightful little free-flowering rose, its very large clusters of small, fully double flowers of clear yellow are suffused red. Foliage small, mid-green and matt-finished. Growth bushy.

[(C) (B) (H) ▽ AL] 1½' × 1½' 45 × 45 cm

'Korona' (Kornita)

Kordes GERMANY 1955
'Obergärtner Wiebicke' × 'Independence'
An outstanding rose from the 1950s whose rich orange-scarlet flowers, double and shaggy when open, come in large clusters on tall stems with deep green, matt foliage. Growth upright and vigorous.

[(C) (P) (B) (H) ▽ AW] 3' × 2' 90 × 60 cm

'Jiminy Cricket' (see text p. 187) and *below:* 'Jocelyn' (see text p. 187)

'Korp', 'Prominent'

Kordes GERMANY 1970
'Colour Wonder' × 'Zorina'
The blooms are borne in small clusters, individually quite large for a Floribunda, cupped and full and vivid orange-red. The foliage is light green on a bushy and upright plant.
[(C) (P) (B) (H) ⛉ ✂ AW]   3′ × 2′   90 × 60 cm

'Korresia', 'Fresia', 'Friesia', 'Sunsprite'

Kordes GERMANY 1977
'Friedrich Wörlein' × 'Spanish Sun'
Rounded buds open flat, large and free and are arranged in large clusters on a sturdy, bushy plant. Foliage lightish green.
[(C) (P) (B) (H) (VF) ⛉ AL]   2′ × 2′   60 × 60 cm

*'La Paloma '85' (Tanamola)

Tantau GERMANY 1985
Parentage unknown
Elegant buds open to shapely, pure white flowers produced freely in large trusses on a plant with clear green foliage. Growth upright.
[(C) (B) (H) (SF) AL]   2½′ × 2′   75 × 60 cm

'Lady Romsey'

Beales UK 1985
('Fragrant Cloud' × 'Pascali') × a seedling
Shapely and high-centred when half-open, the flowers open large, full and flattish, white with cream and pink highlights and scented. The foliage is large, glossy and light green touched pink on a bushy, upright and shortish plant.
[(C) (P) (B) (H) (SF) (Gh) ⛉ ✂ AL]
1½′ × 1½′   45 × 45 cm

'Korresia'

'Lavaglut' *see* 'Intrigue'

'Lavender Pinocchio'

Boerner USA 1948
'Pinocchio' × 'Grey Pearl'
This variety has figured in the parentage of many off-beat-coloured roses since its introduction. The large trusses of fully double flowers are a rather tousled mixture of soft brown, pink and lavender. Foliage mid-green and leathery. Growth bushy.

[(C) (P) (B) (H) (SF) ▽ ✄ AL]   2′ × 2′   60 × 60 cm

'Len Turner' (Dicjeep)

Dickson UK 1984
'Mullard Jubilee' × 'Eyepaint'
The ivory-white to cream flowers, heavily flushed deep pink edged carmine, are full, large and shapely and are carried in large clusters. The foliage is mid-green and glossy, on a shortish, bushy plant. A worthy rose to honour Mr Len Turner, MBE, Secretary of the Royal National Rose Society for eighteen years until his retirement in 1983.

[(C) (P) (B) (H) (SF) ▽ AW]   2′ × 2′   60 × 60 cm

'Lilac Charm'

LeGrice UK 1952
Bred from a *Rosa californica* seedling
A beautiful rose, with large clusters of single, or almost single, soft pastel-mauve flowers which have pronounced gold and red stamens. Foliage dark matt-green. Growth sturdy and bushy.

[(C) (P) (B) (H) (MF) ▽ AL]   2′ × 2′   60 × 60 cm

'Lilli Marlene' (Korlima)

Kordes GERMANY 1958
('Our Princess' × 'Rudolph Timm') × 'Ama'
An outstanding rose whose superbly formed flowers of deep velvety-red are large and well spaced in flattish clusters. Foliage dark green and leathery, the stems very thorny. Growth bushy and upright.

[(C) (P) (B) (H) BS ▥ AW]   2½′ × 2′   75 × 60 cm

'Liverpool Echo'

McGredy NEW ZEALAND 1971
('Little Darling' × 'Goldilocks') × 'München'
The soft salmon-pink blooms, fairly full and large,

'Len Turner'

'Lilli Marlene' and *below:* 'Manx Queen'

are produced in sizeable clusters on a large and upright plant with light green foliage.

[(C) (P) (B) (H) (SF) ▽ ✕ AL]   3′ × 2′   90 × 60 cm

'Living Fire'

Gregory UK 1972
'Super Star' × unknown
Generous clusters of full flowers of rich orange-scarlet and yellow with smallish, plentiful, dark green and leathery foliage, the stems thorny. Growth very upright.

[(C) (P) (B) (H) AL]   2½′ × 2′   75 × 60 cm

'Manx Queen', 'Isle of Man'

Dickson UK 1963
'Shepherd's Delight' × 'Circus'
The large, semi-double flowers are an eye-catching mixture of red, orange, yellow and bronze. The foliage is dark green and leathery on a bushy plant.

[(C) (P) (B) (H) (SF) AL]   2½′ × 2′   75 × 60 cm

'Ma Perkins'

Boerner USA 1952
'Red Radiance' × 'Fashion'
Not widely available, but this variety demands inclusion because it is both beautiful and a representative of the Floribundas of the 1950s. A lively mixture of salmon, shell-pink and cream flowers, large and full, are produced in generous clusters. Foliage glossy and rich green. Growth bushy and upright.

[(C) (B) (H) (Gh) (MF) ▽ ✕ AL]
2′ × 2′   60 × 60 cm

'Margaret Merril' (Harkuly)

Harkness UK 1977
('Rudolph Timm' × 'Dedication') × 'Pascali'
A superb variety, the flowers are white with blushes of soft pink and have pronounced golden stamens when fully open. They are highly scented and are carried in small clusters. Foliage dark green, matt. Growth sturdy and upright.
[(C) (P) (B) (H) (Gh) (VF) ▽ ✂ AW]
2½' × 2'   75 × 60 cm

'Marlena'

Kordes GERMANY 1964
'Gertrud Westphal' × 'Lilli Marlene'
A discreet mixture of red and crimson flowers, semi-double, large and flattish when fully open. Foliage dark green. Growth bushy and compact.
[(C) (P) (B) (H) ▽ AW]   1½' × 1½'   45 × 45 cm

'Masquerade'

Boerner USA 1949
'Goldilocks' × 'Holiday'
A classic from the past, and the forerunner of many brightly coloured Floribundas. Semi-double flowers of bright yellow changing through pink and orange to deep red with age are produced in very large clusters. Foliage small, dark and leathery. Growth upright. The hips set easily and must be dead-headed.
[(C) (P) (B) (H) ▽ AW]   2½' × 2'   75 × 60 cm

'Matangi' (Macman)

McGredy NEW ZEALAND 1974
Seedling × 'Picasso'
The large clusters of bright vermilion-red, double flowers with a white eye and silver reverse are spectacular. Foliage small, mid-green and matt on a bushy and upright plant.
[(C) (P) (B) (H) AW]   3' × 2'   90 × 60 cm

'Megiddo'

Gandy UK 1970
'Coup de Foudre' × 'S'Agaró'
Large sprays of semi-double, bright scarlet flowers on a strong-growing and upright plant with large, olive-green, matt-finished foliage.
[(C) (P) (B) (H) BS ▥AL]   3' × 2'   90 × 60 cm

'Memento' (Dicbar)

Dickson UK 1978
'Bangor' × 'Korbel'
Salmon, red and bright pink blooms of fair size in

'Margaret Merril'

'Marlena' and *right:* 'Matangi'

'Masquerade'

very large clusters, with deep green and leathery foliage on a bushy plant.

[(C) (P) (B) (H) (SF) AW]   2½' × 2'   75 × 60 cm

'Meteor'

Kordes GERMANY 1959
'Feurio' × 'Gertrud Westphal'
Closely packed clusters of many, small, double, orange-scarlet flowers on a compact and upright-growing plant with lightish green foliage.

[(C) (P) (B) (H) ▽ AL]   1½' × 1½'   45 × 45 cm

'Mevrouw Nathalie Nypels' *see* 'Nathalie Nypels'

'Nancy Steen'

Sherwood NEW ZEALAND 1976
'Pink Parfait' × ('Ophelia' × 'Parkdirektor Riggers')
The large, fully double, fragrant flowers are borne in clusters and are blush-pink with hints of salmon, the centre cream. Foliage lush and glossy, dark bronzy-green. Growth bushy and upright.

[(C) (P) (B) (H) (MF) ▽ ✂ AL]
2½' × 2'   75 × 60 cm

'Nancy Steen'

'Nathalie Nypels', 'Mevrouw Nathalie Nypels'

Leenders NETHERLANDS 1919
'Orléans Rose' × ('Comtesse du Cayla' × *Rosa foetida bicolor*)
One of the best and most reliable of the cluster-flowered roses from the past. Large clusters of double, silky-textured, deep pink to salmon flowers are borne on strong stems from a bushy and branching plant with good, dark green foliage.
[(C) (P) (B) (H) ▽ AL]   2½' × 2'   75 × 60 cm

'News' (Legnews)

LeGrice UK 1968
'Lilac Charm' × 'Tuscany Superb'
An unusual colour, beetroot-purple, the flowers are semi-double and arranged in large clusters. Foliage olive-green and semi-glossy. Growth bushy and upright.
[(C) (P) (B) (H) (SF) ▽ ✕ AW]
2½' × 2'   75 × 60 cm

'New Year' *see* 'Arcadian'

'Nina Weibull'

Poulsen DENMARK 1962
'Fanal' × 'Masquerade'
Trusses of semi-double, dark blood-red flowers on a thorny, upright and bushy plant with dark green, semi-glossy foliage.
[(C) (P) (B) (H) ▽ AL]   2½' × 2'   75 × 60 cm

'Norwich Castle'

Beales UK 1979
('Whisky Mac' × 'Arthur Bell') × a seedling
Closely packed clusters of Hybrid-Tea-shaped flowers, flat when fully open, of deep coppery-orange paling to soft apricot. Very free-flowering, with light green, shiny foliage and of upright growth.
[(C) (P) (B) (H) (Gh) ▽ ✕ AL]
2½' × 2'   75 × 60 cm

'Norwich Union'

Beales UK 1975
'Arthur Bell' × (Seedling × 'Allgold')
Large, fully double, cupped flowers of deep clear yellow paling to lemon with age, but losing nothing in doing so, are produced in small, upstanding clusters. Foliage bright green and glossy. Growth stocky and upright.
[(C) (B) (H) (Gh) (VF) ◗ ▽ ✕ AL]
1½' × 1½'   45 × 45 cm

'News'

'Olala', 'Ohlala'

Tantau GERMANY 1956
'Fanal' × 'Crimson Glory'
Blood-red flowers with light red centres, semi-double and large, are carried in very large trusses. Foliage dark green and leathery. Growth bushy and upright.

[(C) (P) (B) (H) ▽ AL]   3′ × 2′   90 × 60 cm

'Old Master' (Macesp)

McGredy NEW ZEALAND 1974
('Maxi' × 'Evelyn Fison') × ('Orange Sweetheart' × 'Frühlingsmorgen')
The flowers are semi-double, their silvery-white petals liberally painted inside with carmine which pales towards the edges to leave brush strokes. Foliage mid-green and semi-glossy. Growth bushy and upright.

[(C) (P) (B) (H) ▽ ✂ AW]   3′ × 2′   90 × 60 cm

'Orangeade'

McGredy UK 1959
'Orange Sweetheart' × 'Independence'
Very large trusses of single, bright vermilion-orange flowers on a vigorous plant with large, leathery and glossy foliage.

[(C) (P) (B) (H) (SF) AL]   3′ × 2′   90 × 60 cm

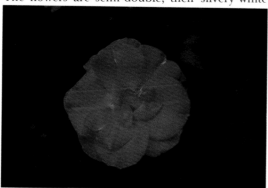

'Olala' and *right:* 'Old Master'

'Orange Sensation' (see text p. 196)

'Orange Sensation'

de Ruiter NETHERLANDS 1961
Parentage unknown
The bright orange, semi-double flowers are well spaced in large trusses. The foliage is mid-green and matt-finished on a rather sprawling but bushy plant.

[(C) (B) (P) (H) (SF) AL]   2½' × 2'   75 × 60 cm

'Orange Silk'

McGredy UK 1968
'Orangeade' × ('Ma Perkins' × 'Independence')
Lots of blooms per cluster, semi-double, orange-vermilion, medium-sized and cupped. Foliage dark green and glossy. Growth bushy.

[(C) (P) (B) (H) (SF) AL]   2½' × 2'   75 × 60 cm

'Orange Triumph'

Kordes GERMANY 1937
'Eva' × 'Solarium'
Individually small, cupped flowers of many petals are borne in large clusters. The name is misleading, as the colour is nearer to clear red. Plentiful, large, dark green and glossy foliage on a robust, upright plant.

[(C) (P) (B) (H) AL]   3' × 2'   90 × 60 cm

'Paddy McGredy' (Macpa)

McGredy UK 1962
'Spartan' × 'Tzigane'
Tubby, Hybrid-Tea-shaped, high-centred individual blooms of carmine to rose-pink are produced in large clusters. Foliage dark green and leathery. Growth bushy and strong.

[(C) (P) (B) (H) (M) ▽ BS ▥ AW]
2½' × 2'   75 × 60 cm

'Paint Box'

Dickson UK 1963
Seedling × 'St Pauli'
Large, semi-double blooms of red and yellow, shedding the yellow with age to become deep red, are carried in large clusters, with dark green, matt foliage. Growth upright and vigorous.

[(C) (B) (H) AL]   3' × 2'   90 × 60 cm

'Penelope Plummer'

Beales UK 1970
'Anna Wheatcroft' × 'Dearest'
Large, semi-double blooms of flamingo-pink to salmon are produced in small, upright clusters. Foliage dark and matt-finished on a short, bushy plant.

[(C) (B) (H) (SF) BS ▥ AL]
1½' × 1½'   45 × 45 cm

'Pernille Poulsen'

Poulsen DENMARK 1965
'Ma Perkins' × 'Columbine'
Semi-double, light pink blooms are borne in large clusters, and are very freely produced. Foliage pointed, light green and profuse. Growth bushy and shortish.

[(C) (P) (B) (H) ✂ AW]   2' × 2'   60 × 60 cm

'Picasso' (Macpic)

McGredy UK 1971
'Marlena' × ['Evelyn Fison' × ('Frühlingsmorgen' × 'Orange Sweetheart')]
Semi-double flowers are produced in clusters, their petals deep rose-pink, the edges and reverse silvery. The foliage is small and dark green on a bushy plant. This was the first of several 'hand-painted' roses, as their raiser calls them.

[(C) (P) (H) ▽ BS ▥ AW]   2½' × 2'   75 × 60 cm

'Pink Parfait'

'Pinocchio' and *below:* 'Plentiful'

*'Piccolo' (Tanolokip)

Tantau GERMANY 1983
Parentage unknown
Small, double, orange-red flowers come in clusters, with dark green, glossy foliage on an upright plant.

[(C) (B) (H) AW]   2½' × 2'   75 × 60 cm

'Pink Parfait'

Swim USA 1960
'First Love' × 'Pinocchio'
Attractive buds open to large, semi-double blooms made up of several shades of pink that are produced in large numbers in clusters of variable size. The foliage is semi-glossy and leathery, the growth upright and bushy. Without any doubt, this is an outstanding rose.

[(C) (P) (B) (H) (SF) (Gh) ▽ ✂ AW]
3' × 2'   90 × 60 cm

'Pinocchio', 'Rosenmärchen'

Kordes GERMANY 1940
'Eva' × 'Golden Rapture'
Small, cupped blooms open rather raggedly but profusely in medium-sized clusters, their colour pink suffused salmon with a hint of yellow in the base, on a bushy plant of leathery foliage. An important rose as a parent in the development of the Floribundas.

[(C) (P) (B) (H) (SF) ▽ AL]   2' × 2'   60 × 60 cm

'Plentiful'

LeGrice UK 1961
Parentage unknown
Large, deep pink and scented flowers packed with

‘Poppy Flash’ and *right:* ‘Radox Bouquet’

petals of different lengths create a very old-fashioned, quartered effect when fully open. Foliage dark green, leathery and veined. Growth angular with many thorns.

[(C) (P) (B) (MF) ▽ ✂ AL] 2½′ × 2½′ 75 × 75 cm

‘Poppy Flash’, ‘Rusticana’ (Meiléna)

Meilland FRANCE 1971
(‘Dany Robin’ × ‘Fire King’) × (‘Alain’ × ‘Mutabilis’)
Large clusters of bright vermilion blooms, fully double, on a vigorous, bushy plant with good, deep green and glossy foliage.

[(C) (P) (B) (H) AL] 3′ × 2′ 90 × 60 cm

‘Princess Michael of Kent’ (Harlightly)

Harkness UK 1981
‘Manx Queen’ × ‘Alexander’
Bright yellow, large and full blooms are carried in small clusters. Foliage mid-green and glossy. Growth bushy.

[(C) (P) (B) (H) (VF) ▽ ✂ AL] 2′ × 2′ 60 × 60 cm

*‘Princess Michiko’

Dickson UK 1966
‘Spartan’ × ‘Circus’
The large clusters of orange-red blooms have a yellow base, are semi-double and of medium size. Dark, glossy foliage on a bushy plant.

[(C) (B) (H) (SF) ▽ BS◫⫶ AL] 2′ × 2′ 60 × 60 cm

‘Priscilla Burton’ (Macrat)

McGredy NEW ZEALAND 1978
[‘Maxi’ × [‘Evelyn Fison’ × (‘Orange Sweetheart’ × ‘Frühlingsmorgen’)]] × [[(‘Little Darling’ × ‘Goldilocks’) × [‘Evelyn Fison’ × (‘Coryana’ × ‘Tantau’s Triumph’)]] × (‘John Church’ × ‘Elizabeth of Glamis’)]
A mixture of red and carmine with a paler, painted reverse, the blooms are semi-double, large and are borne in clusters. Foliage dark green and glossy. Growth upright and vigorous.

[(C) (P) (B) (H) (SF) AW] 2½′ × 2′ 75 × 60 cm

‘Prominent’ *see* ‘Korp’

‘Queen Elizabeth’, ‘The Queen Elizabeth Rose’

Lammerts USA 1954
‘Charlotte Armstrong’ × ‘Floradora’
This outstanding rose has deserved all the attention it has ever received. Long, high-centred buds open to large blooms of clear pink, produced in clusters. The foliage is large, dark green, leathery and glossy on a very vigorous, upright plant.

[(C) (P) (H) (Gh) (SF) ▽ ✂ AW] 5′ × 2½′ 1.5 m × 75 cm

'Radox Bouquet', 'Rosika' (Harmusky)

Harkness UK 1980
('Alec's Red' × 'Piccadilly') × [Southampton × ('Cläre Grammerstorf' × 'Frühlingsmorgen')]
The deep rose-pink flowers, many-petalled with an old-fashioned form, are borne in large clusters on a vigorous, upright plant with good, mid-green, glossy foliage.
[(C) (P) (B) (H) (VF) ▽ ✕ AL]
3½' × 2'   1.05 m × 60 cm

'Ripples'

LeGrice UK 1971
('Tantau's Surprise' × 'Marjorie LeGrice') × (Seedling × 'Africa Star')
The semi-double flowers are lilac-lavender with wavy petals when fully open. Foliage dark green and leathery. Growth bushy.
[(C) (P) (B) (H) (SF) ▽ ✕ AL]   2' × 2'   60 × 60 cm

'Rob Roy' (Corob)

Cocker UK 1970
'Evelyn Fison' × 'Wendy Cussons'
Rich deep red, superbly formed, high-centred flowers of substance are borne in clusters. Good,

glossy and dark foliage. Growth bushy and upright.
[(C) (B) (P) (H) (Gh) (SF) ▽ ✕ AL]
3' × 2'   90 × 60 cm

*'Rosabell' (Cocceleste)

Cocker UK 1986
Seedling × 'Darling Flame'
Full flowers of bright rose-pink, their petals incurved when open to give an old-fashioned look, are very freely produced. Growth short and bushy.
[(C) (B) (H) ▽ AL]   15" × 12"   38 × 30 cm

'Rosemary Rose'

de Ruiter NETHERLANDS 1954
'Grüss an Teplitz' × a Floribunda seedling
The fully double, flattish flowers are crammed, it seems, with petals in *Rosa centifolia* style, and likewise are occasionally quartered. They are carried in large, heavy, carmine-red clusters. Foliage darkish green to maroon, the stems plum-red. Growth, though bushy, is often bent by the sheer weight of flowers.
[(C) (B) (H) ▽ ✕ M〓 AL]   2½' × 2'   75 × 60 cm

*'Royal Occasion' (Montana)

Tantau GERMANY 1974
'Walzertraum' × 'Europeana'
Large clusters of semi-double, orange-scarlet flowers come on a tallish and upright plant. Foliage mid-green and glossy.
[(C) (P) (B) (H) (SF) AL]   3½' × 2'   1.05 m × 60 cm

'Rumba'

Poulsen DENMARK 1958
'Masquerade' × ('Poulsen's Bedder' × 'Floradora')
The medium-sized, fully double blooms of bright yellow are heavily flushed with bright red that

Top left: 'Rosemary Rose' and *top right:* 'Scarlet Queen Elizabeth' (see text p. 200)

'Scented Air

'Scherzo'

'Sexy Rexy'

deepens with age. They are produced in large clusters. Foliage dark green and glossy. Growth bushy and upright.

[(C) (P) (B) (H) ▽ AL]   2′ × 2′   60 × 60 cm

'Scarlet Queen Elizabeth'

Dickson UK 1963
('Korona' × a seedling) × 'Queen Elizabeth'
Globular buds open to loosely formed, cupped, double blooms of bright scarlet and in generous clusters. The foliage, a particular feature, is dark green and leathery, and relatively thornless. Growth upright and tall.

[(C) (P) (B) (H) AW]   3½′ × 2′   1.05 m × 60 cm

'Stargazer' (see text p. 202) and *below:* 'Strawberry Ice' (see text p. 203)

'Scented Air'

Dickson UK 1965
'Spartan' seedling × 'Queen Elizabeth'
Well-formed, very large, double flowers of rich salmon are borne in large clusters, with good, dark green foliage on an upright and vigorous plant.

[(C) (P) (B) (H) ▽ ✄ AW]   3′ × 2′   90 × 60 cm

'Scherzo' (Meipuma)

Paolino FRANCE 1975
'Tamango' × ['Sarabande' × ('Goldilocks' × 'Fashion')]
Full, shapely blooms of bright scarlet-vermilion with paler off-white, splashed crimson on the reverse, are produced in large clusters. Foliage dark green and glossy. Growth bushy and upright.

[(C) (P) (B) (N) ▽ AW]   3′ × 2′   90 × 60 cm

'Sea Pearl', 'Flower Girl'

Dickson UK 1964
'Perfecta' × 'Montezuma'
A delightful combination of soft pink-peach with a soft yellow reverse, the blooms are fully double, shapely, flat when fully open and are carried in

large clusters. Dark, leathery foliage on an upright and vigorous plant.

[(C) (P) (B) (H)·(Gh) ▽ ✄ AL]   3′ × 2′   90 × 60 cm

'Sexy Rexy' (Macrexy)

McGredy NEW ZEALAND 1984
'Seaspray' × 'Dreaming'
Very double flowers opening flat, in large clusters, of pink and soft salmon. Foliage light green and glossy, the growth bushy.

[(C) (B) (H) (SF) ▽ AW]   2′ × 2′   60 × 60 cm

'Southampton'

*'Sheila's Perfume' (Harsherry)

Sheridan UK 1985
'Peer Gynt' × ['Daily Sketch' × ('Paddy McGredy' × 'Prima Ballerina')]
Medium-sized, fairly full blooms are borne in small clusters, clear yellow edged red. Foliage dark green and semi-glossy on a bushy and upright plant.
[(C) (B) (H) (Gh) (VF) ⊽ ✂ AL]
2½' × 2' 75 × 60 cm

*'Shona' (Dicdrum)

Dickson UK 1982
'Bangor' × 'Korbel'
Large clusters of loosely double blooms of soft coral pink. Foliage mid-green and semi-glossy, the growth bushy.
[(C) (P) (B) (H) (SF) AL] 2' × 2' 60 × 60 cm

'Southampton', 'Susan Ann'

Harkness UK 1972
('Ann Elizabeth' × 'Allgold') × 'Yellow Cushion'
Large, fully double blooms of rich apricot flushed orange and scarlet, some yellow in certain weather conditions, are produced in clusters. Foliage dark green and glossy, the growth upright.
[(C) (P) (B) (H) (MF) ⊽ AW] 3' × 2' 90 × 60 cm

'Stargazer'

Harkness UK 1977
'Marlena' × 'Kim'
The flowers are almost single, large, orange-red and are borne in clusters, with mid-green, matt-finished foliage on a bushy plant.
[(C) (B) (SF) ⊽ AL] 1½' × 1½' 45 × 45 cm

*'St Boniface' (Kormatt)

Kordes GERMANY 1980
'Diablotin' × 'Träumerei'
Very double, medium-sized blooms of orange-red are carried in large clusters. Foliage dark green and semi-glossy. Of bushy growth.
[(C) (B) (H) (SF) ⊽ AL] 2' × 2' 60 × 60 cm

'St Bruno' (Lanpipe)

Sealand UK 1985
'Arthur Bell' × 'Zambra'
Large, fully double, deep golden-yellow flowers are borne in sizeable clusters on a bushy plant with mid-green, semi-glossy foliage.
[(C) (B) (H) (VF) ⊽ AL] 2' × 2' 60 × 60 cm

'Sue Lawley'

Top: 'Taora' (see text p. 204) and *bottom:* 'The Times Rose' (see text p. 204)

'Strawberry Ice'

Bees UK 1975
[('Goldilocks' × 'Virgo') × ('Orange Triumph' × 'Yvonne Rabier')] × 'Fashion'
The flowers are large, semi-double and creamy-white, heavily flushed pink and deepening at the edges. Good, dark green foliage on a compact, bushy plant.
[(C) (B) ▽ AL]   2′ × 2′   60 × 60 cm

'Sue Lawley', 'Spanish Shawl' (Macspash)

McGredy NEW ZEALAND 1980
[('Little Darling' × 'Goldilocks') × ['Evelyn Fison' ›('Coryana' × 'Tantau's Triumph')]] × [('John's Church' × 'Elizabeth of Glamis') × ['Evelyn Fison' × ('Orange Sweetheart' × 'Frühlingsmorgen)]]
The semi-double, carmine-red flowers, their edges brushed white and pink, are borne in clusters. The foliage is mid to dark green, the growth bushy.
[(C) (B) (H) (SF) ▽ ✕ AL]   2′ × 2′   60 × 60 cm

'Sue Ryder' (Harlino)

Harkness UK 1983
'Southampton' × [('Highlight' × 'Colour Wonder') × ('Parkdirektor Riggers' × 'Piccadilly')]
The variable salmon-orange to soft vermilion blooms, yellowish on the reverse, are fully double and are carried in large clusters. Foliage mid-green and semi-glossy on a bushy plant.
[(C) (P) (B) (H) ✕ AL]   3′ × 2′   90 × 60 cm

'Sunsilk'

Fryer UK 1974
'Pink Parfait' × a 'Redgold' seedling
Fully double, shapely blooms of soft yellow are produced in medium-sized clusters. Foliage dark green and leathery. Growth upright.
[(C) (P) (B) (H) (SF) ✕ AW]   3′ × 2′   90 × 60 cm

'Sunsprite' *see* 'Korresia'

'Tanamola' *see* 'La Paloma '85'

'Taora' (Tanta)

Tantau GERMANY 1968
'Fragrant Cloud' × 'Schweizer Grüss'
Shapely buds open to double flowers of orange-red. Ample glossy foliage on a bushy plant.

[(C) (B) (SF) ▽ AL]   3' × 2'   90 × 60 cm

'The Times Rose' (Korpeahn)

Kordes GERMANY 1984
'Tornado' × 'Redgold'
Large clusters of fully double, blood-red flowers on a compact and bushy plant with dark green, leathery foliage.

[(C) (B) (H) (SF) ▽ ✂ AL]   2' × 2'   60 × 60 cm

'Tip Top'

Tantau GERMANY 1963
Parentage unknown
The loose, semi-double flowers opening from shapely buds are soft rose-salmon and are produced freely in large clusters. Foliage dark green and matt on a compact, bushy plant. Not to be confused with 'Tip-Top' (Polyantha, Lambert, 1909).

[(C) (B) (H) ▽ BS⬛∷AW]   1½' × 1½'   45 × 45 cm

'Topsi'

Tantau GERMANY 1972
'Fragrant Cloud' × 'Signalfeuer'
Semi-double blooms of orange-scarlet to red are borne in large clusters. Foliage mid-green. Growth bushy and compact.

[(C) (B) (H) ▽ AW]   1½' × 1½'   45 × 45 cm

'Trumpeter' (Mactrum)

McGredy NEW ZEALAND 1977
'Satchmo' × a seedling
Rounded buds open to fully double blooms of bright orange-red, in sizeable clusters. Foliage mid-green and glossy on a bushy, compact plant.

[(C) (B) (H) ▽ AL]   1½' × 1½'   45 × 45 cm

'Violet Carson' (Macio)

McGredy UK 1964
'Mme Léon Cuny' × 'Spartan'
Shapely, full blooms of light peachy-pink with primrose reverses to the petals come in large clusters. Foliage dark green and glossy. Growth bushy.

[(C) (B) (H) (SF) ✂ AW]   2' × 2'   60 × 60 cm

'Warrior'

*'Vital Spark' (Cocacert)

Cocker UK 1982

['Anne Cocker' × ('Sabine' × 'Circus')] × 'Yellow Pages'

Large, full, shapely blooms of rich fiery-red and yellow are produced in large clusters. Foliage dark green and glossy. Of bushy growth.

[(C) (P) (B) (H) (SF) ⊽ ✂ AL]   2' × 2'   60 × 60 cm

'Warrior'

LeGrice UK 1977

'City of Belfast' × 'Ronde Endiablée'

Shapely, full blooms of bright glowing red are carried in large clusters. Foliage light green and semi-glossy. Growth bushy.

[(C) (B) (H) (SF) ⊽ AL]   2' × 2'   60 × 60 cm

'White Queen Elizabeth'

Banner UK 1965

Sport from 'Queen Elizabeth'

See 'Queen Elizabeth', from which this rose differs only in that it is pure white.

*'Wishing', 'Georgie Girl' (Dickerfuffle)

Dickson UK 1984

'Silver Jubilee' × 'Bright Smile'

Deep salmon and shapely blooms are borne in large clusters, with matt-green, semi-glossy foliage on a bushy plant.

[(C) (B) (H) (SF) ⊽ AL]   2½' × 2'   75 × 60 cm

'Woburn Abbey'

Sibley & Cobley UK 1962

'Masquerade' × 'Fashion'

Tight, oval buds open to double, loosely formed blooms of clear orange-yellow, sometimes faintly touched with red. Foliage dark green and leathery, semi-glossy, the stems grained brownish. Growth upright.

[(C) (P) (B) (H) (SF) ⊽ ✂ R❶⫶ AW]
2½' × 2'   75 × 60 cm

'Yellow Queen Elizabeth'

Vlaeminck UK 1964

Sport from 'Queen Elizabeth'

See 'Queen Elizabeth', from which this rose differs only in that it is bright yellow.

'Wishing' and *below:* 'Woburn Abbey'

'Zambra' (Meialfi)

Meilland FRANCE 1961

('Goldilocks' × 'Fashion') × ('Goldilocks' × 'Fashion')

Rounded buds open to small, semi-double blooms of clear orange with a yellow reverse. They are borne in large clusters. Foliage leathery, glossy and light green. Growth bushy.

[(C) (P) (B) (H) (SF) ⊽ BS❶⫶ AW]
2½' × 2'   75 × 60 cm

'Angelina' (see text p. 208)

Shrub Roses

A shrub rose, as distinct from any other type of rose, is difficult to define. In this section I have included 170 varieties that do not qualify for placing elsewhere, for one reason or another. Such roses comprise three distinct groups: species or wild roses, old garden roses and modern shrub roses.

Species
Only those discovered and/or introduced since the year 1900 have been included. Since most species were found long before that date, my list does not necessarily represent the best of this large group.

Old Garden Roses
Most of these pre-date 1900, so I have excluded many varieties that are still widely grown but do not qualify chronologically. Where a variety does qualify, I have placed it into the group of old garden roses to which it belongs, for example 'Adam Messerich' [Bourbon] 1920, 'James Mason' [Gallica] 1982, and so on.

For more details of this group see my previous book, *Classic Roses*.

Modern Shrub Roses
Unlike the classification 'old garden roses', the term 'modern shrub' is less rigid in its definition, the criteria for qualification being based more on usage than origin or progeny. This flexibility enables roses as diverse as 'Golden Chersonese' and 'Alexander' to fall under one heading, although, in all cases, I have tried to place the rose in its rightful group, for example 'Golden Chersonese' [Ecae Hybrid], 'Alexander' [Hybrid Tea], and so forth. There are many uses for shrub roses and one variety or another is usually capable of solving most landscape problems.

Shrub roses are most commonly placed among other shrubs in shrubberies, but some are also excellent specimen shrubs on their own. Others make superb hedging plants, either as a single variety or, with careful choice, as a mixed hedge with others. Most are not averse to growing in urns or tubs and I would like to see many more used in this way. Shrub roses are generally prolific and of considerable vigour, an advantage if a steady flow of cut flowers for the home is required.

'Adam Messerich' [Bourbon]

Lambert GERMANY 1920
'Frau Oberhofgärtner Singer' × ('Louise Odier'
seedling × 'Louis Philippe')
An excellent rose, its clusters of large, initially
cupped and later flat blooms of deep rose-pink
carried on a vigorous, free-branching plant with
good, light green, glossy foliage. It is well scented.

[(C) (P) (VF) ▽ ◑ AL]   5' × 4'   1.5 × 1.2 m

*'Admired Miranda' (Ausmira)
[Modern Shrub]

Austin UK 1983
'The Friar' × 'The Friar'
Large, fully double, light pink blooms opening flat
and reflexing. Foliage mid-green and semi-glossy.
Growth upright.

[(C) (VF) ▽ AL]   3' × 2'   90 × 60 cm

'Agnes' [Rugosa Hybrid]

Saunder CANADA 1900, introduced 1922
R. rugosa × *R. fœtida persiana*
A beautiful rose, the large, fully double blooms
open from discreet buds and are flattish, sometimes quartered, their colour amber-yellow paling
to cream. Dense, crinkled and dark green foliage
on a bushy plant.

[(C) (P) (H) (VF) ▽ ◑ AW]   6' × 5'   1.8 × 1.5 m

'Alexander', 'Alexandra' (Harlex)
[Hybrid Tea]

Harkness UK 1972
'Super Star' × ('Ann Elizabeth' × 'Allgold')
Very large clusters of bright vermilion-red flowers,
sometimes huge, each bloom high-centred when
half open and with loosely arranged petals when
fully open. Good, mid-green, glossy foliage.
Growth upright and bushy.

[(C) (P) (H) (SF) ▽ ✄ AW]   6' × 4'   1.8 × 1.2 m

'Andersonii', *R.* × *andersonii* [Canina Hybrid]

Introduced 1935
Origin and parentage unknown
Said to be a chance cross between *R. canina* and *R.
arvensis*, which is possible, but these two seldom
flower at the same time, *R. arvensis* being later. The
sizeable, single pink flowers have pronounced stamens (larger than the Dog Rose and deeper in colour). Foliage grey-green and matt on an upright
and sprawly plant. Hips oval, orange.

[(S) (H) (T) (SF) (CL) ◑ AL]   8' × 6'   2.5 × 1.8 m

Top: 'Adam Messerich' and *bottom:* 'Alexander'

'Angelina' [Modern Shrub]

Cocker UK 1976
('Super Star' × 'Carine') × ('Cläre Grammserstorf'
× 'Frühlingsmorgen')
The large, almost single flowers of rose-pink, with a
white eye and a paler reverse, are fragrant. Mid-
green foliage on a bushy, slightly spreading plant.

[(C) (P) (H) (MF) ▽ AL]   4' × 3'   1.2 m × 90 cm

'Anna Zinkeisen' (Harquhling)
[Modern Shrub]

Harkness UK 1983
Seedling × 'Frank Naylor'
Plump buds open to fully double flowers of ivory
and yellow, usually in clusters. Leaves numerous,
light green and semi-glossy, and of bushy and
slightly spreading growth.

[(C) (P) (MF) ▽ AL]   4' × 3'   1.2 m × 90 cm

*'Armada' (Haruseful) [Modern Shrub]

Harkness UK 1988
'New Dawn' × 'Silver Jubilee'
The rich clear pink blooms hold their colour well.
They are semi-double and come in large clusters,
leaving handsome hips in the autumn. Foliage
bright green and glossy. Upright, bushy growth.

[(C) (H) (CL) ▽ AL]   5' × 3'   1.5 m × 90 cm

'Arthur Hillier' [Moyesii Hybrid]

Hillier UK 1961
R. macrophylla × R. moyesii
Its large, rose-crimson, single flowers have pronounced yellow stamens. Foliage small and dark
green. Growth vigorous and upright but branching, the stems thorny.

[(S) (P) (MF) (N) ◑ AL]   10' × 6'   3 × 1.8 m

'Autumn Bouquet' [Modern Shrub]

Jacobus USA 1948
'New Dawn' × 'Crimson Glory'
Long, pointed buds open to large and fully double,
carmine to silvery-deep-pink flowers. Foliage

'Autumn Sunset' (see text p. 210)

'Ballerina' (see text p. 210)

leathery and dark green. Growth upright and bushy.

[(C) (P) (VF) (H) ▽ ◍ ✂ AL]
4′ × 3′   1.2 m × 90 cm

'Autumn Delight' [Hybrid Musk]

Bentall UK 1933
Parentage unknown
With trusses of single or almost single flowers of creamy-white with bronzy-red stamens. Foliage mid-green. Growth bushy.

[(C) (P) (MF) (H) ▽ ◍ AL]   4′ × 3′   1.2 m × 90 cm

'Autumn Fire' *see* 'Herbstfeuer'

'Autumn Sunset' [Modern Shrub]

Lowe USA 1987
Sport from 'Westerland'
The medium-sized flowers, fully double, cupped and loosely formed, are apricot with touches of orange and deep yellow. Glossy, mid-green foliage. Growth tall and bushy.

[(C) (P) (MF) (H) ◍ ✂ AL]   6′ × 4′   1.8 × 1.2 m

'Ballerina' [Hybrid Musk]

Bentall UK 1937
Parentage unknown
Large sprays of small, single, pink flowers with a white centre. This is a delightfully showy rose. Foliage mid to dark green and semi-glossy. Growth bushy.

[(C) (P) (H) (B) (SF) ▽ ✂ AW]
4′ × 3′   1.2 m × 90 cm

'Belinda' [Hybrid Musk]

Bentall UK 1936
Parentage unknown
Semi-double flowers of mid-pink borne in trusses on an upright plant with good, clean, dark foliage. A good though lesser known Hybrid Musk.

[(C) (P) (H) (SF) ▽ ◍ AL]   4′ × 3′   1.2 m × 90 cm

'Belle Amour' [Unclassified Shrub Rose]

A foundling at a convent in Elboeuf, France, 1940s
Probably Alba × Damask
Shapely, soft pink, fully double flowers with densely packed petals in the Damask style. Foliage coarse and greyish but plentiful. Stems thorny, growth shrubby.

[(S) (P) (H) (VF) ◍ AL]   5′ × 4′   1.5 × 1.2 m

'Belle Amour'

'Berlin' [Modern Shrub]

Kordes GERMANY 1949
'Eva' × 'Peace'
Large, single blooms of rich orange-scarlet, displayed in very large, erect trusses. Foliage dark green and leathery. Growth upright and tall.

[(C) (P) (H) (SF) (CL) ▽ AL]
5′ × 3′   1.5 m × 90 cm

'Bloomfield Abundance', 'Spray "Cécile Brünner"' [Chinensis type]

Thomas USA 1920
Raiser recorded parentage as 'Sylvia' × 'Dorothy Page-Roberts'
Large pyramidal sprays of small, shell-pink, Hybrid-Tea-like flowers, each with one or two elongated, almost fern-like, sepals. Foliage is sparse on younger plants but its density increases with age. It is small, dark, leathery and semi-glossy, the wood usually brownish-maroon when young, becoming greenish-brown with age. Spindly growth at first becomes bushy and dense on maturity.

There is and has been some controversy about the true identity and origins of this rose. In America, I believe, it is now thought of and listed as 'Spray "Cécile Brünner"'. This name has not been adopted in Britain so far. Climate, without doubt, influences the China roses more than most and the present rose may not be the one originally given this name by its raiser. In my opinion, however, it is not a sport from 'Cécile Brünner', a conclusion reached after observing the behaviour and habits of both varieties in my nursery over the years. It is easy to become dogmatic in matters such as this and I try very hard to keep an open mind, but unless the true 'Bloomfield Abundance' is found

Top: 'Bloomfield Abundance' and *bottom:* 'Bonn' (see text p. 212)

alive and well I see no reason to change the name of the one we have now.

[(C) (H) (P) ▽ AW]   6' × 4'   1.8 × 1.2 m

'Bonn' [Hybrid Musk]

Kordes GERMANY 1950
'Hamburg' × 'Independence'
A bright, carefree rose, its fully double and sizeable orange-scarlet flowers being borne in clusters. Individually the blooms hang their heads but this adds to their attraction. Foliage glossy and lightish green. Growth upright and bushy.

[(C) (P) (H) (MF) (CL) ▽ AL]   6' × 4'   1.8 × 1.2 m

'Buff Beauty' [Hybrid Musk]

Bentall UK 1939 (perhaps earlier)
Said to be 'William Allen Richardson' × unknown
Large, closely packed clusters of buff-yellow to apricot flowers, their centres deeper. The colour varies according to soil and weather, and the weight of clusters sometimes causes branches to arch downwards. Foliage dark green and glossy. Growth bushy and relaxed.

[(C) (P) (H) (MF) (CL) ▽ AW]   5' × 4'   1.5 × 1.2 m

'Butterfly Wings' [Modern Shrub]

Gobbee UK 1976
'Dainty Maid' × 'Peace'
Attractive, semi-double flowers of white edged carmine are produced in clusters on an upright plant with good, large, mid-green foliage.

[(C) (H) (MF) ▽ AL]   4' × 3'   1.2 m × 90 cm

'Canary Bird', R. xanthina spontanea
[R. xanthina Hybrid]

Introduced c. 1907
Probably R. hugonis × R. xanthina
One of the first roses to flower in late spring, its arching branches bear single, bright yellow flowers with attractive soft yellow stamens and small, dark green foliage with many leaflets. Its growth is angular, arching but bushy, the stems mahogany with many wedge-shaped thorns. Oval, brown hips follow in the autumn.

[(SP) (P) (H) ◗ AW]   8' × 6'   2.5 × 1.8 m

'Cantabrigiensis', R. × cantabrigiensis

Cambridge Botanic Gardens UK c. 1931
Thought to be R. hugonis × R. sericea hookeri
Medium-sized pale yellow flowers with primrose stamens are carried in profusion towards midsummer. Its foliage is fern-like, the growth prickly and upright. Small round red hips follow on.

[(SP) (P) ◗ AL]   7' × 5'   2.1 × 1.5 m

'Cerise Bouquet' [Multibracteata Hybrid]

Tantau GERMANY 1958
R. multibracteata × 'Crimson Glory'
The gracefully arching branches bear pendulous

'Buff Beauty' and *right:* 'Canary Bird'

Above: 'Cerise Bouquet'
Below: 'Charles Austin' (see text p. 215)

'Cocktail'

clusters of cerise-crimson, fully double flowers and small, grey-green foliage with many leaflets. Growth vigorous and upright, arching when mature.

[(S) (P) (H) (MS) ◐ AL]   12′ × 12′   3.5 × 3.5 m

'Charles Austin' [Modern Shrub]

Austin UK 1973
'Chaucer' × 'Aloha'
Large, frilly-petalled, cup-shaped flowers of apricot and yellow, paling with age. Large, leathery foliage. Growth vigorous and upright.

[(S) (P) (H) (VF) (CL) AL]   5′ × 4′   1.5 × 1.2 m

'Chaucer' [Modern Shrub]

Austin UK 1970
Seedling × 'Constance Spry'
Globular buds open to fully cupped blooms of rich mid-pink, quartered when fully open. Foliage mid-green. Growth bushy and upright.

[(C) (H) (VF) AL]   3½′ × 3′   1.05 m × 90 cm

'Chianti' [Modern Shrub]

Austin UK 1967
'Dusky Maiden' × 'Tuscany'
Large, semi-double, purplish-maroon flowers are borne in medium-sized clusters, with large – a little coarse – dark green foliage. Growth widish.

[(S) (P) (H) (MF) ◐ ▽ AL]   5′ × 4′   1.5 × 1.2 m

*'City of London' (Harukfore) [Modern Shrub]

Harkness UK 1987
'New Dawn' × 'Radox Bouquet'
Large, shaggy, blush-pink blooms with a heady perfume are produced in clusters. Large, bright green foliage on an upright and bushy plant.

[(C) (P) (H) (VF) (CL) AL]   5′ × 3′   1.5 m × 90 cm

'Cocktail' (Meimick) [Modern Shrub]

Meilland FRANCE 1957
('Independence' × 'Orange Triumph') × 'Phyllis Bide'
Large, upright trusses of single bright red and primrose-yellow flowers. Foliage leathery, dark green and glossy. Growth upright, the stems reddish-brown.

[(C) (P) (H) (MF) (CL) AL]   6′ × 4′   1.8 × 1.2 m

'Complicata' [Gallica or Macrantha Hybrid]

Origin, date and parentage unknown
A superb and useful rose, its large, single, silvery-deep-pink flowers have a white centre and pronounced golden stamens. The foliage is grey-green and matt-finished on a tidy but ultimately rather shaggy plant. It also makes a good climber for small trees.

[(S) (P) (CL) (MF) ◐ AW]   10′ × 6′   3 × 1.8 m

'Conrad Ferdinand Meyer' [Rugosa Hybrid]

Müller 1899
R. rugosa × 'Gloire de Dijon'
The large, cupped, fully double blooms of rich pink are noted for their strong and heady perfume. Foliage coarsely toothed, dark-green and leathery. Growth vigorous and upright, the stems very thorny.

[(R) (H) (CL) (VF) ◐ R❦ AL]
10′ × 8′   3 × 2.5 m

'Copenhagen' [Modern Shrub]

Poulsen DENMARK 1964
Seedling × 'Ena Harkness'
Large, double flowers of bright scarlet come in smallish clusters. Foliage dark green and glossy with coppery overtones. Growth upright, but this rose needs some support when mature.

[(C) (P) (CL) (MF) AL]   8′ × 4′   2.5 × 1.2 m

'Cornelia' [Hybrid Musk]

Pemberton UK 1925
Parentage unknown
Huge conical clusters are borne of smallish double flowers of apricot, strawberry and pink, the clusters sometimes heavy enough to cause branches to arch most attractively. Their colour deepens in the autumn. Foliage bronzy-green and glossy. Growth bushy and slightly arching.

[(C) (H) (VF) ◐ ▽ M❦ AW]
5′ × 5′   1.5 × 1.5 m

'Coryana', R. × coryana

Hurst UK 1926
R. roxburghii × R. macrophylla
Medium-sized, single, pink flowers on a tall shrub with light green leaves of many leaflets, the stems light green. A few stubby thorns only. Growth upright and bushy.

[(S) (P) ◐ AL]   6′ × 4′   1.8 × 1.2 m

'Complicata' (see text p. 215) and *below:*
'Copenhagen' (see text p. 215)

'Corylus' [Rugosa Hybrid]

Hazel le Rougetel UK 1988
R. rugosa × R. nitida
The beautiful, mid-silver-pink and sizeable flowers
are scented and have pronounced stamens. They
are freely produced among dense, feathery, light
green foliage. Bright orange-red hips follow on.
The foliage turns a rich tawny yellow in the
autumn. An upright and dense rose, free-
suckering too, that is good for mass planting.
[(C) (P) (SF) ◑ ▽ AL]   3′ × 3′   90 × 90 cm

*'Cymbaline' (Auslean) [Modern Shrub]

Austin UK 1983
Seedling × 'Lilian Austin'
Its flowers are saucer-like, fully double and grey-
ish-pink, and highly scented. Foliage mid-green
and glossy, the growth bushy and spreading but
not sufficiently so for use as a ground-cover plant.
[(R) (VF) ▽ AL]   4′ × 5′   1.2 × 1.5 m

'Danaë' [Hybrid Musk]

Pemberton UK 1913
'Trier' × 'Gloire de Chédane-Guinoisseau'
The clusters of small, semi-double, buff-yellow

flowers pale to white when in sun. Foliage mid-
green and glossy. Growth upright though slightly
arching.
[(R) (H) (SF) (CL) ◑ AL]   5′ × 4′   1.5 × 1.2 m

'Daybreak' [Hybrid Musk]

Pemberton UK 1918
'Trier' × 'Liberty'
Near-single, golden-yellow blooms are produced
in upward-growing clusters. They pale to lemon
with age. Foliage dark green and semi-glossy.

'Cornelia' (see text p. 215)

Growth upright and bushy, the stems dark, polished and almost thornless.
[(R) (P) (H) (MF) (CL) ◑ AL]
4′ × 3′   1.2 m × 90 cm

'Doncasterii', *R. macrophylla doncasterii* [Macrophylla Hybrid]

Doncaster UK *c.* 1930
R. macrophylla seedling
The medium-sized, single, deep rose-pink flowers have yellow stamens. Plump, elongated, orange-red hips follow in the autumn. Foliage large and dark green, the stems reddish-brown, on a very vigorous, upright plant.
[(S) ◑ AL]   6′ × 4′   1.8 × 1.2 m

'Dorothy Wheatcroft' [Modern Shrub]

Tantau GERMANY 1960
Parentage unknown
Large clusters of orange-red, semi-double flowers, with bright green, semi-glossy foliage on a plant of open growth.
[(C) (P) (H) (SF) ▽ AL]   5′ × 4′   1.5 × 1.2 m

'Dortmund' [Modern Shrub]

Kordes GERMANY 1955
Seedling × *R. kordesii*
Elongated buds open to large, single, bright red flowers, each with a white eye, in clusters. Foliage dark green and polished on a vigorous and upright plant.
[(C) (P) (H) (MF) (CL) AW]   8′ × 6′   2.5 × 1.8 m

'Dr Eckener' [Rugosa Hybrid]

Berger GERMANY 1930
'Golden Emblem' × *R. rugosa* hybrid
The semi-double, large, loosely formed blooms are clear yellow burnished copper. Foliage large, dark green and matt, the growth broad but upright.
[(R) (P) (H) (VF) ◑ AL]   10′ × 8′   3 × 2.5 m

'Eddie's Crimson' [Moyesii Hybrid]

Eddie CANADA 1956
'Donald Prior' × *R. moyesii* hybrid
Deep blood-red, semi-double blooms are borne along arching branches, with dark green foliage.

Hips of 'Doncasterii' (see text p. 217)

Large hips follow in the autumn. Growth upright and vigorous.

[(S) (SF) ◐ AL]   10′ × 6′   3 × 1.8 m

'Eddie's Jewel' [Moyesii Hybrid]

Eddie CANADA 1962
'Donald Prior' × *R. moyesii* hybrid
The large, shapely, semi-double blooms of glowing clear red have prominent stamens when fully open and are produced along arching branches. Foliage light to mid green. Growth upright.

[(S) (P) (H) (SF) ◐ AL]   8′ × 6′   2.5 × 1.8 m

'Ellen' (Auscup) [Modern Shrub]

Austin UK 1984
Parentage unknown
In the style of an old-fashioned rose, with fully double flowers of apricot deepening towards the centre. Foliage mid-green and semi-glossy on an upright plant.

[(C) (H) (MF) ▽ AL]   4′ × 4′   1.2 × 1.2 m

'Elmshorn' [Modern Shrub]

Kordes GERMANY 1951
'Hamburg' × 'Verdun'

The many medium-sized, pompon-like flowers in large trusses are a deep glowing pink. Foliage wrinkled and glossy mid-green. Growth upright.

[(C) (P) (H) (MF) ▽ ✂ AW]   6′ × 4′   1.8 × 1.2 m

'Emanuel' [Modern Shrub]

Austin UK 1985
Parentage unknown
The shapely flowers are in the old-fashioned style and are soft delicate pink with a lemon base. Mid-green foliage on a bushy plant.

[(C) (H) (VF) ▽ AL]   4′ × 3′   1.2 m × 90 cm

Top: 'Eddie's Jewel' and *bottom:* 'Elmshorn'

'English Garden' (Ausbuff) [Modern Shrub]

Austin UK 1987
Parentage unknown
The flat, rosette-like flowers, sizeable and with many petals, are pale yellow deepening towards the centre. Foliage mid-green. Growth compact and upright.

[(C) (H) (VF) ▽ AL]   4' × 3'   1.2 m × 90 cm

'Eos' [Moyesii Hybrid]

Ruys USA 1950
R. moyesii × 'Magnifica'
The medium-sized, initially cupped, semi-double blooms of rosy-red, with a white eye and pronounced stamens, are borne in small bunches along upright branches. Foliage leathery and glossy, but small. Growth upright and very thorny.

[(S) (H) (SF) ◑ AL]   8' × 5'   2.5 × 1.5 m

'Erfurt' [Hybrid Musk]

Kordes GERMANY 1939
'Eva' × 'Réveil Dijonnais'
The large, semi-double blooms of glowing pink and cream, yellowish towards the centre, are freely produced in clusters. Foliage plentiful, bronzy-green and glossy. Growth bushy, free-branching and very thorny.

[(C) (H) (MF) AL]   5' × 4'   1.5 × 1.2 m

'Felicia' [Hybrid Musk]

Pemberton UK 1928
'Trier' × 'Ophelia'
Clusters of soft pink – sometimes deeper – and fully double flowers come on an upright, free-branching shrub with plentiful, glossy, mid-green foliage.

[(C) (H) (P) (MF) ◑ ▽ ✂ AW]
4' × 3'   1.2 m × 90 cm

'Ferdinand Pichard' [Hybrid Perpetual]

Tanne FRANCE 1921
Parentage unknown
One of the most attractive of the striped varieties, its cupped, fully double flowers are pink and crimson heavily striped with silvery-white. Foliage leathery, mid-green and rather coarse. Growth upright and bushy.

[(R) (H) (P) (MF) ▽ ✂ AL]   5' × 4'   1.5 × 1.2 m

'Eos'

*'Fisherman's Friend' (Auschild) [Modern Shrub]

Austin UK 1987
Parentage unknown
Rich crimson flowers, very large and full in the old style. Mid-green foliage on a robust plant.

[(C) (H) (VF) ▽ AL]   4' × 3'   1.2 m × 90 cm

'F. J. Grootendorst' [Rugosa Hybrid]

de Goey NETHERLANDS 1918
R. rugosa rubra × a Polyantha
Large clusters, held upright, of small crimson flowers with frilly edges to their petals, almost like a dianthus. Foliage coarse and mid-green. Growth upright and bushy.

[(C) (H) (MF) ▽ ◑ AW]   4' × 3'   1.2 m × 90 cm

'Fountain', 'Red Prince', 'Fontaine' [Modern Shrub]

Tantau GERMANY 1970
Parentage unknown
The very large flowers, loosely formed from high-centred buds, are rich bright crimson and are borne in clusters. Large and dark green foliage on an upright plant.

[(C) (H) (SF) (CL) ▽ AW]   5' × 4'   1.5 × 1.2 m

Above: 'Erfurt'
Below: 'Felicia'

'Ferdinand Pichard' (see text p. 220)

'Fountain' (see text p. 220)

'Francesca' [Hybrid Musk]

Pemberton UK 1922
'Danaë' × 'Sunburst'
Very large semi-double flowers of rich yellow, produced in clusters on an upright plant with dark glossy foliage.

[(C) (H) (SF) (CL) ⛉ ◑ AL] 4′ × 4′ 1.2 × 1.2 m

'Frank Naylor' [Pimpinellifolia Hybrid]

Harkness UK 1978
Seedling of complex hybridity × ('Cläre Grammerstorf' × 'Frühlingsmorgen')
Clusters of medium-sized single blooms of red and yellow, with small, oval, dark green foliage on a broadly upright plant.

[(C) (H) ⛉ ◑ AL] 4′ × 3′ 1.2m × 90 cm

'Frau Dagmar Hartopp' see 'Fru Dagmar Hastrup'

'Fred Loads'

'Fred Loads' [Modern Shrub]

Holmes UK 1968
'Dorothy Wheatcroft' × 'Orange Sensation'
The very bright, salmon-orange to vermilion flowers are semi-double, large and produced in clusters. Foliage large, dark green and semi-glossy. Growth upright.

[(C) (P) (H) (MF) ⛉ AL] 5′ × 3′ 1.5 m × 90 cm

'Fritz Nobis' [Modern Shrub]

Kordes GERMANY 1940
'Joanna Hill' × 'Magnifica'
Superbly formed, fully double blooms of soft rose-pink with salmon highlights are produced freely in sizeable clusters. Foliage semi-glossy, leathery and dark green. Growth upright and branching.

[(S) (P) (H) (SF) ⛉ ◑ AW] 5′ × 4′ 1.5 × 1.2 m

'Fru Dagmar Hastrup', 'Fru Dagmar Hartopp', 'Frau Dagmar Hartopp' [Rugosa Hybrid]

Hastrup DENMARK 1914
Parentage unknown
The large, single, silvery-pink blooms have pronounced stamens and are freely produced on a compact, wide-growing shrub with dark green, rugose foliage. A special feature are the large, tomato-like hips in the autumn. This rose is of Danish origin and consequently the German 'Frau' is incorrect.

[(C) (P) (H) (P) (SF) ⛉ ◑ AW]
3′ × 4′ 90 cm × 1.2 m

'Frühlingsanfang' [Pimpinellifolia Hybrid]

Kordes GERMANY 1950
'Joanna Hill' × *R. pimpinellifolia altaica*
Large, single, ivory-white blooms, with leathery, dark green foliage on a plant of upright growth.

[(S) (P) (H) (SF) ◑ AL] 10′ × 6′ 3 × 1.8 m

'Frühlingsduft' [Pimpinellifolia Hybrid]

Kordes GERMANY 1949
'Joanna Hill' × R. pimpinellifolia altaica
Large, fully double flowers of ivory-white and golden-yellow, often tinged soft pink. Foliage large and leathery, dark green. Growth angularly upright.

[(S) (P) (H) (VF) ◐ AL]   10' × 6'   3 × 1.8 m

'Frühlingsgold', 'Spring Gold' [Pimpinellifolia Hybrid]

Kordes GERMANY 1937
'Joanna Hill' × R. pimpinellifolia hispida
Probably the best known of Kordes' Scotch rose hybrids, its large, initially cupped but later loosely formed flowers are clear primrose-yellow, the buds tinged red. Foliage mid-green and leathery on an upright, branching plant.

[(S) (P) (H) (VF) ◐ AW]   7' × 6'   2.1 × 1.8 m

'Frühlingsmorgen', 'Spring Morning' [Pimpinellifolia Hybrid]

Kordes GERMANY 1942
('E. G. Hill' × 'Cathrine Kordes') × R. pimpinellifolia altaica
The large, single flowers are ivory-white to cream heavily brushed with cherry-red and have pronounced golden-brown stamens. The foliage is dark green and matt-finished on an upright, branching plant. This rose has served well at stud, being a parent to several unusually coloured modern roses.

[(SP) (P) (H) (VF) ◐ AW]   6' × 5'   1.8 × 1.5 m

'Frühlingsschnee' [Pimpinellifolia Hybrid]

Kordes GERMANY 1954
'Golden Glow' × R. pimpinellifolia altaica
Large, loose, semi-double and creamy-white flowers on a vigorous, upright and arching plant with dark green, greyish foliage.

[(S) (P) (H) (MF) ◐ AL]   6' × 4'   1.8 × 1.2 m

'Frühlingstag' [Pimpinellifolia Hybrid]

Kordes GERMANY 1949
'McGredy's Wonder' × 'Frühlingsgold'
Large clusters of semi-double, rich yellow flowers are carried on a vigorous bush with dark green, matt foliage.

[(S) (P) (H) (SF) ◐ AL]   7' × 4'   2.1 × 1.2 m

'F. J. Grootendorst' (see text p. 220)

'Fru Dagmar Hastrup' (see text p. 222)

'Frühlingszauber' [Pimpinellifolia Hybrid]

Kordes GERMANY 1942
('E. G. Hill' × 'Cathrine Kordes') × *R. pimpinellifolia altaica*
The semi-double, sizeable flowers of ivory-white are splashed and brushed heavily with deep pink. Dark green, leathery foliage on an angular plant.
[(S) (P) (H) (SF) ● M ▥ AL] 7′ × 5′ 2.1 × 1.5 m

'Georg Arends', 'Fortuné Besson' [Hybrid Perpetual]

Hinner GERMANY 1910
'Frau Karl Druschki' × 'La France'
Its shapely, high-centred buds open to large, loosely formed blooms of soft pink brushed deeper. Foliage large, dark green and semi-glossy on an upright, spindly plant.
[(R) (P) (H) (MF) ⁛ AL] 5′ × 4′ 1.5 × 1.2 m

'Geranium' [*R. moyesii* Hybrid]

Royal Horticultural Society UK 1938
R. moyesii seedling
Bright, scarlet, single flowers of perfect form with prominent anthers are produced in small clusters. Large, orange-red, flagon-shaped hips follow in the autumn. Foliage light greyish-green, the stems well endowed with spiky thorns, on a plant of upright, branching growth.
[(P) (SF) (H) ● AL] 8′ × 5′ 2.5 × 1.5 m

'Gertrude Jekyll' (Ausbord) [Modern Shrub]

Austin UK 1987
Parentage unknown
Its deep pink, fully double flowers are in the old style, and are very fragrant. Greyish-green foliage comes on an upright, bushy plant.
[(C) (H) (VF) AL] 4′ × 3′ 1.2 m × 90 cm

'Gipsy Boy', 'Zigeunerknabe' [Bourbon]

Lambert GERMANY 1909
'Russelliana' seedling
The medium-sized, fully double flowers are deep crimson, almost purple, and have primrose-yellow stamens. They sometimes bleach in hot sun. Foliage thick, leathery and heavily veined on a stout, angular plant.
[(S) (P) (VF) (CL) AW] 5′ × 4′ 1.5 × 1.2 m

'Gloire de Guilan' [Damask]

MIDDLE EASTERN ORIGIN
Discovered by Miss Nancy Lindsay 1949
The very double, flat and beautifully quartered flowers are clear pink and fragrant. They are produced early. The foliage is dark green, densely packed on an awkward and rather sprawling plant. This variety has been grown for many years for the production of attar and is much older than the date of introduction given here.
[(S) (P) (VF) ⁛ AL] 6′ × 4′ 1.8 × 1.2 m

'Glory of Edzell' [Pimpinellifolia Hybrid]

Origin, date and parentage unknown
A charmer, the small, single, clear pink to lilac flowers come on a dense shrub with light green, almost fluffy, fern-like foliage.
[(SP) (P) (SF) (H) ● AL] 5′ × 4′ 1.5 × 1.2 m

'Goldbusch' [Eglanteria Hybrid]

Kordes GERMANY 1954
Parentage unknown
Large, semi-double, golden-yellow flowers are produced both singly and in small clusters amid lush, bright green, semi-glossy and scented foliage on a large, free-branching plant which will sprawl unless supported.
[(R) (P) (MF) (CL) ● AL] 8′ × 5′ 2.5 × 1.5 m

'Golden Chersonese' (Hilgold) [Ecae Hybrid]

Allen UK 1967
R. ecae × 'Canary Bird'
Medium to small, rich buttercup-yellow, single blooms are produced in profusion along arching stems in late spring. A lovely shrub with dark green, fern-like foliage and dark brown wood, amply endowed with thorns. Its growth is upright.
[(SP) (P) (SF) (H) ● AL] 6′ × 4′ 1.8 × 1.2 m

'Frühlingsgold' (see text p. 223)

'Golden Wings' [Pimpinellifolia Hybrid]

Shepherd USA 1956

'Soeur Thérèse' × (*R. pimpinellifolia altaica* × 'Ormiston Roy')

The large flowers are single, though sometimes with a few more petals, and are clear sulphur-yellow with prominent, golden-brown stamens. Light green, almost glossy foliage is borne on a bushy plant, the stems dark, rusty-looking and with few thorns. A very good rose in all respects.

[(C) (P) (H) (SF) ◑ AW]   5′ × 4′   1.5 × 1.2 m

'Graham Thomas' (Ausmas)
[Modern Shrub]

Austin UK 1983

Seedling × ('Charles Austin' × 'Iceberg' seedling)

A very good variety, the large, fully double, many-petalled flowers are in the old-fashioned style but with modern colours of rich yellow with a deeper centre and are borne in clusters. Foliage dark green and glossy on a bushy plant.

[(C) (P) (H) (VF) ▽ AW]   4′ × 3′   1.2 m × 90 cm

'Grandmaster' [Hybrid Musk]

Kordes GERMANY 1954

'Sangerhausen' × 'Sunmist'

Sizeable, semi-double blooms of apricot, lemon and pink are produced in clusters. Light green foliage on a plant of upright growth.

[(C) (P) (H) (SF) (CL) ▽ AL]
5′ × 3′   1.5 m × 90 cm

'Hamburger Phoenix' [Modern Shrub]

Kordes GERMANY 1954

R. kordesii × a seedling

Clusters of large, double, rich red flowers on a sprawling plant with good, dark green, glossy foliage. Large red hips follow in the autumn.

[(R) (P) (MF) (CL) ◑ AL]   8′ × 5′   2.5 × 1.5 m

'Hansa' [Rugosa Hybrid]

Schaum & Van Tol NETHERLANDS 1905

Parentage unknown

Very large, many-petalled flowers are borne on rather weak necks. They are purple-red with mauve highlights and have the fragrance of cloves. The dark green, almost glossy, foliage is heavily veined and plentiful. Growth bushy and upright. This is one of the best Rugosas.

[(C) (P) (H) (VF) ▽ ◑ AL]   4′ × 3′   1.2 m × 90 cm

'Headleyensis' [Hugonis Hybrid]

Warburg UK *c.* 1920

R. hugonis × *R. pimpinellifolia altaica*

Fairly large, creamy-yellow, single flowers are produced in early summer on an upright, branching plant with fern-like foliage.

[(S) (P) ◑ AL]   7′ × 4′   2.1 × 1.2 m

'Heather Muir' [Sericea Hybrid]

Sunningdale UK 1957

A form of *R. sericea* found at Kiftsgate Court, Gloucestershire

Abundant, pure white, single flowers along upright panicles are produced over a fairly long period. These are followed by oval orange hips. Foliage fern-like, with greyish-brown, very thorny stems. A plant of upright, branching growth.

[(S) (P) (SF) ◑ AL]   8′ × 6′   2.5 × 1.8 m

'Hebe's Lip', 'Reine Blanche', 'Rubro-tincta' [Eglanteria Hybrid]

Lee UK Prior to 1846

Reintroduced by Paul UK 1912

Probably *R. damascena* × *R. eglanteria*

A rose which qualifies for inclusion because it was reintroduced by William Paul in 1912, and which provokes thought as to how many other good and interesting varieties fell by the wayside during the nineteenth century. Its large, single or semi-double blooms are creamy-white edged pink. Grey-green, scented foliage comes on a bushy plant which is inclined to sprawl.

[(S) (H) (MF) ◑ AL]   4′ × 4′   1.2 × 1.2 m

'Heidelberg', 'Grüss an Heidelberg'
[Modern Shrub]

Kordes GERMANY 1959

'World's Fair' × 'Floradora'

Large, well-packed clusters of double, bright crimson flowers with a lighter reverse. Glossy, leathery, dark green foliage on an upright, bushy plant.

[(R) (P) (SF) (CL) AL]   6′ × 5′   1.8 × 1.5 m

'Helen Knight' [Ecae Hybrid]

Knight UK 1964

R. ecae × *R. pimpinellifolia altaica*

Medium-sized, concave blooms of clear yellow are borne along arching branches. With fern-like, dark green foliage, and of upright, branching growth.

[(R) (P) (SF) (CL) ◑ AL]   5′ × 4′   1.5 × 1.2 m

'Herbstfeuer', 'Autumn Fire' [Modern Shrub]

Kordes GERMANY 1966
Parentage unknown
Large, loosely double, bright red flowers, smudged darker red, are produced in clusters. Large, pear-shaped orange hips follow on. The foliage is large, light green and glossy on a dense and bushy plant. This is an underrated rose.

[(R) (H) (P) (MF) ◐ AL]   6' × 4'   1.8 × 1.2 m

'Heritage' (Ausblush) [Modern Shrub]

Austin UK 1984
Seedling × 'Iceberg' seedling
Cupped, fully double flowers of light pink with deeper centres. Foliage smallish and dark green with a slight gloss. Growth bushy.

[(C) (H) (P) (VF) ▽ AL]   4' × 4'   1.2 × 1.2 m

'Hero' (Aushero) [Modern Shrub]

Austin UK 1983
'The Prioress' × a seedling
The eye-catching mid-pink blooms are cupped and moderately full. Foliage mid-green and semi-glossy. Growth upright and bushy.

[(C) (H) (VF) ▽ AL]   4' × 4'   1.2 × 1.2 m

'Hidcote Gold' [Sericea Hybrid]

Hilling UK 1948
R. sericea seedling
Small clusters of bright yellow, single flowers are borne along arching branches, sometimes in ones

Top: 'Goldbusch' (see text p. 224) and *bottom:* 'Hansa'

or twos. Foliage mid to dark green and ferny, the stems covered in wedge-shaped thorns. An upright and branching plant.

[(S) (P) (H) (SF) ◑ AL]   8′ × 6′   2.5 × 1.8 m

'Highdownensis', *R. moyesii* × *highdownensis* [Moyesii Hybrid]

Hillier UK 1928
R. moyesii seedling
The single, rich crimson flowers have prominent anthers. Large, flagon-shaped reddish-plum hips follow on. The foliage is small and dark green, the stems thorny, maroon when young, on an upright and arching plant.

[(S) (P) ◑ AL]   8′ × 5′   2.5 × 1.5 m

*'Hilda Murrell' (Ausmurr) [Modern Shrub]

Austin UK 1984
Seedling × ('Parade' × 'Chaucer')
Shapely, fully double flowers of clear pink, with mid-green, matt foliage and of bushy growth.

[(R) (H) (MF) AL]   5′ × 4′   1.5 × 1.2 m

'Honorine de Brabant' [Bourbon]

Origin, date and parentage unknown
Cupped, fully double blooms of lilac-pink striped

'Hugh Dickson'

darker pink to red. Foliage plentiful, large and light green with a greyish sheen. Very vigorous, though of sprawling growth.

[(R) (H) (VF) (P) ▽ ◑ AL]   6′ × 5′   1.8 × 1.5 m

'Hugh Dickson' [Hybrid Perpetual]

Dickson UK 1905
'Lord Bacon' × 'Grüss an Teplitz'
The large, deep red, high-centred blooms open blowsily and are produced in clusters, with dark green foliage. Growth upright, needing support when mature.

[(R) (VF) (P) ▽ ✕ AL]   8′ × 5′   2.5 × 1.5 m

'Hunslet Moss' [Moss Rose]

A recent discovery by Mr Humphrey Brooke of Claydon, Suffolk
Introduced by Beales UK 1984
Rich pink and fully double blooms, heavily mossed and scented. Foliage dark green touched bronze. Growth bushy and upright.

[(S) (H) (VF) ▽ AL]   4′ × 3′   1.2 m × 90 cm

'James Mason' [Gallica]

Beales UK 1982
'Scharlachglut' × 'Tuscany Superb'
Large, bright red, almost crimson flowers are produced in profusion in early summer. Dark green foliage on a bushy plant.

[(S) (P) (H) (VF) ◑ AL]   5′ × 4′   1.5 × 1.2 m

'Joseph's Coat' [Modern Shrub]

Armstrong USA 1964
'Buccaneer' × 'Circus'
Aptly named, for its large clusters of semi-double flowers are several shades of orange and yellow, deepening with age. Foliage light green and glossy. Growth upright.

[(C) (P) (H) (SF) (CL) ▽ ✕ AW]
5′ × 4′   1.5 × 1.2 m

'Karl Förster' [Pimpinellifolia Hybrid]

Kordes GERMANY 1931
'Frau Karl Druschki' × *R. pimpinellifolia altaica*
A rose that should be much better known. Its large, fully double, pure white blooms are rather ragged when fully open and are produced on a dense, upright shrub with plentiful greyish-green foliage.

[(R) (P) (H) (SF) ▽ ◑ AL]   5′ × 4′   1.5 × 1.2 m

'Kassel' [Modern Shrub]

Kordes GERMANY 1957
'Hamburg' × 'Scarlet Else'
Large clusters of fully double blooms of rich orange-red are produced very freely on an upright plant. Foliage dark green and glossy.

[(C) (P) (H) (CL) ☐ ✂ AL]   5′ × 4′   1.5 × 1.2 m

'Kathleen' [Hybrid Musk]

Pemberton UK 1922
'Daphne' × 'Perle des Jardins'
Single, blush-pink flowers come in large clusters.

Foliage dark green and semi-glossy on a tall, upright plant.

[(R) (P) (H) (CL) ☐ AL]   8′ × 4′   2.5 × 1.2 m

'Kathleen Ferrier' [Modern Shrub]

Buismann NETHERLANDS 1952
'Gartenstolz' × 'Shot Silk'
The clusters of semi-double flowers are soft pink and salmon, their petals prettily crinkled at the edges. Foliage plentiful, dark green and glossy. Growth upright and widish.

[(C) (H) (P) ☐ ✂ AL]   5′ × 4′   1.5 × 1.2 m

'Lafter' [Modern Shrub]

Brownell USA 1948
['V for Victory' × ('Général Jacqueminot' × 'Dr W. Van Fleet')] × 'Pink Princess'
A vigorous, erect shrub carrying large clusters of salmon, rose and apricot flowers of semi-double form. The foliage is rich bright green and glossy.

[(C) (P) (MF) (CL) AL]   5′ × 4′   1.5 × 1.2 m

Top: 'Joseph's Coat' and *bottom:* 'Karl Förster'

Above: 'Kassel' (see text p. 229)
Below: 'Kathleen' (see text p. 229)

'Kathleen Ferrier' (see text p. 229)

'La Sevillana' (Meigekanu) [Floribunda]

Meilland FRANCE 1978
[('Meibrim' × 'Jolie Madame') × ('Zambra' ×
'Zambra')] × [('Super Star' × 'Super Star') × ('Poppy
Flash' × 'Poppy Flash')]
Very bright vermilion, semi-double flowers are
borne in clusters on a widish plant with rich green
and bronzy foliage.
[(C) (P) (H) (SF) AL]   4' × 4'   1.2 × 1.2 m

'Lavender Lassie' [Hybrid Musk]

Kordes GERMANY 1960
'Hamburg' × 'Mme Norbert Levavasseur'
Large trusses of fully double, lavender-pink flowers with dark green, glossy foliage. Growth upright
and tidy when the branches are not borne down by
the weight of blooms. This is a very good rose.
[(C) (P) (H) (MF) (CL) ⊽ ✕ AW]
5' × 4'   1.5 × 1.2 m

'Lilian Austin' [Modern Shrub]

Austin UK 1973
'Aloha' × 'The Yeoman'
The semi-double flowers of salmon-pink tinged

apricot, deepening towards the centre, open flat
and are produced in clusters. Foliage mid-green
and glossy. Growth bushy and arching.
[(C) (SF) AL]   4' × 4'   1.2 × 1.2 m

'L'Oréal Trophy' (Harlexis) [Modern Shrub]

Harkness UK 1982
Sport from 'Alexander'
Softer in colour than its parent, otherwise identical.
[(C) (P) (H) (SF) ⊽ ✕ AL]   6' × 4'   1.8 × 1.2 m

'Magenta', 'Kordes' Magenta' [Modern Shrub]

Kordes GERMANY 1954
Yellow Floribunda seedling × 'Lavender
Pinocchio'
Shapely, fully double flowers open flat to display a
range of purple, mauve and pink shades. They are
produced in clusters. The foliage is dark green and
leathery on a bushy and upright plant. Needs a
little extra loving to give of its best.
[(C) (VF) ⊽ ✕ AL]   5' × 4'   1.5 × 1.2 m

'Lafter' (see text p. 229)
and *right:* 'Lavender Lassie' (see text p. 231)

'Magnifica' [Eglanteria Hybrid]

Hesse GERMANY 1916
'Lucy Ashton' self-seedling
Lovely, semi-double, purplish-pink flowers are
produced in small clusters, though this is not as
vigorous a rose as some Sweetbriars. The foliage is
dark green and glossy but has little or no scent.
[(S) (P) (SF) ⊽ ◑ AL]   6' × 5'   1.8 × 1.5 m

*'Malcolm Sargent' (Harwharry)
[Modern Shrub]

Harkness UK 1988
'Herbstfeuer' × 'Trumpeter'
Hybrid-Tea-shaped flowers of shining crimson-
scarlet, with rich green and sparkling foliage on a
bushy, upright-plant.
[(C) (H) ⊽ ✕ AL]   4' × 3'   1.2 m × 90 cm

'Märchenland', 'Exception' [Modern Shrub]

Tantau GERMANY 1951
'Swantje' × 'Hamburg'
The very large trusses of semi-double, bright pink
flowers are tinged salmon. Foliage plentiful, dark
green and semi-glossy. Growth bushy.
[(C) (P) (H) ⊽ AL]   5' × 4'   1.5 × 1.2 m

'Marguerite Hilling' [Moyesii Hybrid]

Hilling UK 1959
Sport from 'Nevada'
A bright pink form of 'Nevada', identical to its
parent in all other respects.
[(R) (P) (SF) ◑ AL]   8' × 7'   2.5 × 2.1 m

'Magenta' (see text p. 231)

'Marjorie Fair', 'Red Ballerina', 'Red Yester-
day' (Harhero) [Modern Shrub]

Harkness UK 1978
'Ballerina' × 'Baby Faurax'
Large trusses of small, single flowers of ruby-red
with a white eye, which are individually insignificant but very eye-catching en masse. Foliage light
green and semi-glossy on a bushy, dense plant.
[(C) (P) (B) ⊽ AW]   4' × 3'   1.2 m × 90 cm

'Martin Frobisher' [Rugosa Hybrid]

Svejda CANADA 1968
'Schneezwerg' × unknown
Very pale pink, semi-double blooms with deeper
centres. Foliage large, light green and semi-glossy.
Growth upright and branching.
[(C) (P) (H) (VF) ⊽ AL]   4' × 4'   1.2 × 1.2 m

'Mary Rose' (Ausmary) [Modern Shrub]

Austin UK 1983
Seedling × 'The Friar'
Very double flowers in the old-fashioned form,
warm-mid-pink with a deeper centre and cupped.
Foliage glossy and mid-green. Upright and bushy
growth.

[(C) (B) (VF) ▽ AW]   4′ × 3′   1.2 m × 90 cm

'Master Hugh' [Macrophylla hybrid]

Mason UK 1966
R. macrophylla seedling
The large, rose-pink, single flowers have pronounced pale yellow stamens and are followed by
very large, flagon-shaped, pendulous orange hips.
Foliage dark green and leathery, the stems mahogany. Growth upright.

[(S) (P) ❶ AL]   15′ × 8′   4.5 × 2.5 m

'Micrugosa', *R.* × *micrugosa*

Foundling at Strasbourg Botanical Institute *c.* 1905
R. roxburghii × *R. rugosa*
Large, soft pink, single blooms are produced amid

Above: 'Marguerite Hilling' and *below:* 'Magnifica'

Above: 'Marjorie Fair' (see text p. 232)
Below: 'Mary Rose' (see text p. 233)

an abundance of dark green, rough-textured foliage. Orange-red globular hips follow on. Growth bushy and dense.

[(P) (SF) (H) ⊽ ◖ AL]   5′ × 4′   1.5 × 1.2 m

'Micrugosa Alba', *R.* × *micrugosa alba*

Hurst UK 1900
R. roxburghii × *R. rugosa*
Almost as 'Micrugosa' but with white flowers and slightly taller and broader.

[(P) (H) (SF) ⊽ ◖ AL]   5′ × 4′   1.5 × 1.2 m

'Moonlight' [Hybrid Musk]

Pemberton UK 1913
'Trier' × 'Sulphurea'
Clusters of semi-double, creamy-white flowers with prominent yellow stamens. The foliage is very dark green and glossy, the stems plum-coloured, on a bushy plant.

[(C) (P) (SF) ◖ ✂ ⊽ AW]   5′ × 4′   1.5 × 1.2 m

'Mountbatten' (Harmantelle) [Modern Shrub]

Harkness UK 1982
'Peer Gynt' × [('Anne Cocker' × 'Arthur Bell') × 'Southampton']

Autumn hips of 'Master Hugh' (see text p. 233)

An outstanding shrub, the large, full, clear yellow blooms are borne in clusters, though sometimes singly, on a vigorous plant with rich green, leathery and glossy foliage.

[(C) (P) (H) (B) ⊽ ✂ AW]   5' × 4'   1.5 × 1.2 m

'Mozart' [Hybrid Musk]

Lambert GERMANY 1937
'Robin Hood' × 'Rote Pharisäer'
Small, single, carmine flowers with white centres are produced freely in massive clusters. Foliage mid-green on a dense and bushy plant.

[(C) (P) (B) (H) ⊽ AL]   4' × 3'   1.2 m × 90 cm

'Nevada' [Moyesii Hybrid]

Dot SPAIN 1927
Of uncertain parentage. Usually thought of as a hybrid of *R. moyesii*, but its occasional remontancy suggests the possibility of *R. pimpinellifolia*.
A superb shrub, its large, single, slightly blowsy flowers are soft creamy-yellow flushed pink with pronounced chocolate-brown stamens. Foliage dark green and semi-glossy. Growth vigorous, dense and tidy.

[(R) (P) (SF) ◑ AW]   8' × 7'   2.5 × 2.1 m

'Nova Zembla' [Rugosa Hybrid]

Mees UK 1907
Sport from 'Conrad Ferdinand Meyer'
A white sport from 'Conrad Ferdinand Meyer' with all its parent's characteristics except colour.

[(R) (H) (CL) (VF) R ◉ ◑ AL]
10' × 8'   3 × 2.5 m

'Nymphenberg' [Modern Shrub]

Kordes GERMANY 1954
'Sangerhausen' × 'Sunmist'
Large clusters of fairly large, salmon-pink flowers with tints of yellow and gold, though the colour varies with soil and weather conditions. Foliage rich dark green and glossy. Growth upright and dense.

[(C) (P) (H) ⊽ (CL) AL]   6' × 4'   1.8 × 1.2 m

'Nyveldt's White' [Rugosa Hybrid]

Nyveldt NETHERLANDS 1955
(*R. rugosa rubra* × *R. cinnamomea*) × *R. nitida*
Large, satiny-textured, pure white, single blooms are produced amid very dark green and deeply veined foliage, followed by large red hips. Growth bushy and dense, the stems thorny.

[(C) (P) (H) ◑ AL]   5' × 4'   1.5 × 1.2 m

Above: 'Mountbatten' (see text p. 234)
Below: 'Nymphenberg' (see text p. 235)

'Parkzierde'

'Ohio' [Modern Shrub]

Shepherd USA 1949
R. soulieana × a 'Grüss an Teplitz' seedling
Bright red, semi-double flowers are carried in clus-
ters with bright mid-green foliage on a bushy plant.
An interesting rose from an interesting cross, and
bred especially for hardiness.

[(R) (P) (H) ◑ AL] 4′ × 3′ 1.2 m × 90 cm

'Parkzierde' [Bourbon]

Lambert GERMANY 1909
Parentage unknown
Although not remontant, this is a rose well worth
garden space. It produces large clusters of semi-
double, scarlet-crimson flowers with pronounced
stamens. The foliage is dark green and leathery on
a plant of bushy, upright growth.

[(S) (P) (H) (MF) ◑ ⤬ AL] 5′ × 4′ 1.5 × 1.2 m

'Pax' [Hybrid Musk]

Pemberton UK 1918
'Trier' × 'Sunburst'
Trusses of large, pure white to cream, semi-double
flowers are borne on long, arching stems. Foliage
dark green, leathery. Growth bushy and wide.

[(C) (P) (H) (VF) (CL) ◑ AW] 6′ × 5′ 1.8 × 1.5 m

'Penelope' [Hybrid Musk]

Pemberton UK 1924
'Ophelia' × an unnamed seedling
The clusters of creamy, semi-double flowers
flushed pink are very freely produced. Foliage dark
green and semi-glossy. Growth bushy and wide.

[(C) (P) (MF) (H) ◑ M⬛⦂ AW]
4′ × 4′ 1.2 × 1.2 m

'Pink Grootendorst' [Rugosa Hybrid]

Grootendorst NETHERLANDS 1923
Sport from 'F. J. Grootendorst'
A frilly-petalled, clear rose-pink sport from 'F. J.
Grootendorst'. Identical to its parent in every
respect except colour.

[(C) (P) (H) (MF) ◑ AW] 4′ × 3′ 1.2 m × 90 cm

'Pink La Sevillana', 'Rosy La Sevillana' (Meigeroka) [Modern Shrub]

Meilland FRANCE 1983
Sport from 'La Sevillana'
A pink sport from 'La Sevillana' with all its parent's
characteristics except colour.

[(C) (P) (H) (SF) AL] 4′ × 4′ 1.2 × 1.2 m

'Poulsen's Park Rose' [Modern Shrub]

Poulsen DENMARK 1953
'Great Western' × 'Karen Poulsen'
Large, full, silvery-pink flowers are borne in clusters. Foliage dark green, leathery and rather coarse. Growth very thorny, and tending to sprawl.

[(R) (P) (H) (MF) (CL) ◍ R◧AL]
6′ × 6′   1.8 × 1.8 m

'Prestige' [Modern Shrub]

Kordes GERMANY 1957
'Rudolph Timm' × 'Fanal'
Large, semi-double, light crimson flowers are carried in clusters with plentiful, dark green, matt foliage on a bushy plant.

[(C) (P) (H) (SF) AL]   4′ × 3′   1.2 m × 90 cm

'Prosperity' [Hybrid Musk]

Pemberton UK 1919
'Marie-Jeanne' × 'Perle des Jardins'
One of the nicest of the Pemberton Musks, with its

'Pax' (see text p. 237) and *right:* 'Prosperity'

'Penelope' (see text p. 237)

large, closely packed clusters of fully double, shapely blooms of creamy-white flushed soft pink. Foliage dark green and glossy. Growth bushy and wide.

[(C) (P) (H) (MF) (CL) ● AW]   5′ × 4′   1.5 × 1.2 m

'Robin Hood' [Hybrid Musk]

Pemberton UK 1927
Seedling × 'Miss Edith Cavell'
Large trusses of small, semi-double, cherry-red blooms come on a compact, dense plant with good mid-green foliage. 'Robin Hood' is used extensively by other breeders to bring forth Floribundas.

[(C) (P) (H) (SF) ▽ ● AL]   4′ × 3′   1.2 m × 90 cm

'Robusta' (Korgosa) [Rugosa Hybrid]

Kordes GERMANY 1979
Seedling × R. rugosa
With large, single, scarlet blooms in profusion. Foliage dark green, leathery and glossy on a bushy, upright plant. This is a most welcome new Rugosa.

[(C) (P) (H) (VF) ▽ ● AL]   5′ × 4′   1.5 × 1.2 m

R. × andersonii see 'Andersonii'

R. × cantabrigiensis see 'Cantabrigiensis'

R. × coryana see 'Coryana'

R. davidii

WEST CHINA 1908
Corymbs of smallish pink flowers are followed by long, ovoid, bright red hips. Foliage fern-like and growth upright.

[(S) (P) ● AL]   10′ × 5′   3 × 1.5 m

R. farreri persetosa, 'Threepenny Bit Rose'

NORTHWEST CHINA 1914
Small, soft lilac-pink, single flowers. Foliage fern-like, the stems covered in soft bristles. Of spreading and bushy habit.

[(S) (P) ● ▽ AL]   5′ × 5′   1.5 × 1.5 m

R. forrestiana

WEST CHINA 1918
The small, deep pink, single flowers have pronounced stamens. Foliage small, leathery and dark

green, with dense thorns. Growth spreading and upright.

[(S) (P) ● AL]   7′ × 7′   2.1 × 2.1 m

R. headleyensis see 'Headleyensis'

R. × highdownensis see 'Highdownensis'

R. macrophylla doncasterii see 'Doncasterii'

R. × micrugosa see 'Micrugosa'

R. × micrugosa alba see 'Micrugosa Alba'

R. moyesii

WEST CHINA 1894
Reintroduced 1903
The medium-sized, deep red flowers are variable and have pronounced stamens. They are followed by flagon-shaped, orange-red hips in late summer. Foliage dark green and leathery on a plant of upright, angular growth.

[(S) ● (P) ▽ AW]   10′ × 6′   3 × 1.8 m

R. moyesii 'Geranium' see 'Geranium'

R. moyesii 'Sealing Wax' see 'Sealing Wax'

R. primula, 'Incense Rose'

NORTH CHINA 1910
Its single, soft yellow to creamy-white blooms have matching stamens. The foliage is scented of incense, light green, shiny and fern-like, the stems very prickly with broad reddish thorns. Growth bushy and upright.

[(SP) ● (P) ▽ AL]   5′ × 4′   1.5 × 1.2 m

R. stellata mirifica, 'Sacramento Rose'

NORTH MEXICO 1916
The small mauve to purplish-pink flowers are borne singly. Foliage grey-green, with very bristly stems. A most interesting, pretty rose, not remontant though flowers are produced over a fairly long period. Growth bushy.

[(S) ● (P) ▽ AL]   4′ × 4′   1.2 × 1.2 m

R. sweginzowii macrocarpa

NORTHWEST CHINA 1909
Clear pink single flowers of medium size are followed by large, pendulous, flagon-shaped, orange-

Above: Hips of *R. sweginzowii macrocarpa* (see text p. 239)
Right: 'Roseraie de l'Hay and *below:* 'Ruskin'

red hips. Foliage grey-green, the cane-coloured stems with large thorns. Growth upright and angular.

[(S) ◑ (P) AL]   10′ × 8′   3 × 2.5 m

R. willmottiae

WEST CHINA 1904
Its small, rose-purple, single flowers are produced on short, lateral branches with elongated, plump, orange-red hips later in the year. Foliage bluish-green and fern-like on an upright, branching plant.

[(SP) ◑ (P) AL]   6′ × 6′   1.8 × 1.8 m

R. xanthina lindleyii

NORTH CHINA, KOREA 1906
Medium-sized, double yellow flowers are produced from late spring to early summer. Foliage dark green and fern-like, the growth bushy.

[(P) (H) (VF) ◑ ▽ AW]   10′ × 6′   3 × 1.8 m

'Roseraie de l'Hay' [Rugosa Hybrid]

Cochet-Cochet FRANCE 1901
Parentage unknown
Large, shaggy, wine-red blooms are produced on short flower stalks in small clusters. Foliage dark green. Growth bushy.

[(P) (H) (VF) ◑ ▽ AW]   6′ × 5′   1.8 × 1.5 m

'Roundelay' [Modern Shrub]

Swim USA 1954
'Charlotte Armstrong' × 'Floradora'
The high-centred buds open flat and double, in medium-sized clusters, and are a rich dark red. Foliage dark green and semi-glossy. Growth upright.

[(C) (P) (MF) (B) ▽ ⤢ AL]   4′ × 3′   1.2 m × 90 cm

'Ruskin', 'John Ruskin' [Rugosa Hybrid]

Van Fleet USA 1928
'Souvenir de Pierre Leperdrieux' × 'Victor Hugo'
The very large, full, initially cupped blooms of rich crimson-red are beautifully shaped. Rich green, leathery, semi-glossy and deeply veined foliage.

[(R) (P) (VF) ◑ R⬚ AL]   4′ × 3′   1.2 m × 90 cm

'Sadler's Wells' [Hybrid Musk]

Beales UK 1983
'Penelope' × 'Rose Gaujard'
Semi-double flowers of white heavily laced with cherry-red are borne in large clusters. The red intensifies in the autumn. Foliage dark green and glossy on an upright and bushy plant.
[(C) (P) (H) (SF) ⬤ ▽ ✕ AL]
4′ × 3′   1.2 m × 90 cm

'Sally Holmes' [Modern Shrub]

Holmes UK 1976
'Ivory Fashion' × 'Ballerina'
Large, tightly packed clusters of single, ivory-buff blooms with highlights of soft pink. Foliage dark green and glossy. Growth bushy.
[(C) (P) (H) (SF) ▽ AL]   4′ × 3′   1.2 m × 90 cm

'Sarah Van Fleet' [Rugosa Hybrid]

Van Fleet USA 1926
Parentage unknown
Its rich rose-pink and pointed buds open to attrac-
tive semi-double flowers in clusters. Foliage rugose and leathery, the stems thorny. Growth bushy.
[(C) (P) (H) (VF) ⬤ R⬚ AW]
4′ × 3′   1.2 m × 90 cm

'Scabrosa' [Rugosa Hybrid]

Origin and parentage unknown – prior to 1939
Introduced by Harkness UK 1950
The large, single, mauve-deep-pink to red flowers have prominent soft yellow anthers. Large, round red hips follow them. Foliage dark green, glossy and rugose. Growth upright and bushy.
[(C) (P) (H) (VF) ⬤ AW]   6′ × 4′   1.8 × 1.2 m

Top: 'Sally Holmes' and *bottom:* 'Sarah Van Fleet'

Above: Hips of 'Scabrosa' (see text p. 241)
Below: 'Scharlachglut'

'Scharlachglut', 'Scarlet Fire' [Gallica Hybrid]

Kordes GERMANY 1952
'Poinsettia' × 'Alika'
The large, single, velvety-red flowers have pronounced stamens and are freely produced on a vigorous plant with dark green, semi-glossy foliage. Urn-shaped hips follow in the autumn.
[(S) (P) (SF) (T) ⦿ (CL) AL]   10′ × 6′   3 × 1.8 m

'Schneezwerg', 'Snowdwarf' [Rugosa Hybrid]

Lambert GERMANY 1912
Parentage unknown
Its semi-double, pure white flowers display clear yellow stamens to advantage when fully open. The flowers are often followed by round red hips. Foliage greyish-green, semi-glossy and rugose, the stems very thorny. Growth upright and bushy.
[(R) (P) (H) (MF) ⦿ ▽ AW]   5′ × 4′   1.5 × 1.2 m

'Sealing Wax' [Moyesii Hybrid]

Royal Horticultural Society UK 1938
An *R. moyesii* hybrid
The large, bright red, single flowers have pronounced stamens. Large, flagon-shaped red hips follow on. Foliage grey-green on an upright and vigorous plant.
[(S) (P) (H) ⦿ AL]   8′ × 5′   2.5 × 1.5 m

'Schoener's Nutkana' [Nutkana Hybrid]

Schoener USA 1930
R. nutkana × 'Paul Neyron'
Large, single, clear pink flowers are produced on an arching shrub with plentiful, mid-green foliage. It is almost thornless.
[(S) (P) (H) (VF) ⦿ AL]   6′ × 3′   1.8 m × 90 cm

*'Sir Walter Raleigh' (Ausspry)
[Modern Shrub]

Austin UK 1985
Parentage unknown
Its peony-like flowers, cupped with open centres

Top: 'Sophie's Perpetual' (see text p. 244) and *bottom:* 'Schneezwerg'

'Thérèse Bugnet'

'Vanguard' (see text p. 246)

'Uncle Walter'

'Variegata di Bologna' (see text p. 246)

displaying golden stamens, are clear warm pink. Foliage large and mid-green. Growth bushy.

[(C) (H) (VF) ▽ AL] 4′ × 4′ 1.2 × 1.2 m

'Skyrocket' *see* 'Wilhelm'

'Sophie's Perpetual' [Hybrid China]

Origin and parentage unknown – prior to 1928
Reintroduced by Mr Humphrey Brooke UK 1960
Of soft pink overlaid with deeper pink and cherry-red, the flowers are globular, cupped and are produced in small clusters. Foliage dark green on an upright, almost thornless, plant.

[(C) (SF) (CL) ▽ ✂ AL] 8′ × 4′ 2.5 × 1.2 m

'Sparrieshoop' [Eglanteria Hybrid]

Kordes GERMANY 1953
('Baby Château' × 'Else Poulsen') × 'Magnifica'
Produces clusters of large, single, bright pink blooms with golden stamens and wavy petals. Foliage plentiful, mid-green and leathery. Growth upright and bushy.

[(R) (P) (H) (VF) ◗ AL] 5′ × 4′ 1.5 × 1.2 m

'Spray "Cécile Brünner"' *see* 'Bloomfield Abundance'

'St Nicholas' [Damask]

Found by Mr R. James 1950
Possibly a chance seedling of a Damask rose × a Gallica
The clear rich pink, semi-double blooms come in small clusters with greyish-green, matt foliage on an upright plant.

[(S) (H) (VF) AL] 3′ × 3′ 90 × 90 cm

'The Reeve' [Modern Shrub]

Austin UK 1979
'Lilian Austin' × 'Chaucer'
Its deep pink, very double flowers are in the old-fashioned style and are produced in clusters. Reddish-green foliage. Growth bushy, spreading.

[(R) (H) (VF) ▽ ✂ AL] 4′ × 4′ 1.2 × 1.2 m

*'The Secford Rose' (Korpinrob) [Rugosa Hybrid]

Kordes GERMANY 1987

'Wilhelm' (see text p. 246)

A pink form of 'Robusta' which is identical in all respects except colour.

[(C) (P) (H) (VF) ⊽ ◑ AL] 5′ × 4′ 1.5 × 1.2 m

'The Wife of Bath' [Modern Shrub]

Austin UK 1969
'Mme Caroline Testout' × ('Ma Perkins' × 'Constance Spry')
Its flowers are deep rose-pink with a paler reverse, semi-double and cupped. Foliage small and mid-green. Growth compact and bushy.

[(C) (H) (VF) (B) ⊽ ✕ AW] 3′ × 2′ 90 × 60 cm

'The Yeoman' [Modern Shrub]

Austin UK 1969
'Ivory Fashion' × ('Constance Spry' × 'Monique')
The very full, flattish flowers are salmon-pink and apricot. Mid-green foliage on a compact bush.

[(C) (H) (VF) (B) ⊽ ✕ AL] 3′ × 2′ 90 × 60 cm

'Thérèse Bugnet' [Rugosa Hybrid]

Bugnet USA 1950
[(*R. acicularis* × *R. rugosa kamtchatica*) × (*R. amblyotis* × *R. rugosa plena*)] × 'Betty Bland'

Its fully double flowers, their centre petals muddled, are large and deep rose-pink, and come amid plentiful greyish-green foliage. Growth upright and bushy, with only a few thorns.

[(R) (H) (MF) ◑ ⊽ AL] 6′ × 6′ 1.8 × 1.8 m

'Till Uhlenspiegel' [Eglanteria Hybrid]

Kordes GERMANY 1950
'Holstein' × 'Magnifica'
The single, bright red flowers with white centres are produced in large clusters. Foliage large and glossy, dark green with a reddish tinge. Growth arching and vigorous.

[(S) (P) (H) (MF) (CL) ◑ AL] 10′ × 8′ 3 × 2.5 m

'Uncle Walter' (Macon) [Modern Shrub]

McGredy UK 1963
'Brilliant' × 'Heidelberg'
Shapely, Hybrid-Tea-like, dark red blooms are borne in clusters and very freely produced. They will reach exhibition size if disbudded. The large, leathery, mid-green foliage is tinged copper when young, on an upright plant.

[(C) (P) (H) (B) (E) ⊽ AW] 5′ × 4′ 1.5 × 1.2 m

'Yesterday'

'Vanguard' [Rugosa Hybrid]

Stevens USA 1932
(*R. wichuraiana* × *R. rugosa alba*) × 'Eldorado'
The very large, fully double, orange-apricot to salmon blooms are highly scented. Foliage light green and very glossy. Growth upright, bushy and vigorous.

[(R) (P) (H) (VF) ◑ AL]   8′ × 6′   2.5 × 1.8 m

'Variegata di Bologna' [Bourbon]

Bonfiglioli ITALY 1909
Parentage unknown
Large, globular, cupped blooms of white laced and striped purple. Foliage mid-green, leathery. Growth upright.

[(R) (VF) ▽ ✕ M ◀⊞ AL]   6′ × 5′   1.8 × 1.5 m

'Wilhelm', 'Skyrocket' [Hybrid Musk]

Kordes GERMANY .1934
'Robin Hood' × 'J. C. Thornton'
Its large clusters of dark red, semi-double blooms are very freely produced. Foliage dark green and glossy. Growth vigorous, upright.

[(C) (H) (SF) (CL) ▽ AL]   5′ × 4′   1.5 × 1.2 m

'William and Mary' [Modern Shrub]

Beales UK 1988
Seedling × 'Constance Spry'
With large, fully double, blowsy blooms in the old-fashioned form. They are deep silvery-pink with crimson and carmine highlights, produced singly and in clusters. Foliage greyish-green and matt. Growth bushy and upright.

[(S) (P) (H) (VF) (CL) ✕ AL]   6′ × 4′   1.8 × 1.2 m

*'William Shakespeare' (Ausroyal) [Modern Shrub]

Austin UK 1987
Parentage unknown
Fully double flowers in the old-fashioned style of rich crimson turning to purple with age. Foliage dark green. Growth bushy.

[(C) (H) (VF) (B) ▽ ✕ AL]   4′ × 3′   1.2 m × 90 cm

'Yesterday', 'Topis d'Orient' [Modern Shrub]

Harkness UK 1974
('Phyllis Bide' × 'Shepherd's Delight') × 'Ballerina'
Produces very large clusters of small, semi-double, lilac-pink flowers with golden stamens. Small, dark green foliage on a compact and bushy plant.

[(C) (H) (SF) (B) ▽ AW]   4′ × 4′   1.2 × 1.2 m

Procumbent Shrub Roses (Ground-Cover Roses)

Roses have been planted for ground cover since the nineteenth century. In those days, however, the main source of material were the relaxed ramblers such as the Ayrshires and the Evergreens (the Sempervirens). Later, mostly during the first two decades of this century, the introduction of the flexible Wichuraiana hybrids provided a greater range of colour. The weakness of most ramblers is, of course, their relatively short flowering season, which means that, although they are ideal for covering banks and mounds, they are seldom used for this purpose today; the more's the pity. Since the Second World War, and with landscape gardeners demanding cost-effective plants, ground-cover roses have been in great demand and breeders have not been slow to react, developing a steadily increasing number of both once-flowering and remontant varieties.

Personally, I have never been happy with the term 'ground cover' for roses of any kind. Although I accept that some are suitable for the purpose, very few that I know are sufficiently dense to suppress weeds in the same way as more traditional ground-cover plants such as *Hypericum calcinum* and *Vinca major*. In fact, spreading roses can make weed-infested ground more rather than less difficult to cultivate, and so may create a problem rather than solve one. I prefer the term 'procumbent' which adequately describes their habit with no misleading connotations.

Procumbent roses can be used in a variety of ways. They are most commonly planted for massed displays to give colour to municipal and industrial landscapes. In the garden they can serve useful purposes on banks or in beds where too much height is undesirable. They also look good planted in groups to provide colour lower down in shrubberies and many are excellent grown in tubs, pots or urns, or cascading down from short walls or troughs. One or two smaller varieties make fine rockery subjects.

One clear advantage of this type of rose is that many flourish on their own roots, thus eliminating any difficulties in removing suckers.

Most modern catalogues and, indeed, most decent garden suppliers now offer a considerable range of these roses; it has not been an easy task to choose those for inclusion here. The forty or so selected are, however, a fair cross-section of old and new, and most can be obtained without difficulty.

'Alba Meidiland' (Meiflopan)
[Procumbent Shrub]

Meilland FRANCE 1987
Parentage unknown
With tight, heavy clusters of pure white and fully double flowers, which are good for cutting. Foliage mid-green. Growth dense and spreading.

[(C) (GC) (H) (SF) ◐ ▽ ✕ AL]
3′ × 4′   90 cm × 1.2 m

'Bonica '82' (Meidomonac)
[Procumbent Shrub]

Meilland FRANCE 1982
(*R. sempervirens* × 'Mlle Marthe Carron') × 'Picasso'
Very large clusters of bright pink, fully double flowers paling to soft pink towards the edges of the petals. Foliage plentiful, small, dark green and semi-glossy on a broad, bushy plant. (Not to be confused with 'Bonica', a red rose from Meilland, 1958.)

[(C) (GC) (P) (SF) ▽ ✕ AW]
3′ × 6′   90 cm × 1.8 m

'Candy Rose' (Meiranovi) [Procumbent Shrub]

Meilland FRANCE 1980
(*R. sempervirens* × 'Mlle Marthe Carron') × [('Lilli Marlene' × 'Evelyn Fison') × ('Orange Sweetheart' × 'Frühlingsmorgen')]
Semi-double flowers of deep pink with a reddish reverse. Foliage small, light green and glossy. Growth bushy and spreading.

[(C) (GC) (P) ▽ AL]   4′ × 6′   1.2 × 1.8 m

'Cardinal Hume' (Harregale)
[Procumbent Shrub]

Harkness UK 1984
[[(Seedling × ('Orange Sensation' × 'Allgold')] × *R. californica*)] × 'Frank Naylor'
Small, double, cupped, purple flowers of medium size are carried in large clusters with matt, mid-green foliage. Growth tall and spreading, the stems thorny. Abundant, roundish hips in the autumn.

[(S) (GC) (VF) (P) ◐ AL]   3′ × 4′   90 cm × 1.2 m

'Caterpillar' *see* 'Pink Drift'

'Daisy Hill' [*R. macrantha* Hybrid]

Kordes GERMANY 1906
R. macrantha hybrid
Large, single, pink flowers are produced singly or

'Bonica '82'

'Candy Rose' and *below:* 'Cardinal Hume'

in small clusters, with plentiful round hips in the autumn. Foliage mid-green. Of tall and spreading growth, the stems thorny.

[(S) (GC) (VF) (P) ◐ AL]   5′ × 8′   1.5 × 2.5 m

'Dunwich Rose', *R. dunwichensis*
[Form of *R. pimpinellifolia*]

Discovered growing on sand dunes at Dunwich, Suffolk, 1956

A most useful rose, its medium-sized, soft yellow, single flowers have prominent stamens and are produced singly all along arching branches. Foliage light green and fern-like, with many spiky thorns. There is some evidence that this rose could have been growing as a garden variety in the late nineteenth century.

[(S) (P) (GC) (SF) ◐ AL]   2' × 4'   60 cm × 1.2 m

'Euphrates' (Harunique)

Harkness UK 1986
Hulthemia persica × unknown
Small, single flowers of reddish-pink are borne in small clusters. The foliage is small, variable in shape and light green. Growth prickly, low and spreading. An unusual rose.

[(C) (P) (GC) ◐ AL]   1½' × 3'   45 × 90 cm

'Eyeopener' (Interop) [Procumbent Shrub]

Ilsink NETHERLANDS 1987
(Seedling × 'Eyepaint') × (Seedling × 'Dortmund')

Its bright red flowers have white centres. Foliage dense and mid-green on a vigorous, spreading bush.

[(C) (P) (GC) ◐ AL]   1' × 3'   30 × 90 cm

'Fairy Changeling' (Harnumerous)
[Polyantha-type Procumbent]

Harkness UK 1981
'The Fairy' × 'Yesterday'
Plump little buds open to small, cupped, fully double flowers of clear soft pink in large trusses. Foliage small, dark green and semi-glossy. Growth bushy and spreading.

[(C) (P) (CG) (SF) ▽ AL]   1½' × 2'   45 × 60 cm

'Fairy Damsel' (Harneatly)
[Polyantha-type Procumbent]

Harkness UK 1981
'The Fairy' × 'Yesterday'
Dark red, small, double flowers, cupped at first then flattish in large trusses. Foliage dark green and glossy. Growth bushy and spreading.

[(C) (P) (GC) (SF) ▽ AL]   2' × 5'   60 cm × 1.5 m

'Dunwich Rose'

'Fairy Damsel' (see text p. 249)

'Fairyland' and *below:* 'Fiona'

'Fairyland' (Harlayalong)
[Polyantha-type Procumbent]

Harkness UK 1980
'The Fairy' × 'Yesterday'
Soft pink, cupped, small, fully double flowers
are borne in large trusses. Foliage mid-green and
glossy. Growth bushy and spreading.

[(C) (P) (GC) (SF) ▽ AL]   2′ × 5′   60 cm × 1.5 m

'Ferdy' (Keitoli) [Procumbent Shrub]

Suzuki JAPAN 1984
Climbing seedling × a 'Petite Folie' seedling
It has deep salmon-pink flowers, small and fully
double. Foliage small, plentiful and light green.
Growth bushy, spreading and dense.

[(C) (P) (GC) ▽ AW]   2′ × 3′   60 × 90 cm

'Fiona' (Meibeluxen)

Meilland FRANCE 1982
'Sea Foam' × 'Picasso'
Large clusters of dark red flowers, slightly paler in
the centre. Smallish, dark green and glossy foliage.
Growth bushy and spreading.

[(C) (P) (GC) (MF) (H) ▽ AW]
3′ × 4′   90 cm × 1.2 m

Left: 'Grouse' and *above:* 'Max Graf'

'Grouse', 'Immensee' (Korimro)
[Prostrate Shrub]

Kordes GERMANY 1982
'The Fairy' × an *R. wichuraiana* seedling
Clusters of small, single, white flowers with pink blushes and prominent stamens. Foliage mid-green and glossy on a prostrate, spreading plant.

[(R) (P) (GC) (MF) ❿ AW]   2′ × 10′   60 cm × 3 m

'Harry Maasz' [Procumbent Shrub]

Kordes GERMANY 1939
'Barcelona' × 'Daisy Hill'
The large, single, deep pink flowers have white centres and are cupped, with prominent stamens. Foliage wrinkled, leathery and dark green, the stems thorny. Growth tall and spreading.

[(S) (P) (VF) ❿ AL]   5′ × 8′   1.5 × 2.5 m

'Heidekönigin *see* 'Pheasant'

'Immensee' *see* 'Grouse'

'Harry Maasz'

'Paulii' (see text p. 255) and *below:* 'Paulii Rosea' (see text p. 255)

'Lady Curzon' [Rugosa Hybrid]

Turner UK 1901
R. macrantha × R. rugosa rubra

Its large, single, pink flowers have pronounced stamens. Large, dark green foliage comes on an arching bush, the stems heavily endowed with thorns.

[(C) (P) (VF) (GC) ◐ ▽ AL]   3′ × 6′   90 cm × 1.8 m

'Max Graf' (Prostrate Shrub) [Rugosa Hybrid]

Bowditch USA 1919
Probably *R. rugosa × R. wichuraiana*
Single flowers of bright silvery-pink with golden stamens. Foliage dark green, glossy and rugose, the stems thorny, and of a spreading habit. An important rose which is part of the pedigree of some of the Kordes climbers.

[(S) (GC) (P) ◐ AW]   2′ × 8′   60 cm × 2.5 m

'Nozomi' [Procumbent Shrub]

Onodera JAPAN 1968
'Fairy Princess' × 'Sweet Fairy'
Small, single, star-like flowers of pearly-pink come in small trusses. The foliage is very small, plentiful, dark green and glossy, with arching plum-coloured young stems, the older wood dark green. Growth very dense and spreading.

[(S) (GC) (P) (H) ◐ ▽ AW]   3′ × 6′   90 cm × 1.8 m

'Partridge', 'Weisse Immensee' (Korweirim) [Prostrate Shrub]

Kordes GERMANY 1984
'The Fairy' × an *R. wichuraiana* seedling
Small, single, white flowers come from pink buds in clusters. Foliage small, dark green and glossy, though bronzy when young. Growth prostrate and spreading.

[(R) (P) (GC) (MF) ◐ AL]   2′ × 10′   60 cm × 3 m

'Pearl Drift'

'Pink Bells'

'Paulii', *R. × paulii* [Prostrate Shrub]

Paul UK *c.* 1903

R. arvensis × R. rugosa

The large, single, white flowers have five spaced petals and prominent yellow stamens. Foliage slender, rugose, light to mid-green, the young wood pinkish, and with many thorns. Growth prostrate.

[(S) (GC) (SF) ◐ M⬛⬚ AL]   3′ × 10′   90 cm × 3 m

'Paulii Rosea', *R. × paulii rosea*

Origin unknown *c.* 1912

A possible sport from 'Paulii', but there are many differences

The large, single, soft rose-pink flowers, their petals less spread than 'Paulii', have pronounced yellow stamens. Foliage mid-green and rugose, the stems thorny. Young wood is lime-green. Its growth is prostrate but denser than 'Paulii'.

[(S) (GC) (SF) M⬛⬚ AL]   3′ × 10′   90 cm × 3 m

'Pearl Drift' (Leggab) [Procumbent Shrub]

LeGrice UK 1980

'Mermaid' × 'New Dawn'

Sizeable, semi-double, white flowers flushed pink are borne in large trusses. Foliage dark green and semi-glossy. Growth dense, bushy and spreading.

[(C) (P) (GC) (MF) ◐ ▽ AW]
3′ × 4′   90 cm × 1.2 m

'Pheasant', 'Heidekönigin' (Kordapt) [Prostrate Shrub]

Kordes GERMANY 1986

'Zwerkonig '78' × an *R. wichuraiana* seedling

Modest clusters of small, deep rose-pink, double flowers, with mid-green and glossy foliage on a plant of prostrate, spreading growth.

[(R) (P) (GC) (MF) ◐ AL]   2′ × 10′   60 cm × 3 m

'Pink Bells' (Poulbells) [Procumbent Shrub]

Poulsen DENMARK 1983

'Mini-Poul' × 'Temple Bells'

Small, fully double, bright pink flowers are borne in profusion. Foliage mid-green, semi-glossy, small but plentiful. Growth dense and spreading.

[(S) (P) (GC) (SF) ◐ ▽ AW]   2′ × 4′   60 cm × 1.2 m

'Pink Drift', 'Kiki Rose', 'Caterpillar' (Poulcat) [Procumbent Shrub]

Poulsen DENMARK 1984

'Temple Bells' × a seedling

Large trusses of small, semi-double, light pink

'Raubritter' (see text p. 256)

'Red Blanket'

blooms are freely produced. Foliage plentiful, small, dark green and glossy. Growth bushy and spreading.

[(C) (P) (GC) (MF) ◐ ▽ AL]   2' × 3'   60 × 90 cm

'Pink Meidiland', 'Schloss Heidegg' (Meipoque) [Procumbent Shrub]

Meilland FRANCE 1983
'Anne de Bretagne' × 'Nirvana'
The single flowers of deep pink have a white eye. Foliage smallish, mid-green and semi-glossy. A bushy, spreading habit of growth.

[(C) (GC) (H) (SF) ◐ ▽ AW]   2' × 3'   60 × 90 cm

'Pink Wave' (Mattgro) [Procumbent Shrub]

Mattock UK 1983
'Moon Maiden' × 'Eyepaint'
Soft pink, semi-double flowers are borne in clusters. Foliage mid-green and semi-glossy. Growth bushy and spreading.

[(C) (P) (GC) (MF) ◐ ▽ AL]   2' × 3'   60 × 90 cm

'Raubritter', 'Macrantha Raubritter' [Macrantha Hybrid]

Kordes GERMANY 1936
'Daisy Hill' × 'Solarium'
Numerous small clusters of cupped, fully double, clear rose-pink flowers are produced along slender arching branches, a beautiful sight when in full flush. The greyish-green foliage is rather coarse. Growth bushy and spreading.

[(S) (P) ◐ ▽ M ▥ AL]   3' × 6'   90 cm × 1.8 m

'Red Bells' (Poulred) [Procumbent Shrub]

Poulsen DENMARK 1983
'Mini-Poul' × 'Temple Bells'
Small, fully double, red flowers are produced in great abundance. Foliage mid-green, semi-glossy, small and plentiful. Growth dense and spreading.

[(S) (P) (GC) (SF) ◐ ▽ AL]   2' × 4'   60 cm × 1.2 m

'Red Blanket' (Intercel) [Procumbent Shrub]

Ilsink NETHERLANDS 1979
'Yesterday' × an unnamed seedling
The flowers, semi-double and medium-sized, are

borne in small clusters and are deep pink to almost red. Foliage dark green and glossy. Growth dense and spreading.

[(C) (P) (GC) (SF) ◐ ▽ BS◀▦ AW]
3′ × 4′   90 cm × 1.2 m

'Red Max Graf' (see text p. 258) and *right:* 'Rosy Cushion' (see text p. 258)

'Simon Robinson' (see text p. 258)

'Red Max Graf', 'Rote Max Graf' (Kormax)
[Prostrate Shrub]

Kordes GERMANY 1980
R. kordesii × a seedling
Bright red, medium-sized, single flowers are borne in large clusters. The abundant foliage is matt, dark green and leathery on a coarsely spreading plant.

[(C) (P) (GC) (SF) ◐ AW]   3′ × 6′   90 cm × 1.8 m

'Repens Meidiland' (Meilontig)
[Prostrate Shrub]

Meilland FRANCE 1987
Parentage unknown
Small, single, white flowers come in profusion. Foliage small, mid-green and glossy. Growth very prostrate and vigorous.

[(S) (P) (GC) ◐ AL]   6′ × 10′   1.8 × 3 m

'Rosy Carpet' (Intercarp) [Procumbent Shrub]

Ilsink NETHERLANDS 1983
'Yesterday' × a seedling
Light pink, single blooms are very freely produced in large clusters. Foliage dark green and glossy. Growth prickly, dense and spreading.

[(R) (P) (GC) (MF) ◐ ▽ AL]
2′ × 4′   60 cm × 1.2 m

'Rosy Cushion' (Interall) [Procumbent Shrub]

Ilsink NETHERLANDS 1979
'Yesterday' × a seedling
Soft pink, almost single blooms are borne in large clusters. Foliage dark green and glossy. Growth dense, bushy and spreading.

[(R) (P) (GC) (SF) ◐ ▽ AW]
3′ × 4′   90 cm × 1.2 m

'Scarlet Meidiland' (Meikrotal)
[Procumbent Shrub]

Meilland FRANCE 1987
Parentage unknown
Heavy clusters of bright cherry-red flowers, with dark green, glossy foliage on a dense and spreading bush. Particularly good in the autumn.

[(C) (GC) (H) (SF) ◐ ▽ ✂ AL]
3′ × 4′   90 cm × 1.2 m

'Scintillation' [Procumbent Shrub]

Austin UK 1967
R. macrantha × 'Vanity'
Semi-double, pink blooms in large clusters, with

matt, dark green foliage on a vigorous and spreading plant.

[(R) (P) (GC) (VF) ◐ AL]   4′ × 8′   1.2 × 2.5 m

'Simon Robinson' (Trobwich)
[Procumbent Shrub]

Robinson UK 1982
R. wichuraiana × 'New Penny'
Medium to small, single, mid-pink flowers are borne in clusters. Foliage dark green and glossy. Growth bushy and spreading.

[(C) (P) (GC) (SF) ◐ ▽ AL]
2½′ × 4′   75 cm × 1.2 m

'Smarty' (Intersmart) [Procumbent Shrub]

Ilsink NETHERLANDS 1979
'Yesterday' × a seedling
Large clusters of almost single, smallish blooms of light pink. Foliage bright green and matt-finished. Growth quite thorny, bushy and spreading.

[(R) (P) (GC) (SF) ◐ ▽ AL]   3′ × 4′   90 cm × 1.2 m

'Snow Carpet' (Maccarpe)
[Miniature Spreading Shrub]

McGredy NEW ZEALAND 1980
'New Penny' × 'Temple Bells'
Small, very double, pure white flowers are produced in small clusters. Foliage small, light green and semi-glossy. Growth prostrate and spreading.

[(R) (MF) (GC) ◐ AW]   1′ × 3′   30 × 90 cm

'Swany' (Meiburenac) [Procumbent Shrub]

Meilland FRANCE 1978
R. sempervirens × 'Mlle Marthe Carron'
Yields large clusters of very double, cupped flowers of pure white. Foliage dark green and glossy with bronze overtones. Growth vigorous, bushy and spreading.

[(C) (P) (GC) ◐ ▽ AW]   3′ × 5′   90 cm × 1.5 m

'Tall Story' (Dickooky) [Procumbent Shrub]

Dickson UK 1984
'Sunsprite' × 'Yesterday'
Medium-sized, soft yellow, semi-double flowers come in clusters along arching branches. Foliage light green and semi-glossy on an arching and spreading plant.

[(C) (P) (GC) (VF) ◐ ▽ AL]   2′ × 4′   60 cm × 1.2 m

'Temple Bells' [Prostrate Miniature]

Morey USA 1971

R. wichuraiana × 'Blushing Jewel'

Small, single, white flowers open in profusion at first, then spasmodically. Foliage small and light green. Its hugging, prostrate growth makes this rose well suited to rockeries.

[(R) (GC) ◑ ▽ AW]   2′ × 4′   60 cm × 1.2 m

'The Fairy' [Procumbent Polyantha]

Bentall UK 1932

'Paul Crampel' × 'Lady Gay'

Large trusses of small, double flowers are produced in great abundance on a spreading, bushy plant with plentiful, mid-green, glossy foliage. A superb and useful rose.

[(C) (P) (B) (SF) (GC) ◑ ▽ ✕ AW]
2′ × 4′   60 cm × 1.2 m

'Weisse Immensee' *see* 'Partridge'

'White Bells' (Poulwhite)
[Procumbent Shrub]

Poulsen DENMARK 1983

'Mini-Poul' × 'Temple Bells'

The white, fully double flowers have hints of soft

Top: 'White Bells'

yellow. Foliage small, mid-green and semi-glossy. Growth dense, bushy and spreading.

[(S) (P) (GC) (SF) ◑ ▽ AW]   2′ × 4′   60 cm × 1.2 m

'White Max Graf', 'Weisse Max Graf' (Korgram) [Procumbent Shrub]

Kordes GERMANY 1983

Seedling × an *R. wichuraiana* seedling

Pure white, single flowers, slightly cupped, in clusters. Foliage light green and semi-glossy. Growth vigorous and spreading.

[(C) (GC) (H) (SF) ◑ ▽ AW]
3′ × 6′   90 cm × 1.8 m

'White Meidiland' (Meicoublan)
[Procumbent Shrub]

Meilland FRANCE 1986

Parentage unknown

Bears pure white flowers in clusters on a bushy, spreading plant with plentiful, smallish, mid-green and semi-glossy foliage.

[(C) (GC) (H) (SF) ◑ ▽ AW]
2′ × 4′   60 cm × 1.2 m

Dwarf Polyantha Roses

From the beginning of this century until the early 1940s, Dwarf Polyanthas reigned supreme as bedding roses and many new varieties were introduced. Ironically, they only lost their supremacy when they were put to stud with the Hybrid Teas and became parents to the larger-flowered Hybrid Polyanthas. As their popularity has declined their numbers have inevitably dwindled and several good varieties are now lost for ever. Those that remain are fairly widely available and I have briefly described most of them here. Several are sports from others, mainly 'Orléans Rose'. Their colours are, in fact, rather unstable, and variations can occur within a flower-cluster from time to time.

These little roses are very easy to grow and have numerous uses, from massed display to hedging and edging. In groups, they look most effective among herbaceous plants and are quite at home providing prolonged colour at the front of shrubberies. They also make useful, decorative plants in tubs, urns and other containers, and they are not at all out of place in modern settings; in fact, when planted closely, they readily take on the role of a 'Patio' rose (a term for the 'Compact Floribundas' described in the next section). They also last quite well in water when they are cut and taken indoors.

'Cameo' [Dwarf Polyantha]

de Ruiter NETHERLANDS 1932
Sport from 'Orléans Rose'
Clear salmon-pink, semi-double and cupped flowers are carried in large clusters with bright green foliage on a bushy plant.
[(C) (P) (H) (B) ◕ ▽ AL]   2′ × 2′   60 × 60 cm

'Coral Cluster' [Dwarf Polyantha]

Murrell UK 1920
Sport from 'Orléans Rose'
Similar to 'Cameo' but with coral-pink flowers.
[(C) (P) (H) (B) ◕ ▽ AL]   2′ × 2′   60 × 60 cm

'Gloria Mundi' [Dwarf Polyantha]

de Ruiter NETHERLANDS 1929
Sport from 'Superb'
Striking orange-red semi-double flowers are borne

in large clusters, individual flowers being slightly larger than those of 'Cameo'.
[(C) (P) (H) (B) ◕ ▽ AL]   2′ × 2′   60 × 60 cm

'Golden Salmon Supérieur', 'Golden Salmon Improved' [Dwarf Polyantha]

de Ruiter NETHERLANDS 1929
Sport from 'Golden Salmon', in turn a sport from 'Superb'
With its large trusses of blooms this rose is similar to 'Gloria Mundi' but brighter.
[(C) (P) (H) (B) ◕ ▽ AL]   2′ × 2′   60 × 60 cm

'Katharina Zeimet', 'White Baby Rambler' [Dwarf Polyantha]

Lambert GERMANY 1901
'Etoile de Mai' × 'Marie Pavié'
Small, double blooms are borne in large clusters

'Cameo'

'Golden Salmon Supérieur' (see text p. 260) and *right:* 'Paul Crampel'

'Miss Edith Cavell' and *below:* 'Yvonne Rabier'

on a twiggy, short bush with sparse, light green foliage.

[(C) (P) (H) (B) ◗ ▽ AL]   2' × 2'   60 × 60 cm

'Marie-Jeanne' [Polyantha]

Turbat FRANCE 1913
Parentage unknown
Very large clusters of semi-double, cupped flowers

of creamy-white with hints of soft pink. Good, mid-green foliage. Growth bushy and a little taller than most Polyanthas.

[(C) (P) (H) (B) ◗ ▽ AL]   2½' × 2'   75 × 60 cm

'Miss Edith Cavell', 'Edith Cavell', 'Nurse Cavell' [Dwarf Polyantha]

de Ruiter NETHERLANDS 1917
Sport from 'Orléans Rose'
Large trusses of scarlet-crimson flowers, overlaid with crimson, semi-double and very pretty. Foliage darkish green. Growth bushy.

[(C) (P) (H) (B) ◗ ▽ AL]   2' × 2'   60 × 60 cm

'Paul Crampel' [Dwarf Polyantha]

Kersbergen NETHERLANDS 1930
Parentage unknown
Deep, rich orange bordering on scarlet in large trusses of semi-double, cupped flowers. Foliage mid-green. Growth bushy.

[(C) (P) (H) (B) ◗ ▽ AL]   2' × 2'   60 × 60 cm

'The Fairy' *see* Procumbent Roses

'Yvonne Rabier' [Polyantha]

Turbat FRANCE 1910
R. wichuraiana × a Polyantha
Clusters of pure white, semi-double flowers with soft yellow centres and prominent stamens. The plentiful foliage is light green. Growth bushy and upright.

[(C) (P) (H) (B) ◗ ▽ AL]   2' × 2'   60 × 60 cm

Miniatures and Compact Floribundas

Miniature roses enjoyed brief popularity during the early years of the nineteenth century, but the colour range of the first varieties was limited and they soon fell from favour and disappeared from cultivation until rediscovery in 1918 (see 'Rouletii' page 274). Since then they have established themselves as a very important group and many hundreds of varieties have been raised and introduced; far too many to cover comprehensively, so I have selected 101, including some of the recent 'Patio' varieties (see page 79) – an unofficial classification for which I have substituted the term 'Compact Floribunda'. They are slightly more bushy and taller than Miniatures but shorter and of smaller proportions than the shorter Floribundas.

Both Miniatures and Compact Floribundas grow well on their own roots and, with the advent of micropropagation, more and more are being produced in this way. Own-root Miniatures are usually smaller than those produced by other methods of propagation such as grafting or budding, so it is wise to enquire how they have been grown before purchase. In the garden their uses are several, from close-density bedding and edging to group-planting among other subjects. They also make useful pot plants and will do well in window boxes. They never enjoy growing indoors as house plants.

'Air France', 'Rosy Meillandina', 'American Independence' (Meifinaro) [Miniature]

Meilland FRANCE 1982
'Minijet' × ('Darling Flame' × 'Perla de Montserrat')
Fully double blooms of medium size and clear rose-pink are carried in clusters. Foliage dark green. Growth bushy and upright.
[(C) ⛉ AW]   1′   30 cm

'Amorette' *see* 'Snowdrop'

'Amruda' *see* 'Red Ace'

'Angela Rippon', 'Ocaru', 'Ocarina' [Miniature]

de Ruiter NETHERLANDS 1978
'Rosy Jewel' × 'Zorina'
Largish blooms, fully double and coral-pink to salmon are borne in clusters on a bushy, compact plant with mid-green foliage.
[(C) (MF) ⛉ AW]   1′   30 cm

'Angelita' *see* 'Snowball'

'Anna Ford' (Harpiccolo)
[Compact Floribunda]

Harkness UK 1980
'Southampton' × 'Darling Flame'
Its orange-red flowers, with yellow deep down in their base, are semi-double and come in clusters. Foliage glossy and dark green. Growth dense and bushy, slightly spreading.
[(C) ⛉ ◗ AL]   1½′   45 cm

'Apricot Sunblaze', 'Mark One' (Savamark) [Compact Floribunda]

Saville USA 1984
'Sheri Anne' × 'Glenfiddich'
Bright orange-red blooms are borne profusely in small, compact clusters. Foliage glossy, on a plant of bushy, tidy and dense habit.

[(C) (B) (MF) ⛉ AW]   15″   38 cm

'Baby Darling' [Miniature]

Moore USA 1964
'Little Darling' × 'Magic Wand'
Apricot-orange flowers, quite large and double, come in medium-sized clusters, with mid-green foliage. Growth upright and bushy. Quite nice when cut for miniature flower arrangements.

[(C) (B) (SF) ⛉ ✂ AW]   1′   30 cm

'Baby Gold Star', 'Estrellita de Oro' [Miniature]

Dot SPAIN 1940
'Eduardo Toda' × 'Rouletii'
Sizeable, semi-double flowers of deep yellow bordering on apricot are borne in generous clusters, with plentiful small, mid-green foliage. Growth open and bushy.

[(C) (P) ⛉ BS⬣ AW]   1′   30 cm

'Baby Masquerade', 'Baby Carnaval', 'Tanbakede' (Tanba) [Miniature]

Tantau GERMANY 1956
'Peon' × 'Masquerade'
The almost double blooms, in sizeable clusters, are yellow with red, the red deepening with age. Foliage dark green, almost glossy, and leathery. Growth upright and bushy.

[(C) (P) (B) (SF) ⛉ ✂ AW]   1½′   45 cm

'Baby Sunrise' (Macparlez) [Miniature]

McGredy NEW ZEALAND 1984
'Benson & Hedges Special' × 'Moana'
Smallish, shapely blooms of apricot with coppery overtones, and semi-double, are borne in sizeable clusters. Foliage semi-glossy and mid-green on a bushy plant.

[(C) (SF) ⛉ AL]   1′   30 cm

'Benson & Hedges Special', 'Dorola' (Macshana) [Miniature]

McGredy NEW ZEALAND 1982
'Darling Flame' × 'Mabella'
Deep clear yellow, fully double and shapely flowers are produced in sizeable clusters. Foliage mid-green and semi-glossy. Growth bushy and upright.

[(C) (SF) ⛉ AW]   1′   30 cm

'Bianco' (Cocblanco) [Compact Floribunda]

Cocker UK 1983
'Darling Flame' × 'Jack Frost'
The fully double, pure white flowers come in clusters. The foliage is of fair size, mid-green and semi-glossy. Growth bushy and wide.

[(C) (GC) (SF) ⛉ AL]   1½′   45 cm

'Bit o'Sunshine' [Miniature]

Moore USA 1956
'Copper Glow' × 'Zee'
Semi-double flowers, shapely in bud and bright yellow, are carried in clusters. Foliage mid-green and semi-glossy. Growth upright and bushy.

[(C) (MF) ⛉ AW]   1′   30 cm

'Blue Peter', 'Azulabria', 'Bluenette' (Ruiblun) [Miniature]

de Ruiter NETHERLANDS 1983
'Little Flirt' × a seedling
Its full, lilac-purple blooms are in clusters. Foliage smallish, light green and semi-glossy on a bushy, upright plant.

[(C) (SF) ⛉ AW]   1′   30 cm

'Boys' Brigade' (Cocdinkum) [Compact Floribunda]

Cocker UK 1984
('Darling Flame' × 'Saint Alban') × ('Little Flirt' × 'Marlena')
The small, bright red flowers have a creamy-white eye and are in large clusters. Foliage mid-green and semi-glossy. Growth dense and bushy.

[(C) (P) (B) ⛉ AL]   1½′   45 cm

'Brass Ring' *see* 'Peek a boo'

'Cider Cup' (Dicladida) [Compact Floribunda]

Dickson UK 1988
Parentage unknown
Its shapely, Hybrid-Tea-like flowers of deep

'Air France' (see text p. 263)

'Anna Ford' (see text p. 263)

apricot are produced in clusters. Foliage mid-green and glossy. Growth bushy and wide.

[(C) (B) (H) ⊽ ✂ AL] 1½' 45 cm

'Cinderella' [Miniature]

de Vink NETHERLANDS 1953
'Cécile Brünner' × 'Peon'
Very double, slightly fluffy blooms of white tinged pink. Foliage light green. Growth dense, upright and almost thornless.

[(C) (P) (SF) ⊽ ✂ AW] 1' 30 cm

'Clarissa' (Harprocrustes) [Compact Floribunda]

Harkness UK 1983
'Southampton' × 'Darling Flame'
The shapely, high-centred blooms are very freely produced in large clusters. Foliage dark green and glossy. Growth dense and upright.

[(C) (P) (B) (H) ⊽ ✂ AW] 2' 60 cm

'Colibri' (Meimal) [Miniature]

Meilland FRANCE 1958
'Goldilocks' × 'Perla de Montserrat'
Buff-yellow flushed orange, double flowers come

'Apricot Sunblaze'

in medium-sized clusters. Foliage dark green and glossy on a plant of upright, bushy habit.

[(C) ▽ BS◀▥ AW]   1′   30 cm

'Colibri '79' (Meidanover) [Miniature]

Meilland FRANCE 1979
Parentage unknown
Its yellow flowers, heavily flushed pink and orange, and fully double, are produced in clusters. Foliage semi-glossy and mid-green. Growth upright and bushy.

[(C) (MF) ▽ AW]   1′   30 cm

'Conservation' (Cocdimple)
[Compact Floribunda]

Cocker UK 1986
[('Sabine' × 'Circus') × 'Maxi'] × 'Darling Flame']
The semi-double, shapely, apricot-pink blooms are in clusters. Foliage mid-green and glossy. Growth dense, bushy and wide.

[(C) (B) (SF) (GC) ▽ AL]   1½′   45 cm

'Coralin', 'Carolin', 'Carolyn', 'Karolyn', 'Perla Corail' [Miniature]

Dot SPAIN 1955
'Méphisto' × 'Perla de Alcañada'

Large, full, coral-pink blooms, variable to soft red in some conditions. They are produced in clusters. Foliage mid-green and semi-glossy. Growth upright and bushy.

[(C) (MF) ▽ AW]   15″   38 cm

'Cricri', 'Gavolda' (Meicri) [Miniature]

Meilland FRANCE 1958
('Alain' × 'Independence') × 'Perla de Alcañada'
Clusters of small, fully double, rosette flowers of soft salmon shaded coral on an upright plant with leathery, mid-green foliage.

[(C) (P) (B) ▽ AW]   1′   30 cm

'Dainty Dinah' (Cocamond)
[Compact Floribunda]

Cocker UK 1981
'Anne Cocker' × 'Wee Man'
Soft salmon-pink, semi-double and shapely blooms in clusters. Foliage mid-green and semi-glossy. Growth bushy and wide.

[(C) (B) (SF) ▽ AL]   1½′   45 cm

'Boy's Brigade' (see text p. 264)

'Cider Cup' (see text p. 264)

'Clarissa' (see text p. 265)

'Darling Flame', 'Minuette', 'Minuetto' (Meilucca) [Miniature]

Meilland FRANCE 1971
('Rimosa' × 'Rosina') × 'Zambra'
The double, shapely flowers of orange-red have pronounced yellow stamens when fully open and are borne in large clusters. The foliage is dark green and glossy on an upright, bushy plant. This rose is between a Miniature and a Compact Floribunda in size and it has proved an outstanding parent to other Miniatures.

[(C) (P) (B) (SF) ☑ ✕ AW]   1½'   45 cm

'Dorola' *see* 'Benson & Hedges Special'

'Dresden Doll' [Miniature]

Moore USA 1975
'Fairy Moss' × an unnamed Moss rose seedling
Fairly large, semi-double, shell-pink flowers emerge from heavily mossed buds and are produced in clusters. Foliage plentiful, semi-glossy and leathery. Growth upright and bushy, the stems well mossed.

[(C) (P) (B) (MF) ☑ AW]   1'   30 cm

'Dwarfking', 'Zwergkönig' [Miniature]

Kordes GERMANY 1957
'World Fair' × 'Peon'
Clusters of semi-double, reddish-carmine blooms, which are initially cupped and are occasionally borne singly. Foliage dark green and glossy. Growth upright and slender.

[(C) (SF) ☑]   1'   30 cm

'Easter Morning', 'Easter Morn' [Miniature]

Moore USA 1960
'Golden Glow' × 'Zee'
Its very shapely buds are exquisitely scrolled until fully open, the flowers very full and ivory-white in medium-sized clusters. Foliage glossy. Growth upright and bushy.

[(C) ☑ AW]   1'   30 cm

'Eleanor' [Miniature]

Moore USA 1960
(*R. wichuraiana* × 'Floradora') × (Seedling × 'Zee')
The double, coral-pink flowers deepen with age and are produced in large clusters on an upright, bushy plant with glossy, mid-green foliage.

[(C) (SF) ☑ AW]   1'   30 cm

'Fashion Flame' [Miniature]

Moore USA 1977
'Little Darling' × 'Fire Princess'
Peachy-red to orange blooms, fully double, shapely and in clusters. Good, mid-green, leathery foliage. Growth bushy.

[(C) (S) ☑ AW]   1'   30 cm

'Finstar' *see* 'Mini Metro'

'Conservation' (see text p. 266)
and *right:* 'Cricri' (see text p. 266)

'Fire Princess' [Miniature]

Moore USA 1969
'Baccara' × 'Eleanor'
Full, medium-sized, orange-scarlet flowers. Mid-green and glossy foliage. Upright and bushy growth.
[(C) (SF) ▽ ⚔ AW]   1′   30 cm

'Freegold' *see* 'Penelope Keith'

'Gentle Touch' (Diclulu)
[Compact Floribunda]

Dickson UK 1986
Parentage unknown
Pale pink, the large clusters of shapely double flowers are borne on a compact, widish bush with good mid-green foliage.
[(C) (H) (SF) (GC) ▽ AL]   1′   30 cm

'Gold Coin' [Miniature]

Moore USA 1967
'Golden Glow' × 'Magic Wand'
Rich buttercup-yellow, semi-double to double flowers come in clusters. Foliage mid-green. Growth bushy and upright.
[(C) (MF) ▽ AL]   1′   30 cm

'Golden Angel' [Miniature]

Moore USA 1975
'Golden Glow' × ('Little Darling' × a seedling)
Very double, shapely flowers of deep yellow emerge from tiny round buds. Foliage matt-finished and mid-green on a bushy plant.
[(C) (VF) ▽ AL]   1′   30 cm

'Green Diamond' [Miniature]

Moore USA 1975
Polyantha × 'Sheri Anne'
Greenish soft pink, fully double, small flowers are borne in clusters. Foliage mid-green and leathery. Growth bushy and upright.
[(C) (SF) ▽ AL]   1′   30 cm

'Gypsy Jewel' [Miniature]

Moore USA 1975
'Little Darling' × 'Little Buckaroo'
Its shapely, large blooms are fully double and deep rose-pink. Foliage dark green and glossy. Growth bushy and upright.
[(C) ▽ ⚔ AL]   1′   30 cm

'Happy Hour' (Savanhour) [Miniature]

Saville USA 1983
('Tamango' × 'Yellow Jewel') × 'Zinger'

Semi-double, bright red flowers with a yellow centre are borne in large clusters. Foliage dark green and glossy. Growth bushy and spreading.

[(C) (MF) ▽ AL] 1' 30 cm

'Happy Thought' [Miniature]

Moore USA 1978

(*R. wichuraiana* × 'Floradora') × 'Sheri Anne'
The flowers blend pink, coral and yellow, and are fully double in clusters. Foliage mid-green and glossy on a bushy plant.

[(C) (SF) ▽ AW] 1' 30 cm

'Hombre' [Miniature]

Jolly USA 1982

'Humdinger' × 'Rise 'n' Shine'
The apricot-pink flowers have a paler reverse. They are fully double and high-centred, opening flat in clusters on a plant with mid-green, semi-glossy foliage and of bushy habit.

[(C) (SF) ▽ AW] 1' 30 cm

'Hula Girl' [Miniature]

Williams USA 1975

'Miss Hillcrest' × 'Mabel Dot'
The fully double flowers from long, pointed buds are bright orange-salmon. Foliage mid-green, glossy and leathery. Growth bushy.

[(C) (SF) ▽ AW] 1' 30 cm

'Judy Fischer' [Miniature]

Moore USA 1968

'Little Darling' × 'Magic Wand'
Fully double, deep pink, shapely flowers in clusters. Foliage a bronzy dark green. Growth bushy.

[(C) (SF) ▽ ✕ AW] 1' 30 cm

'June Time' [Miniature]

Moore USA 1963

(*R. wichuraiana* × 'Floradora') × [('Etoile Luisante' seedling × 'Red Ripples') × 'Zee')]
Very double, light pink flowers with a deeper reverse, in large clusters. Foliage mid-green and glossy. Growth bushy.

[(C) (SF) ▽ AW] 1' 30 cm

'Lavender Jewel' [Miniature]

Moore USA 1978

'Little Chief' × 'Angel Face'
Fully double, shapely, high-centred flowers of lavender-mauve. Foliage dark green and semi-glossy. Growth bushy.

[(C) (SF) ▽ AW] 1' 30 cm

'Lavender Lace' [Miniature]

Moore USA 1968

'Ellen Poulsen' × 'Debbie'
Small, fully double, high-centred flowers come in clusters with plentiful, small, mid-green, glossy foliage. Growth bushy, though very short.

[(C) ▽ AL] 9" 23 cm

'Lavender Sweetheart' (Willash) [Miniature]

Williams USA 1984

'Double Feature' × a seedling
Almost double, deep lavender, shapely, high-centred blooms are carried singly on strong stems. Foliage dark green and semi-glossy. Growth upright.

[(C) (E) ▽ ✕ AL] 1' 30 cm

'Lemon Delight' [Miniature]

Moore USA 1978

'Fairy Moss' × 'Gold Moss'
Semi-double, clear lemon flowers come from well-mossed, pointed buds. Foliage mid-green, the stems mossy. Growth upright and bushy.

[(C) (SF) ▽ AL] 1' 30 cm

'Little Artist', 'Top Gear' (Macmanly) [Miniature]

McGredy NEW ZEALAND 1982

'Eyepaint' × 'Ko's Yellow'
Its semi-double flowers, red with an off-white centre and reverse, make this one of McGredy's 'hand-painted' roses. Foliage plentiful, small, mid-green and semi-glossy on a compact, bushy plant. Almost but not quite a Compact Floribunda.

[(C) (B) ▽ AL] 15" 38 cm

'Little Breeze' [Miniature]

McCann EIRE 1981

'Anytime' × 'Elizabeth of Glamis'
Slim buds open to semi-double, orange-red flowers paling to pink. Foliage mid-green and

semi-glossy. Growth upright and bushy.

[(C) ▽ AL]   1'   30 cm

'Little Buckaroo' [Miniature]

Moore USA 1956
(*R. wichuraiana* × 'Floradora') × ('Oakington Ruby'
× 'Floradora')
Double, loosely formed, bright red flowers with
white centres are borne in clusters. Foliage bronzy
and glossy. Growth upright and tallish.

[(C) (B) ▽ ✕ AW]   15"   38 cm

'Little Flirt' [Miniature]

Moore USA 1961
(*R. wichuraiana* × 'Floradora') × ('Golden Glow' ×
'Zee')
Fully double, shapely flowers of rich orange-
yellow, with yellow on the reverse, their pointed
petals giving a star-like appearance. Foliage light
green on a bushy plant.

[(C) (B) ▽ BS ◁≡ AW]   15"   38 cm

'Little Jewel' (Cocabel) [Compact Floribunda]

Cocker UK 1980
'Wee Man' × 'Belinda'
Freely produced, fully double, deep pink and
rosette-shaped flowers are carried in sizeable clusters. Foliage dark green and glossy. Growth bushy
and compact.

[(C) (H) (B) ▽ AL]   1½'   45 cm

'Little Prince' (Coccord) [Compact Floribunda]

Cocker UK 1983
'Darling Flame' × ('National Trust' × 'Wee Man')
The bright orange-red flowers have hints of yellow
deep down in their centre and are semi-double in
large clusters. Foliage small, plentiful, mid-green
and semi-glossy. Growth upright, compact and
bushy.

[(C) (H) (B) ▽ AL]   1½'   45 cm

'Lollipop' [Miniature]

Moore USA 1959
(*R. wichuraiana* × 'Floradora') × 'Little Buckaroo'
Bright red, double flowers are borne in clusters,
with glossy foliage on a plant of vigorous, bushy
habit.

[(C) (SF) ▽ AW]   15"   38 cm

'Mabel Dot' [Miniature]

Dot SPAIN 1966
'Orient' × 'Perla de Alcañada'
Small, fully double, rosy-coral blooms are borne in
clusters. Foliage semi-glossy, bronzy. Growth
upright.

[(C) ▽ ✕ AW]   1'   30 cm

'Magic Carrousel' (Morrousel) [Miniature]

Moore USA 1972
'Little Darling' × 'Westmont'
Its fully double, shapely blooms are white tipped
pink and are produced in small clusters. Foliage
glossy, leathery and mid-green. Growth upright.

[(C) (SF) ▽ ✕ AW]   1'   30 cm

'Mark One' *see* 'Apricot Sunblaze'

'Meillandina' (Meirov) [Compact Floribunda]

Paolino FRANCE 1975
'Rumba' × ('Dany Robin' × 'Fire King')
Currant-red, fully double flowers, cupped. Foliage
matt and deep green. Growth bushy and wide.

[(C) (H) (B) (GC) ▽ AW]   15"   38 cm

'Meirov' *see* 'Meillandina'

'Mini Metro', 'Finstar' (Rufin) [Compact Floribunda]

de Ruiter NETHERLANDS 1979
'Minuette' × a seedling
Shapely, small, orange-salmon blooms are produced in clusters. Foliage mid-green and semi-
glossy on a bushy, upright plant.

[(C) (H) (B) ▽ AW]   15"   38 cm

'Mona Ruth' [Miniature]

Moore USA 1959
[('Soeur Thérèse' × 'Wilhelm') × (Seedling × 'Red
Ripples')] × 'Zee'
Mid-pink, fully double flowers in clusters. Foliage
mid-green and leathery. Growth bushy.

[(C) (SF) ▽ AL]   1'   30 cm

'Mood Music' [Miniature]

Moore USA 1977
'Fairy Moss' × 'Gold Moss'
Very full, orange-pink flowers in small clusters, the

calyx heavily mossed. Foliage plentiful, mid-green and matt, the stems mossed. Growth bushy and upright.

[(C) (B) (H) ▽ AW] 1′ 30 cm

'Mr Bluebird' [Miniature]

Moore USA 1960
'Old Blush' × 'Old Blush'
Small, rounded buds in clusters produce semi-double, lavender-blue flowers in profusion. Foliage dark and matt-finished. Growth upright and bushy.

[(C) ▽ AW] 1′ 30 cm

'My Valentine' [Miniature]

Moore USA 1975
'Little Chief' × 'Little Curt'
Very double, high-centred, deep red flowers are borne in small clusters. Foliage glossy, dark to mid-green tinted bronze. Growth bushy and upright.

[(C) ▽ ✂ AW] 1′ 30 cm

'New Penny' [Miniature]

Moore USA 1962
(*R. wichuraiana* × 'Floradora') × a seedling
Stumpy buds open to double flowers of orange-red paling to coral-pink. Foliage leathery but glossy. Growth bushy and short.

[(C) (MF) ▽ AW] 10″ 26 cm

'Little Buckaroo' and *right:* 'Little Prince'

'Orange Honey' [Miniature]

Moore USA 1979
'Rumba' × 'Over the Rainbow'
High-centred flowers, fully double, orange-yellow and cupped with mid-green, matt-finished foliage. Growth bushy and wide.

[(C) (VF) ▽ AL] 1′ 30 cm

'Orange Sunblaze', 'Orange Meillandina' (Meijikatar) [Compact Floribunda]

Meilland FRANCE 1982
'Parador' × ('Baby Bettina' × 'Duchess of Windsor')
Bright orange-red, double, cupped flowers are borne in profusion in small clusters. Foliage plentiful, light green and matt. Growth bushy and dense.

[(C) (P) (B) (SF) (GC) ▽ AW] 15″ 38 cm

'Para Ti' *see* 'Pour Toi'

'Peachy White' [Miniature]

Moore USA 1976
'Little Darling' × 'Red Germain'
Semi-double flowers come in clusters, white tinted peachy-pink. Foliage leathery and mid-green. Growth bushy and upright.

[(C) (MF) ▽ ✂ AW] 1′ 30 cm

'Peek a Boo', 'Brass Ring' (Dicgrow) [Compact Floribunda]

Dickson UK 1980
'Memento' × 'Nozomi'
Double, flattish flowers of rich copper-orange, paling to pink with age, are borne in large clusters.

Glossy, mid-green foliage. Upright, widish growth.

[(C) (B) (GC) AW]   1½'   45 cm

'Penelope Keith', 'Freegold' (Macfreego)
[Compact Floribunda]

McGredy NEW ZEALAND 1983
'Seaspray' × 'Benson & Hedges Special'
Double, shapely flowers, high-centred, of golden-yellow with a deeper reverse. Foliage light green and semi-glossy. Growth upright and bushy.

[(C) (B) (E) (MF) ▽ ✕ AW]   1½'   45 cm

'Peon', 'Tom Thumb' [Miniature]

de Vink NETHERLANDS 1936
'Rouletii' × 'Gloria Mundi'
Its small, semi-double flowers are deep red with a white centre. Foliage light green and leathery on a bushy, compact plant. A rose with a place in the pedigree of many Miniatures.

[(C) ▽ AL]   9"   23 cm

'Perla de Alcañada', 'Baby Crimson', 'Pearl of Canada', 'Titania', 'Wheatcroft's Baby Crimson' [Miniature]

Dot SPAIN 1944
'Perle des Rouges' × 'Rouletii'

Semi-double, carmine flowers are produced in small clusters or singly. Foliage dark green and glossy, and of bushy, compact habit. This is an important early Miniature, parent to several good varieties and in the pedigree of many more.

[(C) ▽ AL]   9"   23 cm

'Perla de Montserrat' [Miniature]

Dot SPAIN 1945
'Cécile Brünner' × 'Rouletii'
Very shapely blooms are borne in upright sprays reminiscent of its parent, 'Cécile Brünner'. They are of soft pink deepening towards the centre. Foliage darkish green and matt. Growth upright and bushy.

[(C) ▽ ✕ AW]   9"   23 cm

'Petit Four' (Interfour) [Compact Floribunda]

Ilsink NETHERLANDS 1982
'Marlena' seedling × a seedling
Clusters of semi-double, mid-pink blooms. Foliage mid-green, glossy, the shoots very thorny. Growth widish and bushy.

[(C) (B) (H) (MF) ▽ AL]   15"   38 cm

'Mini Metro' (see text p. 270)

'Orange Sunblaze' (see text p. 271) and *right:* 'Peek a Boo' (see text p. 271)

'Pink Posy' (Cocanelia) [Compact Floribunda]

Cocker UK 1982
'Trier' × 'New Penny'
Large sprays of soft pink, almost lilac, fully double flowers on a bushy, wide-growing plant with dark green, matt-finished foliage.

[(C) (B) (H) (MF) ▽ AL]   1½'   45 cm

'Pink Sunblaze', 'Pink Meillandina' (Meijidiro) [Compact Floribunda]

Meilland FRANCE 1983
Sport from 'Orange Sunblaze'
Identical to its parent except in colour, which is bright mid-pink.

[(C) (P) (B) (SF) ▽ AL]   15"   38 cm

'Pixie Rose', 'Pink Pixie' [Miniature]

Dot SPAIN 1961
'Perla de Montserrat' × 'Coralin'
High-centred, cupped, deep pink flowers are carried in clusters of variable size. Dark green, semi-glossy foliage. Growth branching and bushy.

[(C) ▽ AW]   9"   23 cm

'Pot Black' (Peanut) [Miniature]

Pearce UK 1985
Parentage unknown
Small, shapely, fully double and dark velvety-red flowers are borne in clusters. Foliage mid-green and matt. Growth bushy.

[(C) ▽ ✂ AL]   1'   30 cm

'Pour Toi', 'For You', 'Para Ti', 'Wendy' [Miniature]

Dot SPAIN 1946
'Eduardo Toda' × 'Pompon de Paris'
Semi-double flowers, white with yellow deeper in the centre, are produced in small clusters. Foliage mid-green and glossy. Growth short and bushy.

[(C) ▽ AW]   9"   23 cm

'Red Ace', 'Amruda', 'Amanda' [Miniature]

de Ruiter NETHERLANDS 1977
'Scarletta' × a seedling
Shapely, double, deep red flowers are carried in small clusters. Foliage mid-green and semi-glossy. Growth compact and bushy.

[(C) (SF) ▽ AW]   1'   30 cm

'Red Rascal' (Jacbed) [Compact Floribunda]

Warriner USA 1986
Seedling × a seedling
Sprays of fully double, cupped, satiny-red flowers on a compact bush with mid- to dark-green foliage.
[(C) (B) (H) ⏚ AL]   1½'   45 cm

'Regensberg', 'Young Mistress', 'Buffalo Bill' (Macyoumis) [Compact Floribunda]

McGredy NEW ZEALAND 1979
'Geoff Boycott' × 'Old Master'
Its double flowers of soft pink with their petals edged white, and white on the reverse, have prominent yellow stamens. Foliage plentiful and mid-green. Growth compact, spreading and bushy.
[(C) (B) (H) (VF) (GC) ⏚ AL]   1½'   45 cm

'Rise 'n' Shine', 'Golden Meillandina', 'Golden Sunblaze' [Compact Floribunda]

Moore USA 1978
'Little Darling' × 'Yellow Magic'
Clear yellow, shapely, double flowers come in clusters with plentiful, mid-green foliage. Growth upright and bushy.
[(C) (B) (H) (E) ⏚ ✂ AW]   1½'   45 cm

'Robin Redbreast' (Interrob) [Compact Floribunda]

Ilsink NETHERLANDS 1984
Seedling × 'Eyepaint'
Small, single blooms of dark red with creamy-yellow centres and silvery reverses are produced in profusion. Mid-green, glossy foliage, the stems thorny. Growth bushy and spreading.
[(C) (B) (H) (GC) ⏚ AL]   1½'   45 cm

'Rosina', 'Josephine Wheatcroft', 'Yellow Sweetheart' [Miniature]

Dot SPAIN 1951
'Edouardo Toda' × 'Rouletii'
Semi-double, clear yellow flowers are produced in small clusters. Foliage mid-green and glossy. Growth upright and bushy.
[(C) (SF) ⏚ AW]   9"   23 cm

'Rouletii', *R. rouletii* [Miniature]

Correvon SWITZERLAND 1922
Variety of *R. chinensis minima*
The first of the modern Miniatures, discovered growing in pots on window ledges in Switzerland by Major Roulet in 1918. Double flowers of deep rose-pink come singly or in small clusters. Foliage dark green and matt. Growth bushy and compact.
[(R) ⏚ AL]   9"   23 cm

'Royal Salute', 'Rose Baby' (Macros) [Miniature]

McGredy NEW ZEALAND 1976
'New Penny' × 'Marlena'
Double, shapely flowers of rosy-red are carried in small clusters. Foliage dark green and semi-glossy. Growth upright and bushy.
[(C) (SF) ⏚ AL]   1'   30 cm

'Scarlet Gem', 'Scarlet Pimpernel' (Meido) [Miniature]

Meilland FRANCE 1961
('Moulin Rouge' × 'Fashion') × ('Perla de Montserrat' × 'Perla de Alcañada')
Very double, cupped flowers of rich scarlet are borne in clusters. Dark green, glossy foliage on a plant of bushy and upright habit.
[(C) (SF) ⏚ AW]   9"   23 cm

'Sheri Anne' (Morsheri) [Miniature]

Moore USA 1973
'Little Darling' × 'New Penny'
Its semi-double, orange-red flowers with a yellow

'Petit Four' (see text p. 272)

Top: 'Rise 'n' Shine' and *bottom:* 'Robin Redbreast'

base are borne in large clusters. Foliage mid-green and glossy. Growth bushy and upright.

[(C) ▽ ✂ AW]   1'   30 cm

'Silver Tips' [Miniature]

Moore USA 1961
(*R. wichuraiana* × 'Floradora') × 'Lilac Time'
Very double pink flowers with silvery tips to each petal and an even more silvery reverse, paling with age to soft lavender. Foliage mid-green and leathery. Growth dense and bushy.

[(C) ▽ ✂ AW]   1'   30 cm

'Snookie' (Tinsnook) [Miniature]

Bennett USA 1984
'Torchy' × 'Orange Honey'
The double flowers of deep orange turn red with age. Foliage mid-green and semi-glossy Growth bushy and small.

[(C) ▽ AL]   9"   23 cm

'Snowball', 'Angelita' (Macangel) [Miniature]

McGredy NEW ZEALAND 1982
'Moana' × 'Snow Carpet'
Fully double, white, globular blooms are produced in clusters. Foliage light green and dense. Growth bushy.

[(C) ▽ AW]   1'   30 cm

'Snowdrop', 'Amouretta', 'Amorette' (Amoru) [Miniature]

de Ruiter NETHERLANDS 1979
'Rosy Jewel' × 'Zorina'
Its double, white, shapely flowers with ivory centres are usually borne singly. Foliage mid-green and glossy. Growth upright.

[(C) (SF) (Gh) ▽ ✂ AW]   1'   30 cm

'Stacey Sue' [Miniature]

Moore USA 1976
'Ellen Poulsen' × 'Fairy Princess'
Very double, globular blooms of soft pink are borne in small clusters. Foliage mid-green and glossy. Growth bushy and upright.

[(C) (Gh) ▽ AW]   1'   30 cm

'Starina' (Meigabi) [Miniature]

Meilland FRANCE 1965
('Dany Robin' × 'Fire King') × 'Perla de Montserrat'
Orange-scarlet, fully double flowers with mid-green, glossy foliage on a very bushy plant.

[(C) ▽ AW]   1'   30 cm

'Stars 'n' Stripes' [Miniature]

Moore USA 1976
'Little Chief' × ('Little Darling' × 'Ferdinand Pichard')
Double flowers, eye-catchingly striped red and white, shapely and high-centred, are produced in clusters. Foliage mid-green and of bushy, upright habit.

[(C) ▽ ✂ AW]   1'   30 cm

'Sunblaze', 'Sunny', 'Sunny Meillandina' (Meiponal) [Compact Floribunda]

Meilland FRANCE 1985
('Sarabande' × 'Moulin Rouge') × ('Zambra' × 'Meikim')
Orangy-yellow, fully double blooms come in clusters. Foliage plentiful, dark green and matt-finished. Growth bushy and dense.

[(C) (B) (H) ▽ AW]   15″   38 cm

'Sweet Dream' (Fryerminicot) [Compact Floribunda]

Fryer UK 1987
Parentage unknown
Masses of double, peachy-apricot blooms in clusters. Foliage plentiful and mid-green. Growth wide and bushy.

[(C) (B) (H) ▽ AL]   1½′   45 cm

'Sweet Fairy' [Miniature]

de Vink NETHERLANDS 1946
'Peon' × a seedling
Fully double flowers, soft blush-pink and cupped. Foliage dark green and semi-glossy. Growth bushy and very dwarf.

[(C) (Gh) (SF) ▽ AW]   6″   15 cm

Top: 'Sheri Anne' (see text p. 274)

'Sweet Magic' (Dicmagic) [Compact Floribunda]

Dickson UK 1987
Parentage unknown
Semi-double, shapely orange blooms are freely produced in clusters. Foliage mid-green and glossy. Growth bushy, wide and dense.

[(C) (SF) (B) (H) ▽ AW]   1½′   45 cm

'Top Gear' *see* 'Little Artist'

'Toy Clown' [Miniature]

Moore USA 1966
'Little Darling' × 'Magic Wand'
Semi-double flowers open slightly cupped and in clusters, white-edged and shaded pinkish-red. Foliage mid-green and leathery. Growth bushy, dense and upright.

[(C) (Gh) ▽ ✕ AW]   1′   30 cm

'Wee Jock' (Cocabest) [Compact Floribunda]

Cocker UK 1980
'National Trust' × 'Wee Man'
Fully double, bright red flowers are borne in sizeable clusters. Foliage plentiful, mid-green and glossy. Growth compact and bushy.

[(C) (B) (H) ▽ AL]   15″   38 cm

'Sweet Dream'

'Wee Man', 'Tapis de Soie' [Miniature]

McGredy NEW ZEALAND 1974
'Little Flirt' × 'Marlena'
Semi-double flowers of rich scarlet in clusters.
Foliage dark green and glossy. Growth bushy.

[(C) ⊽ BS⬧⠿ AL]   1'   30 cm

'White Meillandina' *see* 'Yorkshire Sunblaze'

'Yellow Doll' [Miniature]

Moore USA 1962
'Golden Glow' × 'Zee'
Its shapely, fully double flowers of creamy-yellow
are not unlike miniature Hybrid Teas. Foliage
mid-green and glossy. Growth vigorous and
bushy.

[(C) (Gh) (SF) ⊽ ✂ AW]   1'   30 cm

'Yellow Sunblaze', 'Yellow Meillandina' (Meitrisical) [Compact Floribunda]

Meilland FRANCE 1980
['Poppy Flash' × ('Charleston' × 'Allgold')] × 'Gold Coin'
Double, yellow flowers edged with pink. Foliage
dark green and semi-glossy. Growth bushy.

[(C) (B) (H) ⊽ AL]   15"   38 cm

'Sweet Magic'

'Yorkshire Sunblaze', 'White Meillandina' (Meiblam) [Compact Floribunda]

Meilland FRANCE 1983
'Katherina Zeimet' × 'White Gem'
Small, densely packed clusters of semi-double
white flowers. Foliage plentiful, light green and
semi-glossy on a compact, bushy plant.

[(C) (MF) (B) (H) ⊽ AL]   1'   30 cm

Climbers and Ramblers

Since 1900 many hundreds, probably thousands, of climbers and ramblers have been raised. Most, if not all of them, are well worth garden space. Whittling my selection down to one hundred or so of the best varieties was not easy; in fact, I feel a little peeved that at least another hundred have had to be omitted, although I have managed to sneak in a few of my personal favourites.

Climbers and ramblers vary considerably in both size and floriferousness. In making my selection, therefore, I have tried to cover the whole range of dimensions together with the widest possible variety of colour. In addition to traditional uses such as adorning walls, fences, arches and pergolas, climbers and ramblers have a variety of other roles, from growing up into trees to acting as ground-cover plants. They are invaluable in giving an extra dimension to any modern garden.

For an explanation of the differences between climbers and ramblers, turn back to pages 82–91.

'Albéric Barbier' [Wichuraiana Rambler]

Barbier FRANCE 1900
R. wichuraiana × 'Shirley Hibberd'
Yellowish buds open to large double to semi-double flowers of creamy-white flushed lemon-yellow. Foliage rich dark green and very glossy. Growth pliable, with dark green wood and few thorns of consequence. A superb older variety.

[(P) (T) (N) (S) (MF) ⏺ AW]   15′ × 10′   4.5 × 3 m

'Albertine' [Wichuraiana Rambler]

Barbier FRANCE 1921
R. wichuraiana × 'Mrs Arthur Robert Waddell'
Its flowers are produced in small clusters, the shapely buds opening to muddled full blooms of lobster-pink with gold deep down in the base. The foliage is glossy dark green, burnished coppery-red, the stems barbed with hooked thorns. Growth angular and vigorous.

[(P)′(T) (S) (VF) M⏺ AW]   15′ × 10′   4.5 × 3 m

'Alchemist' [Modern Climber]

Kordes GERMANY 1956
'Golden Glow' × *R. eglanteria*
The flowers are large, opening flat, and often quartered in the old-fashioned style. Their colour is a pleasing variable mixture of soft yellow and egg-yolk-orange. Foliage is rich green, semi-matt and leathery, the stems well arched. Growth rather stiff and vigorous.

[(P) (S) (T) (VF) ⏺ AW]   12′ × 8′   3.5 × 2.5 m

'Alexander Girault' [Wichuraiana Rambler]

Barbier FRANCE 1909
R. wichuraiana × 'Papa Gontier'
Very double flowers, opening flat with muddled centres, of deep rose-pink and copper with hints of yellow, and in clusters. Dark green, glossy foliage on a vigorous plant, though prostrate unless trained.

[(R) (P) (SF) ⏺ AL]   12′ × 12′   3.5 × 3.5 m

Above: 'Albéric Barbier'
Below: 'Albertine'

'Alchemist' (see text p. 278)

'Alida Lovett' [Wichuraiana Rambler]

Van Fleet USA 1905
'Souvenir du Président Carnot' × *R. wichuraiana*
Very large shapely flowers of soft shell-pink, with
yellow deep down in the base, are borne sometimes in clusters, sometimes singly. Foliage dark
green and glossy, the stems relatively thornless.
Growth relaxed and sturdy.

[(P) (T) (S) (MF) AL]   12′ × 10′   3.5 × 3 m

'Allen Chandler' [Climbing Hybrid Tea]

Chandler USA 1923
'Hugh Dickson' × unnamed seedling
The large, bright red, semi-double flowers have
pronounced golden stamens. Foliage dark green,
matt and plentiful. Growth upright and sturdy.

[(P) (R) (SF) AL]   12′ × 8′   3.5 × 2.5 m

'Allgold' [Climbing Floribunda]

Gandy UK 1961
Sport from 'Allgold'
Bush form, LeGrice UK 1956
'Goldilocks' × 'Ellinor LeGrice'
Shapely buds open to almost double, clear,
unfading yellow blooms that are borne in clusters
on a plant of strong, upright growth with rich dark
green foliage.

[(S) (P) (MF) ✕ AL]   15′ × 10′   4.5 × 3 m

'Aloha' [Modern Climber]

Boerner USA 1949
'Mercedes Gallart' × 'New Dawn'
The freely produced, very large and shapely flowers are packed with petals, in colour rose-pink with
a deeper reverse and shadings of magenta and
highlights of salmon. They have a lovely perfume.
Foliage lush dark green with a bronzy overlay, and
glossy, on a plant of upright habit.

[(C) (P) (VF) ✕ ▽ AW]   10′ × 6′   3 × 1.8 m

'Altissimo' (Delmur) [Modern Climber]

Delbard-Chabert FRANCE 1966
'Ténor' × unknown
Very large single flowers of bright red are carried in
clusters or singly, and have prominent stamens.
Foliage dark green and semi-glossy. Growth angu-
lar and upright.

[(C) (SF) AW]   10′ × 6′   3 × 1.8 m

'Aloha'

'Alexander Girault' (see text p. 278)

'American Pillar' [Wichuraiana Rambler]

Van Fleet USA 1902
(*R. wichuraiana* × *R. setigera*) × 'Red Letter Day'
Single flowers are produced in clusters, and are reddish-pink with off-white centres paling to rose-pink with age. Rain mottles them. Its foliage is plentiful, deep green and glossy. Growth coarse and robust.
[(P) (S) (T) ❶ AW]   15' × 10'   4.5 × 3 m

'Arthur Bell' [Climbing Floribunda]

Pearce UK 1979
Sport from 'Arthur Bell'
Bush form, McGredy UK 1965
'Cläre Grammerstorf' × 'Piccadilly'
Clusters of deep yellow, double flowers paling to soft yellow with age on a tall, upright plant with exceptionally glossy, deep green foliage.
[(S) (P) (VF) ✕ AL]   12' × 8'   3.5 × 2.5 m

'Auguste Roussel' [Macrophylla Hybrid]

Barbier FRANCE 1913
R. macrophylla × 'Papa Gontier'
Its semi-double, bright pink flowers are widely spaced in clusters. Foliage dark greyish-green. Growth angular, spreading and vigorous.
[(P) (S) ❶ AL]   15' × 8'   4.5 × 2.5 m

'Autumn Sunlight' [Modern Climber]

Gregory UK 1965
'Danse de Feu' × 'Goldilocks'
Large clusters of fully double, orange-vermilion flowers. Foliage rich mid-green. Growth upright and tall.
[(C) (P) (SF) AL]   12' × 8'   3.5 × 2.5 m

'Aviateur Blériot' [Wichuraiana Rambler]

Fauque FRANCE 1910
R. wichuraiana × 'William Allen Richardson'
Large trusses of well-scented, double, golden-yellow flowers, paling to creamy-yellow with age. Foliage dark green and glossy. Growth relatively thornless and upright.
[(P) (S) (T) (MF) AL]   12' × 6'   3.5 × 1.8 m

'Bantry Bay' [Modern Climber]

McGredy UK 1967
'New Dawn' × 'Korona'
The large, loosely semi-double flowers, quite shapely in bud, are deep pink with quieter reflections and golden stamens. Foliage dark green and glossy. An outstanding long-flowering climber.
[(P) (C) (MF) ✕ AW]   12' × 8'   3.5 × 2.5 m

'Bleu Magenta' [Multiflora Rambler]

Origin unknown *c.* 1900
Parentage unknown
Rich purple flowers with muddled petals and golden stamens are borne in clusters. Foliage mid-green and glossy. Growth lax and tall.
[(S) (P) (N) ❶ M ▦ AL]   12' × 10'   3.5 × 3 m

'Bobbie James' [Rambler]

Sunningdale UK 1961
Probably related to *R. multiflora*
Cupped flowers of soft creamy-white are produced in very large cascading clusters, and very freely when the plant is established. Foliage lush mid-green, glossy and large. Growth noticeably vigorous.
[(S) (P) (T) (N) ❶ AW]   30' × 20'   9 × 6 m

'Breath of Life' (Harquanne)
[Modern Climber]

Harkness UK 1982
'Red Dandy' × 'Alexander'
Full, shapely blooms of pinky-apricot are carried

'Auguste Roussel'
in clusters with mid-green, glossy foliage on an upright and vigorous plant.

[(C) (P) (MF) ✄ AL]   10′ × 6′   3 × 1.8 m

'Casino', 'Gerbe d'Or' (Macca) [Modern Climber]

McGredy UK 1963
'Coral Dawn' × 'Buccaneer'

Large, clear yellow, fully double flowers are borne singly or in clusters. Foliage large, deep green and glossy. Growth upright, spreading and good for pillar work.

[(R) (P) (MF) AW]   10′ × 8′   3 × 2.5 m

'Chaplin's Pink', 'Chaplin's Pink Climber' [Wichuraiana Rambler]

Chaplin UK 1928
'Paul's Scarlet' × 'American Pillar'
Its large trusses of clear pink, semi-double flowers are very striking. Foliage mid to dark green and glossy. Growth vigorous and wide.

[(S) (P) (T) (SF) ◑ AL]   15′ × 10′   4.5 × 3 m

'Clair Matin' (Meimont) [Modern Climber]

Meilland FRANCE 1960
'Fashion' × [('Independence' × 'Orange Triumph') × 'Phyllis Bide']
Large clusters are produced of exquisite, medium-sized, light pink blooms, with deeper, sometimes bronzy, highlights. Foliage dark green and glossy, the growth relaxed and upright. Its stems occasionally arch with the weight of flowers.

[(R) (P) (H) (MF) (CL) ◑ AL]   8′ × 4′   2.5 × 1.2 m

'Bantry Bay'

Top: 'Compassion' and *bottom:* 'Coral Dawn'

'Comtesse Vandal' [Climbing Hybrid Tea]

Jackson & Perkins USA 1936
Bush form Leenders NETHERLANDS 1932
('Ophelia' × 'Mrs Aaron Ward') × 'Souvenir de Claudius Pernet'
A very beautiful and elegant rose, with classically high-centred blooms. Pointed, orange-toned buds open to loosely formed flowers of pinky-apricot with deeper shadings in the centre. Ample, dark green, coppery-tinted and semi-glossy foliage comes on a vigorous plant. This is an outstanding old variety.
[(S) (MF) (P) (E) AL]   15′ × 8′   4.5 × 2.5 m

'Compassion', 'Belle de Londres' [Modern Climber]

Harkness UK 1973
'White Cockade' × 'Prima Ballerina'
The shapely, high-centred blooms of apricot-copper and cream have yellow highlights. Foliage dark green and glossy. Growth upright and angular.
[(R) (VF) ✕ BS AW]   10′ × 6′   3 × 1.8 m

'Constance Spry' [Modern Shrub]

Austin UK 1961
'Belle Isis' × 'Dainty Maid'
Breathtakingly beautiful at their best, the large, fully double, cupped blooms of rich pink are in the old-fashioned style. They have a strong, myrrh-like scent. Foliage rather coarse, leathery and mid-green on a vigorous but sprawling plant which needs support when grown as a shrub.
[(S) (CL) (VF) ◍ AW]   20′ × 10′   6 × 3 m

'Coral Dawn' [Modern Climber]

Boerner USA 1952
'New Dawn' × an unnamed yellow Hybrid Tea
Plumpish buds open to large, full, coral-pink flowers in small clusters. Foliage dark green and glossy. Growth upright and wide.
[(R) (MF) ◍ ✕ AW]   12′ × 8′   3.5 × 2.5 m

'Crépuscule' [Noisette]

Dubreuil FRANCE 1904
Parentage unknown
Attractively muddled flowers of rich apricot are borne in clusters. Lush and mid-green foliage on

'Danse de Feu' and *right:* 'Dublin Bay' (see text p. 286)

an upright grower which needs protection in colder districts.

[(R) (Gh) (MF) ∷ AL] 12′ × 5′ 3.5 × 1.5 m

'Crimson Conquest' [Climbing Hybrid Tea]

Chaplin UK 1931
Sport from 'Red Letter Day'
Bush form, Dickson UK 1914
Parentage unknown
Its semi-double, almost single flowers of rich crimson have golden stamens. Foliage glossy and dark green. Growth upright and angular.

[(S) (P) ❶ AL] 15′ × 8′ 4.5 × 2.5 m

'Crimson Glory' [Climbing Hybrid Tea]

Jackson & Perkins USA 1946
Sport from 'Crimson Glory'
Bush form, Kordes GERMANY 1935
'Cathrine Kordes' seedling × 'W. E. Chaplin'
Superbly shaped velvety-crimson flowers are produced in small clusters and are highly scented. Foliage dark green and semi-glossy. Growth stiff, upright and sturdy.

[(S) (P) (VF) ✂M❶∷ AL] 15′ × 8′ 4.5 × 2.5 m

'Cupid' [Climbing Hybrid Tea]

Cant UK 1915
Parentage unknown
The beautiful, large, single flowers of soft peachy-pink have pronounced stamens, though this rose is a little reluctant to flower in profusion at times. Foliage large, greyish-green and matt. Growth upright and stiffish.

[(R) (P) (SF) ❶ AL] 12′ × 6′ 3.5 × 1.8 m

'Danse de Feu', 'Spectacular'
[Modern Climber]

Mallerin FRANCE 1953
'Paul's Scarlet' × an *R. multiflora* seedling
The very bright orange-red, sometimes brick-red, blooms are shapely, high-centred and double, and are produced in clusters. Foliage mid-green and semi-glossy.

[(C) ❶ BS◆∷AW] 12′ × 8′ 3.5 × 2.5 m

'Dorothy Perkins' [Wichuraiana Rambler]

Jackson & Perkins USA 1901
R. wichuraiana × 'Mme Gabriel Luizet'
Clusters of double, small, clear pink flowers

'Emily Gray' (see text p. 288)

'Excelsa' (see text p. 288)

'François Juranville' (see text p. 289)

cascade in profusion from a vigorous, pliable plant with glossy, dark to mid-green foliage.

[(S) (P) (G) (SF) M❁⁝⁝⁝ AW]   10′ × 8′   3 × 2.5 m

'Dublin Bay' (Macdub) [Modern Climber]

McGredy NEW ZEALAND 1975
'Bantry Bay' × 'Altissimo'
Fully double, medium-sized, rich blood-red flowers come in clusters. Foliage large, dark and glossy. Growth upright. Makes a good pillar rose.

[(C) (P) (SF) ✂ AL]   7′ × 5′   2.1 × 1.5 m

'Easlea's Golden Rambler', 'Golden Rambler' [Rambler]

Easlea UK 1932
Parentage unknown
Large, shapely, golden-yellow and fully double flowers are borne in small clusters held on strong, long stems. Foliage rich dark green and glossy. Growth vigorous and rambling.

[(S) (P) (T) (N) (MF) ◉ ✂ AW]   20′ × 15′   6 × 4.5 m

'Eden Rose '88' (Meiviolin) [Modern Climber]

Meilland FRANCE 1987
Parentage unknown
Its fully double flowers are in the old-fashioned style, their creamy-white shaded with lavender-pink at the base of the petals. Foliage dark green and glossy. Growth upright and bushy.

[(C) (SF) AL]   8′ × 6′   2.5 × 2 m

'Elegance' [Wichuraiana Rambler]

Brownell USA 1937
'Glen Dale' × ('Mary Wallace' × 'Miss Lolita Amour')
Shapely, at first high-centred, blooms of clear yellow paling to soft yellow with age. Foliage plentiful, mid to dark green and semi-glossy. Growth widish and upright.

[(R) (P) (N) ◉ ✂ AL]   10′ × 8′   3 × 2.5 m

'François Juranville' (see text p. 289) growing at Leeds Castle

'Emily Gray' [Wichuraiana Rambler]

Williams UK 1918
'Jersey Beauty' × 'Comtesse du Cayla'
A beautiful, semi-double rose of rich yellow with golden stamens. Foliage dark green and very glossy. Growth wide and relatively thornless.

[(S) (P) (T) (SF) (N) ◑ AW]   15′ × 10′   4.5 × 3 m

'Ena Harkness' [Climbing Hybrid Tea]

Murrell UK 1954
Sport from bush form, Norman UK 1946
'Crimson Glory' × 'Southport'
With its bright velvet-crimson flowers, very shapely and free-flowering, this is an outstanding climber and well worth garden space. Foliage dark green and matt on an upright plant.

[(S) (P) (VF) ✂ ☺ AW]   15′ × 8′   4.5 × 2.5 m

'Ethel' [Wichuraiana Rambler]

Turner UK 1912
Seedling from 'Dorothy Perkins'
Large, cascading clusters of mauve-pink, fully double, cupped flowers. Foliage mid-green and glossy, the stems with several thorns. Growth scrambling and wide.

[(S) (P) (T) (N) (SF) (GC) ◑ AL]
20′ × 15′   6 × 4.5 m

'Etoile de Hollande' [Climbing Hybrid Tea]

Leenders NETHERLANDS 1931
Bush form, Verschuren NETHERLANDS 1919
'General MacArthur' × 'Hadley'
Shapely flowers of cloudy red, velvety in texture and highly scented. Foliage dark green and matt. Growth upright and stout.

[(S) (VF) M◁ ✂ AL]   12′ × 8′   3.5 × 2.5 m

'Excelsa', 'Red Dorothy Perkins' [Wichuraiana Rambler]

Walsh USA 1909 Parentage unknown
Large clusters of small, double, crimson flowers come in profusion in midsummer. Foliage dark green and matt. Growth pliable and relaxed.

[(S) (P) (GC) (N) (T) ◑ M◁ AW]
15′ × 12′   4.5 × 3.5 m

'Fragrant Cloud' [Climbing Hybrid Tea]

Collin UK 1973
Sport from bush form, Tantau GERMANY 1963
Seedling × 'Prima Ballerina'
Its shapely blooms are coral-red, though variable. Foliage dark reddish-green. Growth upright, sturdy.

[(S) (VF) ✂ BS◁ AL]   12′ × 8′   3.5 × 2.5 m

'Gardenia'

'Goldfinch' (see text p. 290)

'Francis E. Lester' [Multiflora Rambler]

Lester USA 1946
'Kathleen' × a seedling
Large trusses of shapely, single flowers, white with splashes of pink at the edges of each petal. Foliage coppery, though tinted dark green, on a plant of shrubby, vigorous habit.

[(S) (P) (VF) (T) (N) ◐ AL]   15′ × 10′   4.5 × 3 m

'François Juranville' [Wichuraiana Rambler]

Barbier FRANCE 1906
R. wichuraiana × 'Mme Laurette Messimy'
Its beautiful flowers, made up of a tangle of well-proportioned, clear silky-pink petals, are usually produced in small clusters. This is a more refined form of 'Albertine'. Foliage dark green, burnished bronze and semi-glossy. Growth pliable and dense, though with very few thorns.

[(S) (P) (GC) (SF) (N) ◐ AL]   15′ × 10′   4.5 × 3 m

'Galway Bay' (Macba) [Modern Climber]

McGredy UK 1966
'Heidelberg' × 'Queen Elizabeth'
Large, shapely, fully double flowers of salmon-pink are carried in clusters. Foliage dark green and glossy on a vigorous, upright plant. This is a good pillar rose.

[(C) (P) (N) ◐ ✕ AL]   12′ × 8′   3.5 × 2.5 m

'Gardenia' [Wichuraiana Rambler]

Manda USA 1899
R. wichuraiana × 'Perle des Jardins'
I could not resist including this rose despite its date of introduction. It has really beautiful, fully double flowers of creamy-white, together with rich dark green and glossy foliage. Growth relaxed and vigorous, with few thorns.

[(S) (P) (T) (GC) (MF) ◐ AL]   20′ × 15′   6 × 4.5 m

'Ghislaine de Féligonde' [Multiflora Rambler]

Turbat FRANCE 1916
'Goldfinch' × unknown
Very large clusters of fully double, orange-yellow flowers are produced in profusion all summer long. Foliage plentiful, mid to light green and glossy. Growth bushy and upright. An excellent though little known variety that also makes a fine shrub.

[(C) (P) (N) (SF) ◐ AL]   8′ × 8′   2.5 × 2.5 m

'Guinée' and *below:* 'Handel'

'Golden Glow' [Wichuraiana Rambler]

Brownell USA 1937
'Glen Dale' × ('Mary Wallace' × a Hybrid Tea)
It has clusters of shapely, cupped, double flowers of clear golden-yellow, with plentiful, crisp, darkish green foliage on a strong and wide plant.
[(S) (P) (N) (SF) ⏸ ✂ AL]   10' × 8'   3 × 2.5 m

'Golden Showers' [Modern Climber]

Lammerts USA 1957
'Charlotte Armstrong' × 'Captain Thomas'
The clusters of large, loosely formed, rather ruffled flowers of deep golden-yellow pale quickly to cream. Foliage dark green and glossy. Growth upright. This rose also makes a good shrub.
[(C) (P) (SF) ⏸ AW]   10' × 6'   3 × 1.8 m

'Goldfinch' [Multiflora Rambler]

Paul UK 1907
'Hélène' × unknown
Its small, cupped, semi-double flowers are golden-yellow fading to cream and are borne in large, tightly packed clusters. Foliage mid-green and glossy, almost thornless. Growth bushy and upright – to medium height.
[(S) (P) (N) (SF) ⏸ AL]   8' × 4'   2.5 × 1.2 m

'Grand Hotel' (Mactel) [Modern Climber]

McGredy UK 1972
'Brilliant' × 'Heidelberg'
Semi-double, sizeable flowers of rich scarlet come in clusters. Foliage dark green and semi-glossy. Growth upright and bushy.
[(C) (P) (SF) AL]   8' × 4'   2.5 × 1.2 m

'Kathleen Harrop' (see text p. 292) and *below:* 'Lawrence Johnston' (see text p. 293)

'Grandmère Jenny' [Climbing Hybrid Tea]

Meilland FRANCE 1958
Sport from bush form, Meilland FRANCE 1950
'Peace' × ('Julien Potin' × 'Sensation')
Long, pointed buds open to sizeable, high-centred flowers of soft yellow brushed pink, sometimes a deeper flush of burnt orange. Foliage semi-glossy, leathery and dark green. Growth strong and upright.

[(S) (P) (MF) ✂ AL]   18′ × 10′   5.5 × 3 m

'Guinée' [Climbing Hybrid Tea]

Mallerin FRANCE 1938
'Souvenir de Claudius Denoyel' × 'Ami Quinard'
Its very deep crimson, double flowers have a velvety texture. They open flat and muddled, displaying golden-brown anthers. Foliage dark green overlaid with maroon. Growth angular.

[(R) (P) (VF) ✂ AL]   15′ × 8′   4.5 × 2.5 m

'Handel' (Macha) [Modern Climber]

McGredy UK 1965
'Columbine' × 'Heidelberg'
Large, semi-double flowers, silvery-white with pinkish or reddish markings on the petal edges.

Foliage large and dark green, with a purplish tinge. Growth upright and bushy.

[(C) (P) (SF) ✂ AW]   12′ × 8′   3.5 × 2.5 m

'Hiawatha' [Multiflora Rambler]

Walsh USA 1904
'Crimson Rambler' × 'Paul's Carmine Pillar'
Single, deep pink to crimson flowers with a white centre are borne in clusters. Foliage dark green and semi-glossy. Growth bushy and spreading.

[(S) (P) (T) (N) ◐ AL]   15′ × 12′   4.5 × 3.5 m

'Iceberg', 'Schneewittchen', 'Fée des Neiges' (Korbin) [Climbing Floribunda]

Cant UK 1968
Sport from 'Iceberg'
Bush form, Kordes GERMANY 1958
'Robin Hood' × 'Virgo'
Clusters of shapely, white flowers are carried in profusion, with bright green, plentiful foliage on a vigorous, upright, bushy plant.

[(S) (P) (N) (T) ◐ ⚔ AW]   18′ × 10′   5.5 × 3 m

'Josephine Bruce' [Climbing Hybrid Tea]

Bees UK 1952
Sport from 'Josephine Bruce'
Bush form, Bees UK 1949
'Crimson Glory' × 'Madge Whipp'
The shapely, high-centred flowers are of deep velvety-crimson. Foliage dark green and matt.

Growth stiff, angular and rather awkward.

[(S) (P) (VF) M ⚔ AL]   15′ × 10′   4.5 × 3 m

'Kathleen Harrop' [Bourbon]

Dickson UK 1919
Sport from 'Zéphirine Drouhin' Bizot FRANCE 1868
Parentage unknown
With its soft pink, semi-double flowers produced all summer long, this has all the attributes and few of the drawbacks of its famous parent. Foliage matt, grey-green and smooth, the stems thornless. Growth upright and bushy.

[(C) (N) (P) (VF) ◐ M ⚔ AL]   10′ × 6′   3 × 1.8 m

'Kiftsgate', R. filipes 'Kiftsgate' [Climber]

Murrell UK 1954
Sport from R. filipes
A foundling at Kiftsgate Court, Gloucestershire
Fragrant, single, creamy-white flowers are borne in huge trusses, with rich green, glossy foliage. Of extremely vigorous growth, this is an excellent rose for climbing into tall trees or covering eyesores of whatever size. It has attractive foliage and fruit in the autumn, too.

[(S) (P) (GC) (T) (N) ◐ AW]   30′ × 20′   9 × 6 m

'Korizont' see 'Summer Wine'

'Madeleine Selzer' (see text p. 294)

'Korona' (Kornita) [Climbing Floribunda]

Kordes GERMANY 1957
Sport from bush form, Kordes GERMANY 1955
'Obergärtner Wiebicke' × 'Independence'
Its clusters of semi-double, orange-scarlet flowers open somewhat ragged. Foliage dark green and matt. Growth dense and upright.

[(S) (P) (N) ◑ AL]   15′ × 10′   4.5 × 3 m

'Maigold' (see text p. 294)

'Malaga' (see text p. 294)

'Lady Hillingdon' [Climbing Hybrid Tea]

Hicks UK 1917
Sport from bush form, Lowe UK 1910
'Papa Gontier' × 'Mme Hoste'
Semi-double, blowsy flowers of rich egg-yolk-yellow, and very dark greyish-green foliage with heavy bluish tones, the stems plum-coloured and with few thorns. Growth upright and branching. Needs protection in cold climates.

[(R) (P) (Gh) (VF) ✂ ☼ AL]   15′ × 8′   4.5 × 2.5 m

'Lady Sylvia' [Climbing Hybrid Tea]

Stevens UK 1933
Bush form, Stevens UK 1926
Sport from 'Mme Butterfly'
Shapely buds open to high-centred flowers of soft flesh-pink with deeper undertones. This is an excellent climber with greyish-green foliage and vigorous, upright, branching growth.

[(S) (P) (Gh) (VF) ✂ AW]   15′ × 10′   4.5 × 3 m

'Lawrence Johnston', 'Hidcote Yellow' [R. foetida Climber]

Pernet-Ducher FRANCE 1923
'Mme Eugène Verdier' × R. foetida persiana
The early-flowering clusters of large, semi-double, clear yellow flowers have prominent stamens. Foliage lime-green and semi-glossy. Growth angular.

[(R) (P) (N) (SF) ◑ AL]   25′ × 20 ′   7.5 × 6 m

'Leverkusen' [Kordesii Hybrid]

Kordes GERMANY 1954
R. kordesii × 'Golden Glow'
Its almost double, lemon-yellow flowers have attractively ragged edges when open. They are produced in profusion. The foliage is glossy, serrated and lightish green on a bushy, wide plant with several thorns. Exceptionally hardy and healthy.

[(C) (P) (N) (SF) ◑ AL]   10′ × 8′   3 × 2.5 m

'Lykkefund' [Hélènae Hybrid]

Olsen DENMARK 1930
R. hélènae seedling
With huge trusses of fragrant, creamy-yellow flowers tinged pink. Foliage lush, light green tinted bronze. Growth thornless, vigorous and bushy. A fine variety, though not widely known, that is ideal for growing up into small trees.

[(S) (P) (T) (VF) ◑ AL]   25′ × 15′   7.5 × 4.5 m

'Madeleine Selzer' [Multiflora Rambler]

Walter FRANCE 1926
'Tausendschön' × 'Mrs Aaron Ward'
Trusses of shapely, fully double flowers of soft
lemon to white are produced in great profusion.
Foliage bronzy mid-green. Growth almost
thornless, bushy and upright. A most useful rose.

[(S) (P) (MF) AL]   10′ × 6′   3 × 1.8 m

'Maigold' [Pimpinellifolia Hybrid]

Kordes GERMANY 1953
'Poulsen's Pink' × 'Frühlingstag'
One of the first climbers to flower each season, it
has clusters of rich golden-yellow flowers flushed
orange. Foliage rich mid-green and very glossy, the
stems prickly with reddish thorns. Growth angular
and upright.

[(S) (P) (N) (SF) 🌓 AW]   12′ × 8′   3.5 × 2.5 m

'Malaga' [Modern Climber]

McGredy UK 1971
('Hamburger Phoenix' × 'Danse de Feu') ×
'Copenhagen'
Large, deep rose-pink flowers are borne in sizeable
clusters, with dark green, semi-glossy foliage on an
upright, bushy plant.

[(R) (P) (MF) ✂ AL]   8′ × 4′   2.5 × 1.2 m

'Masquerade' [Climbing Floribunda]

Gregory UK 1958
Sport from 'Masquerade'
Bush form, Boerner USA 1949
'Goldilocks' × 'Holiday'
Its clusters of semi-double flowers of soft primrose
change with age to deep reddish-crimson. Foliage
dark green and leathery. Growth upright and
branching.

[(S) (P) AW]   18′ × 10′   5.5 × 3 m

'Meg' [Modern Climber]

Gosset UK 1954
Thought to be 'Paul's Lemon Pillar' × 'Mme
Butterfly'
The large, almost single, flowers of buffish-yellow
have flushes of apricot and highlights of peach, and
pronounced anthers. Foliage dark green and semi-
glossy. Growth upright and bushy. A superb rose.

[(R) (P) (SF) AW]   8′ × 4′   2.5 × 1.2 m

'Mermaid' [Bracteata Hybrid]

Paul UK 1918
R. bracteata × a double yellow Tea rose
A most useful and beautiful climber, its scented
flowers are large and single, lemon-yellow in colour and with prominent golden-brown stamens.
The foliage is almost evergreen, a rich glossy dark
green, the stems armed with many vicious hooked
thorns. Growth vigorous, wide and branching.

[(C) (N) (MF) (T) 🌓 AW]   30′ × 20′   9 × 6 m

'Minnehaha' [Wichuraiana Rambler]

Walsh USA 1905
R. wichuraiana × 'Paul Neyron'
Clusters of cascading, scented pink flowers come

Top left: 'Minnehaha' and *top right:* 'New Dawn' (see text p. 296)

in profusion in midsummer. Foliage small, matt and greyish-green. Growth relaxed and vigorous.

[(S) (P) (N) (GC) (T) (MF) ◍ M◁⫶ AL] 15′ × 8′   4.5 × 2.5 m

'Mme Butterfly' [Climbing Hybrid Tea]

Smith UK 1926
Sport from bush form, Hill USA 1918
Sport from 'Ophelia'
The shapely, high-centred flowers are pale soft pink with darker colouring and some yellow deep

down in the bloom. Foliage greyish-green and matt. Growth upright and branching.

[(S) (P) (Gh) (VF) ✂ AW]   15′ × 10′   4.5 × 3 m

'Mme Grégoire Staechelin', 'Spanish Beauty' [Climbing Hybrid Tea]

Dot SPAIN 1927
'Frau Karl Druschki' × 'Château de Clos Vougeot'
Its very large, almost double flowers are pale pink with a deeper reverse and edges to their petals. If not dead-headed, this rose will produce some superb, large, urn-shaped hips in autumn. Foliage dark green and matt. Growth vigorous and wide.

[(R) (N) (P) (VF) ◍ AW]   15′ × 10′   4.5 × 3 m

'Mrs Herbert Stevens' [Climbing Hybrid Tea]

Pernet-Ducher FRANCE 1922
Sport from bush form, McGredy UK 1910
'Frau Karl Druschki' × 'Niphetos'
Shapely, high-centred flowers of pure white are produced singly in profusion. Foliage mid-green and matt. Growth sturdy, upright and branching with a good constitution.

[(R) (P) (N) (MF) ◍ ✂ AW]   12′ × 8′   3.5 × 2.5 m

Top: 'Parkdirektor Riggers' (see text p. 298) and *bottom:* 'Paul Lédé' (see text p. 298)

'Mrs Sam McGredy' [Climbing Hybrid Tea]

Buisman NETHERLANDS 1937
Sport from bush form, McGredy UK 1929
('Donald McDonald' × 'Golden Emblem') ×
(Seedling × 'The Queen Alexandra Rose')
Large, shaggy flowers emerge from shapely buds,
fiery coppery-orange in colour with golden
centres. Foliage very dark green, copper-tinted, the
younger leaves reddish-maroon. Growth vigorous,
branching and awkward, but this rose is still an
exceptionally good climber.

[(R) (P) (N) (SF) ◍ ✕ AL]   20′ × 15′   6 × 4.5 m

'New Dawn', [Wichuraiana Rambler]

Somerset USA 1930
Sport from 'Dr W. Van Fleet'
Van Fleet USA 1910
(R. wichuraiana × 'Saffrano') × 'Souvenir du
Président Carnot'
Tubby buds open to semi-double blooms of soft
blush-pink, usually in clusters. The foliage is plentiful, greyish-green and semi-glossy on a wide,
bushy plant. This is an outstanding rose, probably
the most useful sport ever discovered, and is an
important parent to many modern climbers.

[(C) (P) (N) (MF) ◍ ✕ AW]   10′ × 8′   3 × 2.5 m

'Night Light' (Poullight) [Modern Climber]

Poulsen DENMARK 1982
'Westerland' × 'Pastorale'
With sizeable sprays of large, double, deep yellow
flowers. Foliage dark green and glossy. Growth
upright.

[(C) (SF) AL]   10′ × 8′   3 × 2.5 m

'Ophelia' [Climbing Hybrid Tea]

Dickson UK 1920
Sport from bush form, Paul UK 1912
Said to be a chance seedling of 'Antoine Rivoire'

Top: 'Paul's Scarlet' (see text p. 299) and *bottom:* 'Paul Transon' (see text p. 299)

Above: 'Phyllis Bide' (see text p. 301)
Below: 'Pink Perpétue' (the centre rose, on a pillar; see text p. 301)

Shapely, high-centred flowers of flesh-pink with deeper shadings and yellow in the base. Foliage greyish-green and matt. Growth upright and branching.

[(S) (P) (Gh) (VF) ✂ AL] 15′ × 10′ 4.5 × 3 m

'Parade' [Modern Climber]

Boerner USA 1953
'New Dawn' seedling × 'World's Fair'
Fully double, cerise-red to crimson flowers are borne in clusters, with glossy, profuse, mid-green foliage on a plant of upright, bushy habit.

[(C) (P) (N) ◍ ✂ AW] 10′ × 8′ 3 × 2.5 m

'Parkdirektor Riggers' [Kordesii Hybrid]

Kordes GERMANY 1957
R. kordesii × 'Our Princess'
It has large clusters of deep red to crimson flowers, dark green, glossy and leathery foliage and is of branching, upright and sturdy growth. Very hardy.

[(C) (P) (N) ◍ AW] 10′ × 6′ 3 × 1.8 m

'Paul Lédé' [Climbing Hybrid Tea]

Lowe UK 1902
Bush form, Pernet-Ducher FRANCE 1902
Parentage unknown
Very large, full flowers of soft pink with peachy highlights and a yellow base. Plentiful, mid-green foliage. Growth upright and branching. A good, free-flowering older variety.

[(R) (P) (VF) ☺ AL] 12′ × 8′ 3.5 × 2.5 m

'Paul's Himalayan Musk' [Moschata Hybrid]

Paul UK Date and parentage unknown
Drooping clusters of pinkish-lavender, small, semi-double, cupped flowers come in profusion in mid-July. Foliage semi-glossy, dark green and plentiful. Growth very vigorous and scrambling.

[(S) (P) (T) (N) (MF) ◍ AL] 20′ × 12′ 6 × 3.5 m

Top: 'Réveil Dijonnais' (see text p. 301) and *bottom:* 'Rosy Mantle' (see text p. 301)

'Royal Gold' (see text p. 301)

'Sander's White' (see text p. 302)

'Paul's Lemon Pillar' [Climbing Hybrid Tea]

Paul UK 1915
'Frau Karl Druschki' × 'Maréchal Niel'
Its massive, shapely blooms are creamy-white suffused lemon and are tolerant of changeable weather. Foliage large and greyish to light green. Growth sturdy, upright and branching. Well armed with stubby thorns.

[(S) (N) (MF) ◑ ✂ AW]   15′ × 10′   4.5 × 3 m

'Paul's Scarlet', 'Paul's Scarlet Climber' [Climber]

Paul UK 1916
'Paul's Carmine Pillar' × 'Rêve d'Or'
A rose that is difficult to classify, though probably of Multiflora ancestry. Semi-double, initially cupped flowers of bright glowing scarlet are produced in clusters. Foliage dark green, matt. Growth upright and wide, and sparsely thorned.

[(S) (P) (N) ◑ AL]   10′ × 8′   3 × 2.5 m

'Paul Transon' [Wichuraiana Rambler]

Barbier FRANCE 1900
R. wichuraiana × 'L'Ideal'

'Senateur Amic' (see text p. 302)

Clusters of flat, fully double flowers of salmon with coppery tones and a creamy yellow base. Mid-green, coppery foliage on a relaxed plant.

[(R) (P) (SF) ◑ AL]   10′ × 8′   3 × 2.5 m

'Schoolgirl' (see text p. 302)

'Phyllis Bide' [Chinensis Climber]

Bide UK 1923
'Perle d'Or' × 'Gloire de Dijon'
Its pyramidal clusters of semi-double flowers are a combination of yellow, cream, pink and orange becoming deeper with age. Foliage small, light green and plentiful. Growth vigorous and upright, though twiggy.
[(R) (P) (N) (SF) ❶ AW]   10′ × 6′   3 × 1.8 m

'Pink Perpétue' [Modern Climber]

Gregory UK 1965
'Danse de Feu' × 'New Dawn'
Clusters of deep pink, semi-double, cupped flowers are produced continuously throughout the summer. Foliage dark green with purple overtones. Growth upright and wide.
[(C) (P) (N) (SF) ❶ BS⬤☰ AW]
12′ × 8′   3.5 × 2.5 m

'Réveil Dijonnais' [Modern Climber]

Buatois FRANCE 1931
'Eugène Fürst' × 'Constance'
Large, semi-double flowers of vivid orange, yellow

and red, with plentiful mid-green foliage, the stems thorny. Of bushy growth.
[(R) (P) (N) (MF) ❶ BS⬤☰ AL]   10′ × 6′   3 × 1.8 m

'Rose-Marie Viaud' [Multiflora Rambler]

Igoult FRANCE 1924
'Veilchenblau' seedling
Clusters of very double flowers of lavender-purple with light green foliage on a vigorous, wide plant.
[(S) (P) (N) (SF) ❶ M⬤☰ AW]
12′ × 6′   3.5 × 1.8 m

'Rosy Mantle' [Modern Climber]

Cocker UK 1968
'New Dawn' × 'Prima Ballerina'
Plump, high-centred, silvery-deep-pink flowers are freely produced in clusters. Foliage large, glossy and dark green. Growth wide and dense.
[(C) (N) (MF) ❶ ✂ AL]   8′ × 8′   2.5 × 2.5 m

'Royal Gold' [Modern Climber]

Morey USA 1957
'Goldilocks' × 'Lydia'
The shapely, high-centred, deep golden-yellow blooms open blowsily, with dark green and glossy

'Sir Cedric Morris' (see text p. 302)

'Swan Lake'

foliage on a plant of upright, angular and wide habit. This variety needs protection in winter in colder climates.

[(C) (VF) ✕ ∴ AL]   8′ × 8′   2.5 × 2.5 m

'Sander's White', 'Sander's White Rambler' [Wichuraiana Rambler]

Sander UK 1912
Parentage unknown
Abundant, rosette-shaped, pure white flowers come in cascading clusters. Foliage plentiful, mid-green, semi-glossy. Growth vigorous and relaxed.

[(S) (P) (T) (G) (C) (N) ◐ AW]   12′ × 8′   3.5 × 2.5 m

'Schoolgirl' [Modern Climber]

McGredy UK 1964
'Coral Dawn' × 'Belle Blonde'
Its rich coppery-orange flowers are Hybrid-Tea-shaped and open loose and semi-double. Foliage large, dark green and matt-finished, though not very plentiful. Growth upright and branching.

[(C) (MF) ✕ BS ▮⸬ AW]   10′ × 8′   3 × 2.5 m

'Seagull' [Multiflora Rambler]

Pritchard UK 1907
R. multiflora × 'Général Jacqueminot'
Bright yellow stamens surrounded by a double layer of white petals characterize this rose, and its flowers are produced in great profusion in large trusses. Foliage plentiful, grey-green and soft to the touch. Growth vigorous, dense and spreading.

[(S) (P) (T) (VF) (GC) ◐ AL]   25′ × 15′   7.5 × 4.5 m

'Sénateur Amic' [Climbing Hybrid Tea]

Nabonnand FRANCE 1924
R. gigantea × 'General MacArthur'
Its shapely, high-centred flowers open loosely semi-double, a rich, silvery deep pink with hints of yellow in the base. Foliage large, mid-green and semi-glossy. Growth upright, branching and bushy.

[(R) ∴ ✕ AL]   12′ × 8′   3.5 × 2.5 m

'Shot Silk' [Climbing Hybrid Tea]

Knight AUSTRALIA 1931
Sport from 'Shot Silk'
Sport from bush form, Dickson UK 1924
'Hugh Dickson' seedling × 'Sunstar'
Fully double, cupped flowers of soft cherry-cerise with a yellow base, their petals with a silky texture. Foliage lush dark green and glossy. Growth upright and branching.

[(R) (P) (N) (VF) ✕ ● AL]   18′ × 10′   5.5 × 3 m

'Silver Moon' [R. laevigata Hybrid]

Van Fleet USA 1910
Probably (R. wichuraiana × 'Devoniensis') × R. laevigata
Very large and beautiful pure white single flowers with golden stamens are produced singly, sometimes reluctantly. Foliage large, dark green semi-glossy. Growth vigorous, wide and branching.

[(R) (T) (N) (MF) ● AL]   15′ × 8′   4.5 × 2.5 m

'Sir Cedric Morris' [Vigorous Climber]

Morris UK Introduced Beales UK 1979
Thought to be R. glauca × R. mulliganii
Very large trusses of small, single, star-like flowers of pure white with hints of cream and rich golden stamens are followed by small, oval, orange hips in the autumn. Foliage glaucous, the stems very thorny. Growth very vigorous, branching and dense.

[(S) (T) (P) (VF) ◐ AL]   30′ × 20′   9 × 6 m

'Sparkling Scarlet', 'Iskra' (Meihaiti) [Modern Climber]

Meilland FRANCE 1970
'Danse des Sylphes' × 'Zambra'
Clusters of semi-double, very bright scarlet flowers, with large, mid-green, semi-glossy foliage on an upright, branching plant.
[(C) (P) (VF) AL]   10′ × 8′   3 × 2.5 m

'Spectacular' *see* 'Danse de Feu'

'Summer Wine' (Korizont) [Modern Climber]

Kordes GERMANY 1985
Parentage unknown
Its large, semi-double, deep pink flowers have red stamens and come in clusters. Foliage mid-green and semi-glossy. Growth upright and bushy.
[(C) (P) (MF) AL]   10′ × 6′   3 × 1.8 m

'Super Star', 'Tropicana' (Tangostar) [Climbing Hybrid Tea]

Blaby UK 1965 and Boerner USA 1971
Sport from 'Super Star'
Bush form, Tantau GERMANY 1960
(Seedling × 'Peace') × (Seedling × 'Alpine Glow')

The large, full, shapely blooms of coral-vermilion are high-centred in bud. Foliage matt and grey-green. Growth upright and branching.
[(S) (P) (MF) M AW]   12′ × 8′   3.5 × 2.5 m

'Sutter's Gold' [Climbing Hybrid Tea]

Weeks USA 1950
Sport from 'Sutter's Gold'
Bush form, Swim USA 1950
'Charlotte Armstrong' × 'Signora'
Slim buds held on long stems open loosely to deep yellow flowers brushed orange and pink. Foliage mid-green and semi-glossy. Growth upright.
[(S) (P) (VF) AW]   12′ × 8′   3.5 × 2.5 m

'Swan Lake', 'Schwanensee' [Modern Climber]

McGredy UK 1968
'Memoriam' × 'Heidelberg'
Shapely buds open to large and fully double white flowers with pale pink flushes, especially in the centre. Foliage rounded, dark green and glossy. Growth upright and bushy.
[(C) (P) (MF) AL]   10′ × 8′   3 × 2.5 m

'Violette' (see text p. 304)

'White Cockade'

'Veilchenblau', 'Violet Blue', 'Blue Rambler', 'Blue Rosalie' [Multiflora Rambler]

Schmidt GERMANY 1909
'Crimson Rambler' × 'Erinnerung an Brod'
Its large trusses of semi-double lavender-purple flowers are sometimes flecked white and pale to lilac-grey. They go well with creamy-white colours elsewhere in the garden. Foliage glossy and mid-green. Growth bushy, upright and branching.
[(S) (T) (N) (SF) ⓪ AW]   15' × 12'   4.5 × 3.5 m

'Violette' [Multiflora Rambler]

Turbat FRANCE 1921
Parentage unknown
With clusters of rich violet-purple double flowers, which display truly golden stamens when fully open, and good dark green foliage. Growth bushy and wide.
[(S) (T) (SF) ⓪ ✂ AL]   15' × 10'   4.5 × 3 m

'Wedding Day' [Sinowilsonii Hybrid]

Stern UK 1950
R. sinowilsonii × unknown
Its single white flowers have prominent yellow stamens and come in large clusters. Foliage bright green and glossy. Growth vigorous and spreading.
[(S) (N) (T) (GC) (MF) ⓪ AL]   30' × 15'   9 × 4.5 m

'Whisky Mac' (Andmac) [Climbing Hybrid Tea]

Anderson UK 1985
Sport from 'Whisky Mac'
Bush form, Tantau GERMANY 1967
Parentage unknown
Shapely blooms of rich golden-amber, with dark green, semi-glossy foliage on an upright plant.
[(S) (VF) ✂ AL]   12' × 8'   3.5 × 2.5 m

'White Cockade' [Modern Climber]

Cocker UK 1969
'New Dawn' × 'Circus'
Its pure white, fully double flowers sometimes open in rather triangular shapes, and are very free-flowering. Foliage dark green and matt. Growth bushy and upright.
[(C) (SF) ✂ AW]   10' × 6'   3 × 2 m

'Veilchenblau'

Appendix A

World Climatic Map

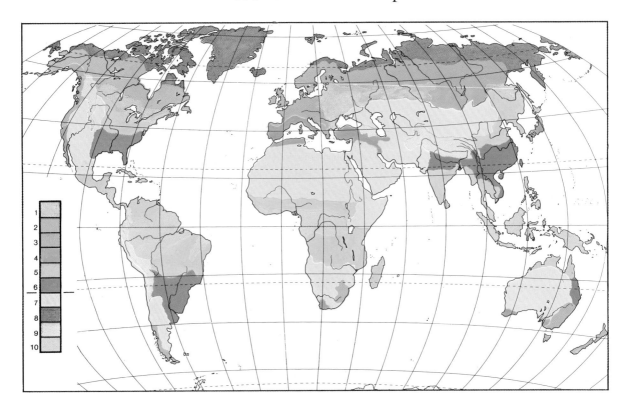

The following are brief notes on the main climatic regions of the world where roses can be grown. Temperature ranges are only an average and from time to time can be far exceeded, and terrain, and therefore the influence of climate upon roses, can vary dramatically over even a small area. Wild, species roses are found widely across Central Asia, but for the main in less arid and less mountainous parts. Areas of desert, arctic waste, high mountains and humid jungle – numbers 7, 8, 9 and 10 respectively on the map colour key – are not conducive to growing roses.

1 Temperature range −3 °C (26 °F) (Winter) to 22 °C (72 °F) (Summer)

Most roses require winter protection, except for Pimpinellifolia hybrids, *kordesii* hybrids and the very hardy species. Most other types will grow well in summer, but the less hardy ramblers and climbers seldom reach their full potential.

2 Temperature range −25 °C (−13 °F) (Winter) to 16 °C (61 °F) (Summer)

Roses will require winter protection. Avoid all Teas, Chinas, Noisettes and less hardy Hybrid Teas and Floribundas.

3 Temperature range 0 °C (32 °F) (Winter) to 23 °C (73 °F) (Summer)

All roses enjoy such conditions, though Teas, Noisettes, Chinas and some less hardy Hybrid Teas and Floribundas may suffer some frost damage in more severe winters.

4 Temperature range 10 °C (50 °F) (Winter) to 23 °C (73 °F) (Summer)

All roses will flourish in such conditions, except for some hybrid Rugosas, Centifolias, Gallicas and hybrid Pimpinellifolias which will not enjoy the heat of summer and may struggle, especially in areas of low rainfall.

5 Temperature range 10 °C (50 °F) (Winter) to more than 30 °C (86 °F) (Summer)

Almost all roses will grow reasonably well where rainfall is sufficient. In these conditions hybrid Rugosas, Pimpinellifolias and *kordesii* hybrids will suffer in the heat of the summer, as will some Hybrid Perpetuals, Bourbons and older types such as Centifolias and Gallicas.

6 Temperature range 5 °C (41 °F) (Winter) to 25 °C (77 °F) (Summer)

Most roses will grow well, especially Teas, Chinas and Noisettes. Rugosa and Pimpinellifolia hybrids will dislike the heat of summer, as will older roses such as Centifolias, Damasks and Gallicas.

Appendix B

Rose Societies of the World

Rose lovers in many countries can join societies and associations specifically set up to promote and encourage the growing and enjoyment of roses. Most, if not all, of these organizations have display gardens to show large collections of roses at their best and trial grounds to test new varieties. They also issue periodicals, some annually, others quarterly. Almost all organize rose shows at least twice a year and arrange conferences or conventions where rosarians can keep abreast of developments and exchange views on all aspects of the subject.

There are no boundaries or frontiers in the rose world and most of the national societies are affiliated to the World Federation of Rose Societies. This organization operates internationally and among other liaison work arranges conventions in various countries every three years. The last two were held in Canada and Australia. The Rose Society of Northern Ireland are hosts in 1991 and India in 1994.

ROSE SOCIETIES OF THE WORLD

ARGENTINA

THE ROSE SOCIETY OF ARGENTINA
Solis, 1348 Hurlingham, Buenos Aires, Argentina

AUSTRALIA

THE NATIONAL ROSE SOCIETY OF AUSTRALIA
271 Belmore Road, North Balwyn, Victoria 3104, Australia

AUSTRALIAN STATE SOCIETIES

NEW SOUTH WALES
279 North Rocks Road, North Rocks, New South Wales 2151

QUEENSLAND
Box 1866, GPO Brisbane, Queensland 4001

SOUTH AUSTRALIA
18 Windybanks Road, Happy Valley, South Australia 5159

TASMANIA
263 Main Road, Austins Ferry, Tasmania 7011

VICTORIA
40 Williams Road, Blackburn, Victoria 3130

WESTERN AUSTRALIA
105 Hemsmans Street, South Perth, Western Australia 6151

AUSTRIA

OSTERREICH GEPRUFTE ROSE
Baden Bei Wien, Vienna

BELGIUM

LA SOCIETE ROYALE NATIONALE DES AMIS DE LA ROSE
Vrijheidslaan 28, B-9000 Ghent, Belgium

BERMUDA

THE BERMUDA ROSE SOCIETY
BOX PG162, Paget 6, Bermuda

CANADA

THE CANADIAN ROSE SOCIETY
20 Portico Drive, Scarborough, Ontario

CHINA

THE BEIJING ROSE SOCIETY
97 Mu-nan Road, Tianjin, People's Republic of
China

CZECHOSLOVAKIA

ROSA KLUB PRAHA
Hradec Kralove, Czechoslovakia

DENMARK

THE VALBY PARK ROSE GARDEN
Copenhagen, Denmark

EIRE

THE CLONTARF HORTICULTURAL SOCIETY
20 Chapel Street, Dublin 1, Eire

FRANCE

LA SOCIETE FRANCAISES DES ROSES
Parc de la Tête d'Or, 69459 Lyon, France

GERMAN FEDERAL REPUBLIC
(West Germany)

VEREIN DEUTSCHER ROSENFREUNDE
Mainaustrasse 198A, 775A Konstanz, West
Germany

GREAT BRITAIN

THE ROYAL NATIONAL ROSE SOCIETY
Chiswell Green, St Albans, Hertfordshire
AL2 3NR, England

INDIA

THE ROSE SOCIETY OF INDIA
1-267 Defence Colony, New Delhi 17, India

ISRAEL

THE ISRAEL ROSE SOCIETY
Ganot-Hadar, PO Netanya, Israel

ITALY

ASSOCIAZIONE ITALIANA DELLA ROSA
Villa Reale, 20052 Monza, Milano, Italy

JAPAN

THE JAPANESE ROSE SOCIETY
4-12-6 Todoroki Setagaya-ku, Tokyo, Japan

NETHERLANDS

NEDERLANDSE ROSENVERENIGING
Mildestraat 47, 2596 SW, S'Gravenhage,
Netherlands

NEW ZEALAND

THE NATIONAL ROSE SOCIETY
PO BOX 66, Bunnythorpe, New Zealand

NORTHERN IRELAND

THE ROSE SOCIETY OF NORTHERN IRELAND
36A Myrtlefield Park, Belfast, Northern Ireland

NORWAY

THE NORWEGIAN ROSE SOCIETY
c/o Hageselskatet, PB 9008 Vaterland, N-0134,
Oslo, Norway

SOUTH AFRICA

THE ROSE SOCIETY OF SOUTH AFRICA
PO BOX 65217, Bensmore, Transvaal 2010,
South Africa

SWITZERLAND

GESELLSCHAFT SCHWEITZERISCHER ROSENFREUNDE
Haus Engelfried, 8158 Regensberg, Switzerland

UNITED STATES
OF AMERICA

THE AMERICAN ROSE SOCIETY
PO BOX 30,000, Shreveport, Louisiana, USA

URUGUAY

THE ROSE ASSOCIATION OF URUGUAY
Blanes Viale 6151, Montevideo, Uruguay

Appendix C

Rose Gardens of the World

In addition to the gardens of the various rose societies around the world, many parks, private gardens and commercial nurseries have displays and collections of roses which can be visited by the public either throughout the year or in the flowering season. The following are the most important and well known. Most include both older historical roses and modern varieties.

AUSTRALIA

NEW SOUTH WALES, The Botanic Gardens, Rumsey Nurseries, Swanes Nurseries, all in Sydney

SOUTH AUSTRALIA, The Botanic Gardens, Adelaide; The Ruston Rose Garden, Renmark; The Ross Rose Gardens and Nursery, Willunga

VICTORIA, The Benalla Rose Gardens, Benalla; The Rose Gardens, Canberra; The Rose Gardens, Melbourne

WESTERN AUSTRALIA, The Peace Memorial Gardens, Nedlands

AUSTRIA

BADEN, Osterreichisches Rosarium

LINZ, The Rose Garden

VIENNA, Donau Park; Baden Bei Wien

BELGIUM

HAINAULT, Rosarium du Roeulx

LIMBURG, Ghent Rozentium Koningin, Astridpark

MELLE, Rosarium de Rijksstation

STEENWEG, International Rozentium

BERMUDA

Camden House; many other small but interesting collections

CANADA

HAMILTON, The Ontario Royal Botanic Gardens

MONTREAL, The Floralies Rose Garden

NIAGARA, The Canadian Horticultural Society Rose Garden

OTTAWA, The Dominion Arboretum and Botanic Gardens

ONTARIO, Hortico, Inc. (Nursery), Waterdown; Pickering Nurseries, Pickering

DENMARK

COPENHAGEN, The Valby Park Rose Garden

EIRE

DUBLIN, The Parks Department, St Anne's

FRANCE

ALSACE, Roseraie de Saverne

LYON, Roseraie du Parc de la Tête d'Or

ORLEANS, Roseraie du Parc Floréal de la Source

PARIS, Roseraie de l'Hay-les-Roses; Roseraie du Parc de Bagatelle

POITIERS, Roseraie de Poitiers Parc Floral

GERMAN DEMOCRATIC REPUBLIC (East Germany)

LAUSITZ, The Forst Rose Garden

SANGERHAUSEN, The Rosarium

TORGAU, The Castle Rose Garden

GERMAN FEDERAL REPUBLIC (West Germany)

BADEN-BADEN, Kurgarten Lichtentaler, Allee

DORTMUND, Deutsches Rosarium, Westfalenpark

FRANKFURT AM MAIN, Palmengarten

HAMBURG, Planten und Blomen

KARLSRUHE, Rosengarten

LAKE KONSTANZ, Rosengarten, Insel Mainau

SAARBRUCKEN, Rosengarten

UETERSEN, Rosarium

ZWEIBRUCKEN, Rosengarten

GREAT BRITAIN

BERKSHIRE, Saville Gardens, Windsor

BUCKINGHAMSHIRE, Cliveden (National Trust), Maidenhead

CAMBRIDGESHIRE, Anglesey Abbey Gardens, Lode; The Botanic Gardens, Cambridge

CHESHIRE, C. and K. Jones (Nursery), Chester; Fryer's Nursery, Knutsford; Sealand Nurseries, Sealand

CLEVELAND, Borough Park, Redcar

DEVON, Castle Drogo, Drewsteignton; Rosemore Gardens, Torrington

GLOUCESTERSHIRE, Hidcote Manor (National Trust), Chipping Camden; Kiftsgate Court, Chipping Camden

HAMPSHIRE, Hillier's Arboretum, Winchester; Mottisfont Abbey (National Trust Historic Collection), Romsey

HERTFORDSHIRE, Harkness Rose Gardens, Hitchen

KENT, Sissinghurst Castle, Maidstone

LEICESTERSHIRE, Gaudy Roses (Nursery), Lutterworth; Rearsby Roses (Nursery), Rearsby

LONDON, The Queen Mary Rose Gardens, Regent's Park

NORTHERN IRELAND, Dickson Roses (Nursery), Newtownards; Lady Dixon Park, Belfast

NOTTINGHAMSHIRE, Gregory Roses (Nursery), Rosemary Roses (Nursery), The Arboretum (Rose Gardens), Wheatcroft Roses (Nursery), all near Nottingham

NORFOLK, Heigham Park Rose Gardens, Norwich; LeGrice Roses (Nursery and Display Gardens), North Walsham; Mannington Hall Rose Gardens, Saxthorpe; Peter Beales Roses (Nursery and Display Gardens), Attleborough

SCOTLAND, Brodick Castle, Isle of Arran; City of Roses, Aberdeen; Cocker Roses (Nursery and Display Gardens), Aberdeen; Craithes Castle Gardens, Branchory; Malleny House, Ballerno, near Edinburgh; The Botanic Gardens, Edinburgh; Tyninghame Rose Gardens, East Lothian

SOMERSET, Scott Nurseries, Merriott; Vivary Park Rose Gardens, Taunton

STAFFORDSHIRE, David Austin Roses (Nursery and Display Gardens), Albrighton; Wolesley Rose Gardens (a large collection opening in 1989), Rugeley

SUFFOLK, Lime Kiln Rose Gardens, Claydon; Notcutts' Nurseries, Woodbridge

SURREY, Henry Street Nurseries, The Gardens of the Royal Horticultural Society, Wisley Gardens, all near Woking

WALES, Bodnant Gardens, Gwynedd; Queen Park Gardens, Colwyn Bay; Roath Park Gardens, Cardiff

WARWICKSHIRE, Warwick Castle Gardens, Warwick

WEST SUSSEX, Charleston Manor, West Dean; Nyman's Gardens (National Trust), Handcross

WILTSHIRE, Sheldon Manor, Chippenham

YORKSHIRE, Castle Howard Gardens, York; Harlow Court Gardens (the Gardens of the Northern Horticultural Society), Harrogate

INDIA

NEW DELHI, The Rose Society of India Gardens

PUNJAB, The Zakir Rose Gardens, Chandigarh

ISRAEL

JERUSALEM, The Wohl Rose Park

JAPAN

CHOFU, The Botanic Gardens

TOKYO, Yatsu-Yuen Rose Gardens

NETHERLANDS

AMSTERDAM, Amstelpark Rosarium

THE HAGUE, Westbroekpark Rosarium

NEW ZEALAND

AUCKLAND, The Parnell Rose Gardens, The Nancy Steen Gardens, Bell's Roses

CHRISTCHURCH, Mona Vale Rose Gardens

HASTINGS, Frimley Rose Gardens

INVERCARGILL, The City Gardens

MOTUEKA, Tasman Bay Roses

NAPIER, The Kennedy Park Rose Gardens

OPOTIKI, The Rose Gardens

PALMERSTON NORTH, The Rose Trial Gardens

ROTORUA, The Murray Linton Rose Gardens

TAUPO, The Rose Gardens

TE AWAMUTU, The Rose Gardens

TIMARU, Trevor Griffiths Roses

WAIKATO, The Rose Gardens

WELLINGTON, The Lady Norwood Rose Gardens

NORWAY

VOLLEBEKK, Agricultural College

PAKISTAN

QUETTA, Department of Agriculture, Baluchistan

SOUTH AFRICA

SWELLENDAM, Western Cape Province

JOHANNESBURG, The Botanical Gardens

SPAIN

MADRID, Parque de Oeste

SWEDEN

NORRKOPING, Horticultural College

GOTEBORG, A newly planted rose garden

SWITZERLAND

GENEVA, Parc de la Grange

ST GALL, Rapperswill Gardens

SCHAFFHAUSEN, Neuhausen am Rheinfall Gardens

UNITED STATES OF AMERICA

CALIFORNIA, The Rose Gardens, Berkley; The Rose Acres Nursery, Diamond Springs; Descanso Gardens, La Canada; The Exposition Park Rose Gardens, Los Angeles; The Municipal Rose Garden, Oakland; The Tournament House and Wrigley Gardens, Pasadena; Ligett's Rose Nursery, The Municipal Rose Garden, San José; The Huntingdon Botanical Gardens, San Marino; Armstrong's Roses (Nursery), Somis; Moore's Miniature Roses (Nursery), Visalia; Roses of Yesterday and Today, Watsonville; The Pageant of Roses Garden, Whittier

CONNECTICUT, The Elizabeth Park Rose Gardens, Hartford

INDIANA, The Lakeside Rose Garden, Fort Wayne; Krider Nurseries, Inc., Middlebury

KANSAS, The Rose and Trial Garden, Topeka

LOUISIANA, The American Rose Center, Donovan's Nursery, Shreveport

MARYLAND, Rosehill Farm Nursery, Galena

MASSACHUSETTS, The Municipal Rose Gardens, Boston; The Arnold Arboretum, Jamaica Plain; Nor-East Miniatures (Nursery), Rowley

MISSOURI, The Capana Park Rose Display Gardens, Cape Girardeau; The Municipal Rose Gardens, Kansas City; The Missouri Botanic Gardens, St Louis

NEVADA, Idlewild Park, Reno

NEW HAMPSHIRE, Lowe's Roses (Nursery), Nashua

NEW JERSEY, The Rudolf van der Groot Rose Gardens, Colonial Park Arboretum, East Millstone

NEW YORK, The Botanic Gardens, Brooklyn; Kelly Bros Nurseries, Dansville; The Queens Botanic Gardens, Flushing; The Maplewood Park Rose Gardens, Rochester

OHIO, The Park of Roses, Columbus; The Michael H. Hovath Garden of Legend and Romance, Wooster

OKLAHOMA, The Municipal Rose Garden, Tulsa

OREGON, Oregon Miniature Roses (Nursery), Beaustrom; Jackson & Perkins (Nursery), Medford; The International Rose Test Garden, Portland

PENNSYLVANIA, The Rose Gardens, Hershey; The Gardens, Kennett Square, Longwood; The Marion W. Revinus Rose Garden (in the Morris Arboretum), Philadelphia

SOUTH CAROLINA, Wayside Gardens (Nursery), Hodges; Edisto Gardens, Orangeburg

TEXAS, The Municipal Rose Garden, Tyler

WASHINGTON, The Manito Gardens, Spokane

WEST VIRGINIA, The Ritter Park Gardens, Huntington

WISCONSIN, The Boerner Botanical Gardens, Hales Corner

Bibliography

Plenty of reading material is available to those who wish to obtain a wider knowledge of this fascinating family of plants. I have yet to pick up a book on roses for a serious read, or even a casual browse, without learning something new or finding different, thought-provoking views on aspects of their behaviour and cultivation. I have dipped into many books while writing *Twentieth-Century Roses*; in fact it would have been difficult, if not impossible, to write this book without them. Many to which I constantly referred are now out of print, but, depending upon where you live, the following should be generally obtainable from book shops, libraries or by mail order from the publishers. I recommend them all.

Beales, P. *Classic Roses* Collins Harvill, London, and Henry Holt, New York (USA) 1985

Dobson, B. R. *Roses in Commerce and Cultivation* published annually by Beverly R. Dobson, New York (USA)

Fisher, J. *The Companion to Roses* Viking 1986

Gault, S. M., and Singe, P. M. *The Dictionary of Roses in Colour* Michael Joseph and Ebury Press 1970

Gibson, M. *Growing Roses* Croom Helm, London, and Timber Press, Portland (USA) 1984

Griffiths, T. *My World of Old Roses* (Volumes I and II) Whitcoulls, Christchurch (New Zealand) 1983 and 1986

Griffiths, T. *The Best of Modern Roses* Pacific, Auckland (New Zealand) 1987

Haglund, G. *Rosen Blommornas Drotting* Haglund, Göteborg (Sweden) 1986

Harkness, J. *Roses* J. M. Dent & Sons 1978

Harkness, J. *The Makers of Heavenly Roses* Souvenir Press 1985

Harkness, P. *Modern Roses* Century Hutchinson 1987

Hessayon, D. *The Rose Expert* PBI Publications 1981

Hillier's *Manual of Trees and Shrubs* (4th edition) 1974

Krüssman, G. *Roses* Batsford, London 1982, and Timber Press, Portland (USA) 1981

LeGrice, E. B. *Rose Growing Complete* (Revised Edition) Faber & Faber 1976

McCann, S. *Miniature Roses for Home and Garden* David & Charles 1985

McFarland, J. H. *Modern Roses 8 and 9* The McFarland Co. and the American Rose Society (USA) 1980 and 1986

Money, K. *The Bedside Book of Old-Fashioned Roses* Degamo 1986

Notle, T. *Growing Old-Fashioned Roses in Australia and New Zealand* Kangaroo Press (Australia) 1983

Ross, D. *Rose Growing for Pleasure* Lothian 1985

Testu, C. *Les Roses Anciennes* Flammarion (France) 1984

Thomas, A. S. *Growing Roses in Australia* Nelson 1983

Thomas, G. S. *Shrub Roses of Today* J. M. Dent & Sons 1974

Thomas, G. S. *The Old Shrub Roses* J. M. Dent & Sons 1978

Thomas, G. S. *Climbing Roses Old and New* J. M. Dent & Sons 1979

Warner, C. *Climbing Roses* Century Hutchinson 1987

Index

Notes on the Indexes

INDEX OF ROSES

This index lists in one alphabetical sequence the names of roses, species and hybrids. Synonyms and raisers' trademark names are cross-referred to the name by which each rose is most commonly known and under which it appears in the Dictionary section and elsewhere.

GENERAL INDEX

In this index will be found entries referring to the first three parts of the book, together with the classifications by which roses are arranged in the Dictionary section – Procumbent shrub roses, Dwarf Polyantha roses, and so on.

Page numbers in **bold type** refer to illustrations. Where the only page number given is in bold type and that number is for pages 131 to 305 a description of the rose illustrated will be found on the same page. All entries are arranged 'letter-by-letter'.

INDEX OF ROSES

GENERAL INDEX